The
LOUVRE

Edited and Produced
for Chartwell Books Inc. by
The Vendome Press
New York   Paris   Lausanne

The LOUVRE

by Jean Clay and Josette Contreras
in collaboration with
The Editors of Réalités-Hachette

Chartwell Books Inc.

pages 1 and 2: The so-called Colonnade serves as the exterior façade on the east wing of the Cour Carrée, facing the medieval church of Saint-Germain l'Auxerrois. Commissioned by Louis XIV and built in 1667–70, this most important part of the 17th-century Louvre was abandoned as a roofless, empty shell once the King turned all his interest to Versailles and moved the court there. The design conceived by Perrault, Le Brun, and Le Vau is considered to be one of the first authentic triumphs of French Classicism. Indeed, the flat, balustraded roof, and the pedimented portico flanked by long sequences of paired Corinthian columns make the facade look like a Roman temple with all four sides extended along a single axis. As the engraving by Blondel shows, the original conception called for a largely "blind" front, with medallions and niches instead of the windows that now pierce the wall. Louis XV ordered the Colonnade completed in the third quarter of the 18th century, only after disgusted Parisians protested the eyesore that the squatter-infested building had become. Even so, the tympanum was not carved until the time of the Empire (1805–14). Finally, in the 1960s, Malraux arranged for the moat to be dug, thereby giving the Colonnade the high, handsome base and the proportions its architects had envisioned.

This book was produced by the editors of Réalités-Hachette
under the direction of Jean Clay
Layout by Jean-Louis Germain

Originally published in French under the title *Les Merveilles du Louvre*
copyright ©1970 by Librairie Hachette
This edition copyright ©1980
English Translation copyright ©1980 by Hachette-Vendome

Printed and bound in Hong Kong by South China Printing Co.

ISBN: 0-89009-370-9
Library of Congress Catalog Card Number: 80-66935

Contents

The Louvre: History and Architecture

The Louvre is a vast complex of structures facing, on various sides, the Seine, the Tuileries Gardens, the Rue de Rivoli, and the splendid medieval church of Saint-Germain l'Auxerrois. The most beautiful approach to the palace lies through the gardens, laid out in the 17th century by the great André Le Nôtre, designer of the gardens at Versailles. The name of this delightful realm—with its *grande allée*, its parterres and patterned plantings, its sculptures, fountains, and groves of majestic chestnuts—comes from Catherine de' Medici's Renaissance palace that until 1871 fronted on the gardens, spanning the space between the present Louvre's Pavillon de Flore and Pavillon de Marsan. So intimate was the relationship between the Louvre and the Tuileries that the history of neither can be traced without the other.

The origins of the Louvre date back to 1190, when, as part of his general plan for reinforcing the defenses of Paris, King Philippe Auguste (r. 1180–1223) built a keep and a *château fort* on the right bank of the Seine. Long vanished except for a few vestigial pillars, the old Louvre occupied a site now corresponding to the southwest quadrant of the Cour Carrée. The early sovereigns did not live in the Louvre but, rather, maintained their official residence in the Palais de la Cité, a seat of government since Roman times. The Louvre itself functioned mainly as a place of safekeeping for the royal treasury, the state archives, and fine furniture. To render it more habitable and palatial, Saint Louis (r. 1226–70) added an enormous hall suitable for receptions and festivities. Then, in the 14th century, Charles V (r. 1364–80) installed his famous library, thereby taking the first fortuitous step toward the museological purpose the Louvre eventually would serve. This monarch civilized the old bastion still further by razing the militaristic towers and by commissioning Raymond du Temple to build a vast circular stairway embellished with ten large statues portraying members of the royal family.

For some fifty years after the death of Charles V, the Louvre rarely sheltered royalty, most of whom, from Charles VII to François I, preferred to reside either at the Hôtel des Tournelles in Paris' Marais district or in their châteaux on the banks of the Loire.

In 1527 François I, having seen the great urban cultures and palaces of Italy, decided to bring the court back to Paris and the Louvre. After destroying Philippe Auguste's keep, he set himself up, for better or worse, in the *corps de logis* built by Saint Louis. He even had it sumptuously decorated for the reception of Emperor Charles V. More important, François commissioned Pierre Lescot and Jean Goujon to replace the whole medieval hodgepodge with a new palace designed with all the Classical order and elegance dictated by a recently acquired Renaissance taste. Alas, the walls of François' Louvre had scarcely begun to rise when the King died in 1547. But in his lifetime this art-loving monarch had imported from Italy not only such masters as Leonardo da Vinci, Sebastiano Serlio, Rosso Fiorentino, Andrea del Sarto, and Primaticcio, but also some of the finest masterworks ever to grace the Louvre's collections. And while amassing canvases by Titian and Raphael, as well as by Leonardo, he also sponsored a major new style—the School of Fontainebleau—whose Mannerist qualities can be seen in the bronze relief by Cellini reproduced on page 8.

Henri II, François' son and successor, continued the construction already under way at the Louvre, which gave the Cour Carrée the two right-angle wings forming its southwest corner. Here the revived language of Greco-Roman antiquity—as articulated in the architecture of Lescot and the sculptural reliefs of Goujon—is spoken fluently, albeit with a strong French accent. But small as François I's Louvre may be, relative to the total, it witnessed vast amounts of history. It was here, in the Salle des Cariatides decorated by Goujon, that Mary Stuart and François II celebrated their marriage in 1559. Five years later, the Queen Mother, Catherine de' Medici, asked Philibert Delorme to build nearby—at a distance of 500 meters—a separate palace for her own use. This became the Tuileries, an enormous and much more Italianate structure that also remained largely unfinished at its sponsor's death. What was completed in the 16th century consisted of the central pavilion and two adjacent wings, plus a long, narrow gallery along the Seine embankment intended to provide a protected passage between the Louvre and the Tuileries.

In 1572, at the height of France's Religious Wars, another marriage took place in the Louvre, this time between a Protestant—Henri, King of Navarre—and Marguerite de Valois, the daughter of Henri II and Catherine de' Medici. Since the event brought all of France's leading Huguenots to the capital, it served to

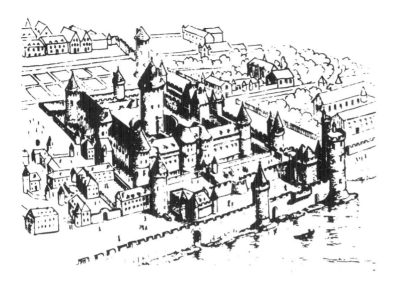

left: This reconstruction made by Paris' Musée Carnavalet suggests how the Gothic Louvre appeared in the time of Charles V (r. 1364–80), almost two hundred years after Philippe Auguste (r. 1180–1223) had built it on the right bank of the Seine as part of the French capital's defense system. Although still very much a militaristic complex of stout walls and towers enclosing a square courtyard and a tall, round *donjon*, or "keep," the old bastion had by the 15th century begun to acquire certain internal characteristics of royal comfort and civility. See also page 12.

below: By 1846, when this bird's-eye view was made of the Tuileries and the Louvre, the Cour Carrée had been completed, and so had Napoleon I's wing (on the left running parallel to the Seine), along with the Arc de Triomphe du Carrousel. But the two great palaces remained separate entities, connected only by the long, relatively narrow gallery-passageway bordering the Seine, commenced in the third quarter of the 16th century by Catherine de' Medici and finished at the end of the century by Henri IV. It was in this part of the Louvre that so much of France's artistic life unfolded in the 17th and 18th centuries, with artists living on the lower floors and the regular "salons" held under the high tunnel vault of the 442-meter Grande Galerie on the top floor. Hardly had vast new construction made the Louvre and the Tuileries a single palace when the latter burned during the Communard insurrection of 1871. See also pages 12, 13 and 312.

spark the notorious Saint Bartholomew's Day Massacre. But when the Valois line died out with the murder of Marquerite's brother Henri III (1574–89), Henri de Navarre became the first Bourbon monarch of France, gaining the throne only by abjuring Protestantism in favor of the Catholic faith.

The new dynasty also began at the Louvre, where Henri IV moved in 1594 and shortly thereafter recommenced work on the Tuileries. To the palace itself he added the Pavillon de Flore, now the southwesternmost terminus of the Louvre, and completed the long gallery parallel to the Seine. As finished, this provided space for shops and ateliers at the first two levels and above them the covered passage originally desired by Catherine. In the lower accommodations Cardinal Richelieu installed the royal mint and printing works. Later in the 17th century, however, Louis XIV assigned the spaces to the army of artists employed in his service—painters, sculptors, architects, furniture makers—which gave the Louvre a kind of direct association with the living arts that it would retain until the Napoleonic Empire in the early 19th century. Among the palace's most illustrious inhabitants must be counted Le Moyne, Pigalle, Boucher, Chardin, Fragonard, Greuze, David, and

left: The Louvre's Salle des Cariatides takes its name from the female figures carved by Jean Goujon in 1550 as supports for the musicians' gallery in what Pierre Lescot designed to be the ballroom in that part of the Louvre built under Henri II. Obviously inspired by the caryatids on the Athenian acropolis, the column-figures witness the extent to which France had abandoned its Gothic heritage in favor of Renaissance Classicism. So do the round-headed vaults, which replaced the exposed beams *(plafond à la française)* that originally supported the ceiling. The bronze relief above the gallery — entitled *Diana the Huntress* — was made by Benvenuto Cellini as the tympanum over the Porte Dorée at Fontainebleau. In the end, however, it went into the main gate at the Château d'Anet, the home of Henri II's mistress, Diane de Poitiers, who was Catherine de' Medici's great rival and one of the most powerful women in 16th-century France. The attenuated lines of the reclining nude reflect the Mannerist style of the School of Fontainebleau. See also pages 188, 189.

right: As elsewhere in the 16th-century Louvre, Jean Goujon was responsible for the sculptural work on the barrel vault of Henri II's staircase.

Prud'hon. Living in the Louvre meant official recognition, in addition to the material benefit of quarters furnished and maintained by the crown.

Upon his accession to the throne, Louis XIII decided to enlarge the Valois Louvre and commissioned Lemercier to double the size of the Cour Carrée. The architect accomplished his task by extending the western wing constructed by Lescot—actually repeating it—and by connecting the two parts with a magnificent, imperial-domed clock tower. This established the basic module for the dimensions finally given the ancient heart of the Louvre. It also doomed all that remained of the Gothic structure, including the much-admired staircase built by Raymond du Temple for Charles V.

Louis XIII and his Prime Minister, Richelieu, also undertook to embellish the 442-meter passageway-gallery leading along the Seine from the Louvre to the Tuileries. Here, on the wall sections between windows, Jacques Fouquières painted 96 views of France's principal towns. For the long barrel vault, Poussin was summoned from Rome in 1641. Unfortunately, intrigue at the French court drove 17th-century France's greatest painter back to Rome after only a year in the Louvre. His designs were finally carried out much later by Boulogne, but the whole decorative program fell into neglect and finally disappeared at the end of the 18th century.

When the twenty-one-year-old Louis XIV took up residence in the Louvre in 1659, the palace entered a brief period of exceptional brilliance. As early as 1653 Anne of Austria, the Queen Mother and Regent during Louis' minority, had begun to prepare two magnificent apartments, one for winter (now disappeared) and another for summer. Installed in the Petite Galerie built by Catherine de' Medici at the outer angle of the two Lescot wings, the Petite Galerie with its ceiling painted by Romanelli survives as the ground floor under the present Galerie d'Apollon. This majestic hall came about after 1661, when a fire ruined the original Galerie des Rois. As decorated by Le Brun, it provided a preview of the splendor that its royal and artistic creators would achieve at Versailles.

While at the Louvre, the young Louis XIV began his long career as a prodigious lover of women and as the powerful patron of Molière, one of the true geniuses of French civilization. For fifteen years, beginning in 1658, Molière would dazzle the court with endlessly inventive diversions, among them his own enduring comedies of wit and social satire. On January 17, 1671, *Psyché*, which Molière wrote in collaboration with Lully, Quinault, and Corneille, served to inaugurate the Salle des Machines, a vast hall (seating an audience of 6,000!) whose name suggests the elaborate engineering needed to mount the productions the King's theatrical tastes demanded.

In 1662 the open area outside the Salle des Machines, lying between the Tuileries and the Louvre, be-

left: From the 17th-century Louvre survive the ceilings in the apartment that Anne d'Autriche, mother of Louis XIV, had prepared in 1653–55 for her own use. The themes from Classical mythology, the stucco enframements by Michel Anguier, and the trompe-l'oeil pictorial composition by Romanelli all had their inspiration in Italy and would, in turn, inspire the great decorative programs at Versailles.

science, painting, and sculpture. It was also in the Louvre that Le Brun organized the royal picture collection, numbering some 423 works in 1692, from which the King would draw for the decoration of Versailles and his other residences, such as Marly. Installed in the Galerie d'Apollon and neighboring spaces, this depository could not be called a museum in the strictest sense, but permission to visit and view the collection was scarcely more difficult to obtain than in a public institution.

When Louis XIV mounted the throne, he owned fewer than 200 paintings. The holdings expanded rapidly, however, when Colbert, Louis' astute Finance Minister, took advantage of the banker Jabach's difficulties to acquire, for the sum of 220,000 *livres,* both his hoard of 5,542 master drawings, which Bernini admired so much, and 101 paintings that Jabach had bought when the English Parliament sold off Charles I's art collection, which included the collection originally assembled by the Dukes of Mantua, once considered the most beautiful in Italy. Colbert then enriched these acquisitions with the works that Jabach had sold to Mazarin, Louis' Prime Minister until the Cardinal's death in 1661. From him came the sensual *Antiope* by Correggio (page 183).

The life of art penetrated still more deeply into the Louvre when the long water-side gallery connecting the palace to the Tuileries became, from 1699 to 1725, the site of the annual exhibitions of painting and sculpture sponsored by the Académie des Beaux-Arts. From 1726 until 1848 the event took place in the Louvre's Salon Carré, whence the name "Salon" for the official exhibitions that did so much to give France its primacy in art.

Under the Regency, Louis XV (r. 1715–74) lived in the Tuileries from 1716 to 1722, before following the precedent of his great-grandfather and taking up residence at Versailles. The Salle des Machines was demolished in 1725 to make way for a hall designed for "spiritual concerts," performed during Lent while the Opéra was closed. But another theatre came to the site in 1760, which housed first the Opéra itself and then, temporarily in 1770, the Comédie-Française. Here too was held the historic "apotheosis" of the aged Voltaire, crowned with laurel and proclaimed for his living genius.

At the insistence of disgusted Parisians, the Marquis de Marigny, Louis XVI's fine arts advisor and the brother of Mme de Pompadour, concluded the long-interrupted work on the Cour Carrée, ridding the Colonnade and its side wings of the population of squatters who had been encamped there for generations.

On October 6, 1789, royalty once again took up residence in the Tuileries, this time forced there by the Revolutionary mob, who to assuage their hunger brought

came known as the Place du Carrousel, for the entertainment offered there in celebration of the new Dauphin, born to Louis XIV and his Queen, Marie-Thérèse of Spain.

Two years later Louis commissioned the architect Le Vau to transform and enlarge the Tuileries to suit the monarch's growing sense of himself as *le Roi Soleil.* From this modification came the present Louvre's Pavillon de Marsan. Meanwhile, Le Nôtre gave the Tuileries Gardens the superb form they retain even today. In a further campaign, initiated in 1665, the Cour Carrée acquired its definitive, grandiose dimensions. Now the talents of Bernini, Rainaldi, François Mansart, Cottard, and Le Vau were all consulted, but in the end it was Claude Perrault, Le Vau, and Le Brun who devised the majestic west façade known as la Colonnade, built from 1667 to 1670. Here the French realized their ultimate formulation of Renaissance Classicism—monumental, sober, and serene. To accommodate the grandeur of the new elevations, the attic of Lescot's west wing was replaced on its east façade by a full story embellished with columns and pilasters.

Sadly, much of the new construction remained open to the sky until the third quarter of the 18th century. The abandonment of the Louvre resulted from the King's determination to build Versailles and to transfer the court there, a move that took place in 1683. With this the Louvre itself—apart from the Tuileries—ceased to be a royal residence and began to assume its cultural role. From 1672 to 1699 it housed, successively, the French Academy and the academies for architecture, from Versailles "the baker, his wife and the little apprentice." Now Marie-Antoinette returned to the small apartment that in 1784 the great *ébéniste* Riesener had furnished for her—to what purpose remains a mystery. Thus, it was from the Tuileries that Louis XVI and his family set off on the ill-fated flight that ended with their arrest at Varennes on June 20, 1791. In the confused aftermath the mob stormed and attacked the Tuileries on August 10, 1792, killing 600 of the 900 Swiss guards employed by the royal family. While the King and Queen languished in the Temple and ultimately went to the guillotine (1793), the Revolutionary Convention sat in the Tuileries theatre and the Comité du Salut Public occupied the royal suites, decorating them with pikes and phrygian caps!

The Revolutionary government also put into effect a project envisioned by the *ancien régime* as early as 1776—the transformation of the long passageway-gallery of Catherine de' Medici and Henri IV into a public museum. Opened on April 10, 1793, the museum displayed the great wealth of the former royal collections. Once augmented by the war booty brought by Napoleon Bonaparte from his campaigns in Italy and elsewhere in Europe, the Louvre indeed became the premier museum of the world, a status it did not lose even when the confiscated treasures were returned to their rightful owners.

The all-conquering Napoleon installed himself in the Tuileries, where he served as First Consul, beginning in 1800, and then, from 1804, as Emperor of France. For his coronation in Notre-Dame, the parvenu monarch brought Pope Pius VII from Rome, lodging him in the Pavillon de Flore. On April 2, 1810, the marriage of the Emperor to the Archduchess Marie-Louise of Austria was celebrated in the Louvre's Salon Carré, following a long procession made by the wedding party through the old gallery—the Grande Galerie—now a well-stocked museum.

Napoleon used the Tuileries as his official residence until the Battle of Waterloo in 1815 made him Emperor of nothing but the tiny, remote island of Saint Helena. Meanwhile, the Eagle had a profound impact on both the Tuileries and the Louvre, which became the center of the Imperial court. With the aid of architects Percier and Fontaine, he built the beautiful Arc de Triomphe du Carrousel precisely where Louis XIV had erected the temporary carousel in 1662. It once bore a quadriga formed by the famed gilt-bronze horses taken from Saint Marc's in Venice. More important, Napoleon had the same architects draw up plans for the unification of the two palaces. Of this project only one wing was completed, now an extension of the arm that reaches, along the Rue de Rivoli, to the Pavillon de Marsan. In addition, the Cour Carrée was finally brought to conclusion and the Grande Galerie redecorated. In the Tuileries, Percier and Fontaine arranged a new theatre and a chapel, while also fitting out the Salle des Maréchaux.

Under the Restoration, Louis XVIII moved into Napoleon's rooms and even slept in his bed, bothering only to change the arms. There he died in 1824. During his feeble reign, Louis XVI's brother had about 300 paintings redistributed from the Louvre to various churches and provincial musems. He also ordered that the *Venus de Milo* be placed in the Louvre just as it had been discovered. In the interim, the third brother of Louis XVI, the Comte d'Artois, found accommodations in the Pavillon de Marsan, which gave its name to the ultrarightists who attached themselves to the future Charles X, their extreme policies finally bringing an end to the long Bourbon dynasty in 1830.

If the July Monarchy of Louis-Philippe proved bourgeois and lackluster, the court led by Napoleon III and Empress Eugénie from 1852 to 1870 became its total antithesis. Brilliant and lavish, it ushered in an era that gave Paris its enduring reputation for lights and gaiety. In addition to commissioning Baron Haussmann to make the French capital the most beautiful city in the world, the Second Empire also brought the Louvre and the Tuileries together at last and from the Tuileries side gave the complex the appearance it has today.

Earlier, the Second Republic had undertaken the restoration of the Galerie d'Apollon, where Delacroix painted the central medallion, *Apollo Slaying the Python.* Also at this time, Duban redecorated the Salon Carré. But a major overhaul got underway once Napoleon III came to the throne. With Visconti in charge, the gaggle of houses that had long cluttered the large inner court separating the Louvre and the Tuileries were demolished. This cleared the way for the first stone of the new Louvre to be laid on July 25, 1852. When Visconti died a year later, Lefuel continued his plans but modified them to create the ornate façades sometimes characterized as "a confectioner's masterpiece." Not content merely to build, Napoleon III and his architects decided to rebuild, often destroying old, stylistically authentic structures so as to replace them with modern pastiches. They even rehabilitated completely Lemercier's Clock Tower in the Cour Carrée. On the interior of the Tuileries, Lefuel created on one of Le Vau's terraces three famous salons—Rose, Blue, and Green—all triumphs of a revivalist, synthetic manner called "Louis XVI-Impératrice."

Hardly had the Louvre and the Tuileries been joined when the latter was put to the torch on the evening of May 24, 1871, the victim of the Communard insurrection that broke out in the aftermath of the Franco-Prussian War, which humiliated France and forced Napoleon III to abdicate. Although gutted, the palace could have been reconstructed from the walls that remained standing. However, the Third Republic preferred to demolish. Only the Pavillon de Marsan was rebuilt, from Lefuel's plans for its counterpart opposite, the Pavillon de Flore. With the Tuileries gone, the great arms that were extended westward from the Louvre now embrace, not Catherine de' Medici's palace, but rather the world public that the modern museum receives in vastly increasing numbers every day.

As a public museum, the Louvre has continued to build its collections both by purchase and by legacy. Among the most famous bequests are those of Sauvageot, La Caze, de la Salle, Caillebotte, Rothschild, David-Weill, and Gachet. In the realm of antiquities, the Clercq-de-Boisgelin estate alone added 3,500 treasures to the museum's holdings. The National Museum Board and

above: Nothing remains above ground of the Gothic Louvre portrayed in the early 15th century by the Limbourg brothers in *Les Très Riches Heures du Duc de Berry.* The *enceinte* of the old *château fort* occupied a site that is now the southwest quadrant of the Cour Carrée (the near right quadrant in the photograph below). See also page 312.

right: The new Louvre was commissioned by François I, one year before his death in 1547. With full justice, the façade reproduced here is considered to be one of the great masterworks of the French Renaissance. Pierre Lescot prepared the design, but while adopting the new Greco-Roman vocabulary of the Italian *rinascimento,* he articulated it with a pronounced French accent. Rhythmically punctuated by three lightly projecting bays, one at either end and another at the center, the elevation rises to three stories, each endowed with its own variation upon the Corinthian order: at the ground level, arches flanked by pilasters and paired columns, on the *pre-mier étage,* alternating triangular and round-headed pediments, in addition to Ionic volutes integrated with Corinthian capitals; and for the attic, richly sculptural reliefs bracketing low windows separated by unfluted pilasters.

below: The Louvre, which was commenced in 1190, assumed its final form only in the late 19th century, after Napoleon I and Napoleon III had extended the long arms that reach forward from the Cour Carrée, built on the site of the original Louvre, and after the Tuileries had been put to the torch by a Communard mob in 1871. This palace, the masterwork of Philibert Delorme, the greatest of France's Renaissance architects, spanned the space now left open in the foreground between the Pavillon de Marsan on the left and the Pavillon de Flore on the right. Although rebuilt in the 19th century, these westernmost terminals of the Louvre were, like the far side of the Cour Carrée (see pages 1, 2), constructed in the 17th century. See also page 312.

the Friends of the Louvre oversee and guide the fortunes of an institution that is a living tribute to the glory of France.

The resources of the Louvre are such that a lifetime of study would only scratch their surface. On the following pages appears a sample of first the palace itself and then the painting and sculpture it contains, the various pieces chosen to convey the essence of the major periods in the history of art. Of course, the Louvre also serves as a treasure house of crown jewels, precious enamels, porcelain, furniture, textiles, and master drawings. The selection of masterpieces reproduced here can be regarded merely as an invitation to visit, revisit, and experience directly the world's greatest art museum.

The Ancient Civilizations of the Mediterranean East

Mesopotamia, Egypt, Crete. These were the regions in the ancient world whose artistic and intellectual values made the eastern Mediterranean the cradle of Western civilization.

Whether nourished by the fertile valleys of the Nile, Tigris, and Euphrates rivers, as in Egypt and Mesopotamia, or by the sea, as in Crete, the art produced among the earliest civilizations of the eastern Mediterranean shared one common characteristic: a magical and commemorative function. Inseparable from religion, objects and images were not created either for self-expression or for aesthetic pleasure. Rather, they were believed to possess "power." The Sumerian statues, for example, found at the Ishtar Temple in Mari reproduce the features of the donor so as to place him under divine, eternal protection (page 16). In the same way, the objects represented on the walls of Egyptian tombs are substitutes for the real things that the deceased would need in the world beyond.

Commemorative art provided perpetual reminders of important events—battles and hunts—that occurred in the life of a great personage.

As the least of its objectives, art could be ornamental. Artists, once they had served the gods, the dead, and their sovereign, had the opportunity to abandon rules and conventions and simply address themselves to the embellishment of homes and ordinary objects. Free of the hieratism required in official art, they could indulge private fantasies, choose their own subjects, and treat them as they wished.

Each country, of course, had its own resources and customs, and to a large degree these determined that nation's artistic personality and development.

Mesopotamia

The Sumerians were the first people to settle in Mesopotamia in the region lying between the Tigris and Euphrates. The oldest Sumerian art, found at Susa, dates back to the 4th millennium B.C., but the high period extended from the first Ur dynasty (c. 2700 B.C.) to the first Babylonian dynasty, which from 1830 to 1530 B.C. constituted a climactic moment.

The absence of stone in Mesopotamia imposed certain limitations on the art of the Sumerians. Obliged to use sun-dried brick, they built walls thick enough to resist bad weather and allowed only small openings so as not to weaken the structure. But even with such material, they learned to vault interior spaces. For sculpture, however, the Sumerians had to import stone, which restricted them to small-scale works. It also resulted in figures with disportionately small bodies relative to the heads (page 16).

Around the middle of the 2nd millennium B.C., Mesopotamia and adjacent regions suffered a series of incursions from the East. Of all the invaders, it was the Hittites who would play a significant role in the history of art. Indo-Europeans established in Anatolia from the early 2nd millennium, they seized Babylonia and put an end to its first dynasty, led by Hammurabi. In their art, the Hittites followed Sumerian models but added an Asian touch, which made them the connecting link between eastern and western Asia, a link that in time would connect even with Greece by way of Egypt and Achaeminid Persia.

Under the Kassites, who succeeded the Hittites and held power in Mesopotamia for five centuries, artists did little more than repeat old Sumerian themes. Somewhat to the north, the Hurrites founded the Kingdom of Mitanni, which would challenge Egypt until royal intermarriage allied the rival nations and produced an artistic exchange.

Then, in the 12th century B.C., new Indo-European invasions made a clean sweep of the Mediterranean basin. This brought the People of the Sea, by way of Libya and the Mediterranean islands and into northern Syria, Asia Minor, and even Europe. Related to this migration was the capture of Hellas by the Dorians. An invincible force, the People of the Sea overwhelmed the Hittite empire, destroyed Troy, ravaged Sidon on the Phonecian coast, and left a contingent in Palestine—the Philistines.

Still another power would rise—Assyria—this time in Akkad north of Babylonia. Progressively, the Assyrians asserted their authority until, around the 9th century B.C., they became the masters of the Mesopotamian world, from the Persian Gulf to the mouth of the Nile. Finding its model in Sumerian tradition, Assyrian art began to bloom during the 9th-century reign of Assurnasirpal and reached full flower two centuries later under Assurbanipal. A royal, official art, it served mainly to decorate vast palaces with endless series of bas-reliefs, the whole scheme of palace and embellishment designed to glorify the monarch and his exploits, these being for the most part war and hunting (page 50). Thematically, it is the animals, both real and fantastic, that dominate this art (pages 48, 49, 50). As in old Sumeria, the human figures fell into what had become a classic mould, requiring that the details of hair and harness be treated with extreme care. Quite apart from its realistic elements, Assyrian art seems animated with the very breath of life, reflecting the aggressive spirit and energy of the sovereigns who sponsored it.

Egypt

The earliest dynasties that unified Egypt into a single nation also established the aesthetic principles by which Egyptian art would be governed throughout the Old

Neolithic Times—7th Century B.C.

Kingdom (2720–2065 B.C.) and on to the end of the Middle Kingdom (2065–1580 B.C.)

Funerary in purpose, Egyptian art reflects its creators' obsessive preoccupation with death, which, for Egyptians, marked the beginning of true life, a life justifying the construction of the most beautiful dwellings—tombs—furnished with the most essential of everyday objects.

The belief of the Egyptians in immortality, their rigid system of religion, and a strongly hierarchical social structure gave the art of the Old and Middle Kingdoms an immobile and hieratic quality. All statues depict their subjects in repose, realistically rendered yet idealized.

The New Kingdom dates from 1580 B.C., when the Hyksos invaded and occupied the country for a century and a half. The 18th Dynasty that resumed power then undertook the conquest of neighboring territory so as to gain a protective barrier against further invasion. Around 1450 B.C., the Pharaohs succeeded in extending Egypt's frontiers south as far as the Nile's Fourth Cataract and to the Euphrates in the northeast. At the same time, Egyptian art entered its last great period and the most sumptuous of all. But the triumphant luxury of this art, reflecting influence from Egypt's new Oriental subjects, witnessed the advent of a taste that would lead to decadence.

The New Kingdom also produced builders as formidable as those of the Old Kingdom. But while the Pharaohs of the 4th Dynasty had each constructed a single great monument—the pyramid enclosing the tomb—with an attached funerary temple, the New Kingdom monarchs would separate the two elements, the tomb carved out of the rock wall in a valley near Luxor and the temple placed at some distance in the desert. Constructed on a vast scale, the latter—such as the monuments at Thebes and Karnak—were designed to accommodate religious feasts observed with long processions.

Statuary assumed all the grandeur of the architectural ensembles it was meant to adorn, taking the form of colossal portraits of the King, sphinxes with the sovereign's face, and effigies of favorites permitted to share the sanctuary and the offerings brought there.

A notable feature of New Kingdom art is its aestheticism. For the first time, beauty was sought for itself, resulting in a stylized attenuation that endows bodies with remarkable grace and delicacy.

But overproduction and narrow conventions led to an occasional loss of power. No doubt these tendencies would also have brought serious decline, but for the arrival of that singular monarch—Amenophis IV (Akhenaton)—who suddenly changed everything. Around 1370 Akhenaton undertook a revolution that was both religious and artistic. The so-called Amarna style that it produced gave Egypt some of its most unforgettable masterpieces (pages 40,41,43,44). The whole experience, however, was deemed heretical and would not survive Akhenaton's own reign, even though it did reinvigorate the Egyptian creative spirit. Indeed, the art that came in the immediate aftermath of Amarna is unquestionably the most admired in the entire history of ancient Egypt. Once again classic in manner, it now displayed a new freedom and warmth not seen before the heretical interlude.

Fifty years after the death of Akhenaton, in the reign of Ramses II (1301–1235 B.C.), Egyptian decoration began to lose both its truth and its fantasy. While still possessed of a striking grace, Ramsid statuary reveals the germs of decadence. Genuine decline set in before 1200, at the end of the 19th Dynasty, and would accelerate from then on.

Crete

Cretan civilization began to take form in the 4th millennium B.C. but reached its mature, historic phase later than Mesopotamia and Egypt. Meanwhile, Crete played a major role in the Mediterranean by making its influence felt not only in Greece but even in the land of the Pharaohs. The art of Crete differs from that of the last two regions by its freedom and decorativeness, both of which qualities can be seen in numerous pottery vessels made for everyday use. While borrowing certain motifs from Egypt and the ancient Cycladic civilizations (pages 22, 23), Cretan artists interpreted them with a liveliness all their own. Native themes, meanwhile, appeared wherever the Cretans carried on trade—mainly the bull representing the famous Minotaur, which had long formed the heart of Minoan (Cretan) civilization. Movement and brilliant fantasy are the salient features of Minoan art.

Around 1600 B.C, with the prodigious spread of its commerce and art, Crete entered a golden age. Greek Argolis, on the Peloponnesus, succumbed to Minoan art without having suffered military conquest. Thus, the palaces at Mycenae and Tiryns rivaled the wealth of the immense, labyrinthine palace at Knossos. Eventually, Cretan civilization could claim all of continental Greece, while also reinforcing long-established relations with Cyprus, Syria, and Egypt. Then, in 1400 B.C., in the aftermath of events still not fully understood—insurrection or an earthquake succeeded by foreign invasion—Crete disappeared from the artistic map. However, its civilization continued in Argolis and at Mycenae, which assumed leadership in the Aegean world, establishing outposts everywhere in the Mediterranean. But deprived of its source of inspiration, Mycenaean art weakened and merely survived for the two centuries that elapsed between the destruction of the palace at Knossos and the Dorian invasion.

15

From the earliest times
the worshiper
and the worshiped
assume aesthetic forms
expressive of
primitive society's
profound sense
of the magical forces
that seem
to govern all life
and all death

Steward Ebil-il. c. 3000–2500 B.C.
Mari, Mesopotamia. Alabaster, height o.525m/1'8¾".

left: The statue *Steward Ebil-il* was carved for the only purpose a human representation had throughout the history of Sumer. A sacred image placed in the sanctuary, it was meant to perpetuate an individual's adoration of his god. But that "eternal life" of the devout was irrevocably lost whenever the image suffered mutilation, which is why, in time of war, the victors never failed to attack the effigies of the vanquished. And the statue of Ebil-il did not altogether escape such vandalism. Early in antiquity it was thrown down the temple steps onto the stone courtyard below. Modern archaeologists participating in the excavations conducted by André Parrot, director of the Louvre, found the fragments of the broken form in the very spot where the impact had scattered them. Miraculously, the head had not been hammered, and even the nose, the feature most vulnerable to desecrators' vindictiveness, remained intact. A unique offering and a human evocation like no other, the statue is probably a realistic portrayal. Certainly, it cannot be mistaken for any other high official of the kingdom of Mari, where Ebil-il served in all likelihood as a chief minister. But while the sculptor retained his subject's most salient and identifying features, he treated them in a vigorously schematic fashion, as in the strongly projected nose and in the dilation of those enormous pupils, whose intensity makes the eyes seem as fascinated as they are fascinating. The attitude of the body, on the other hand, conforms to an established convention for the representation of the pious. Fixedly immobile and seated upon a wicker stool, Ebil-il wears the *kaunakes*—the ritual vestment of the Sumerians—whose tiers of "tongues" represent a sheep's skin. This wooly skirt, by contrast, brings out the smoothness of the flesh, with all its delicate modeling in an alabaster of extremely fine grain. The very simplicity of the prototype imposed a certain economy of means that the artist used with superb skill so as to obtain an effect of great monumentality. As the bulging mass of the knees rhymes with the spherical volume of the shaved head, the slope of the shoulders echoes the shape of the hands joined in a sign of devotion. The statue of Ebil-il constitutes a wondrous witness to a civilization that knew how to ally power with delicacy, strength with softness. The ineffable charm of the smile sketched upon the lips endows the steward with an essential characteristic of Mari art—sensitivity.

Anatolian Idol. c. 5500 B.C.
Glazed terra-cotta, height 0.28m/11".

right: Dating from about 5500 B.C., the *Anatolian Idol* fascinates as much by its extreme antiquity as by its artistic quality. In 1960 a team of English archaeologists working near Haçilar, Turkey, uncovered the remains of a civilization that had flourished in the 6th and 5th millennia B.C. It was a remarkable discovery that brought to light one of the oldest of all known cultural centers. Unfortunately, this archaeological feat gave rise to clandestine digging, and whole lots of objects began to appear on the market. No doubt the piece reproduced here, which the Louvre acquired only recently, had such a provenance. It possesses the same characteristics as those of the glazed terra-cotta figurines and anthropomorphic vases found by the English, which permits the present work to be dated with reasonable security. Enveloped in the mystery that still surrounds our knowledge and imagination concerning the remote reaches of the neolithic age, the *Anatolian Idol* seems to retain something of the magical power that its creators would have attributed to it. In order to make the most effective representation of the mother goddess symbol of fertility, the carver emphasized the amplitude of the breasts and the swelling of the abdomen, as if these portions of the anatomy contained the promise of all generations to come.

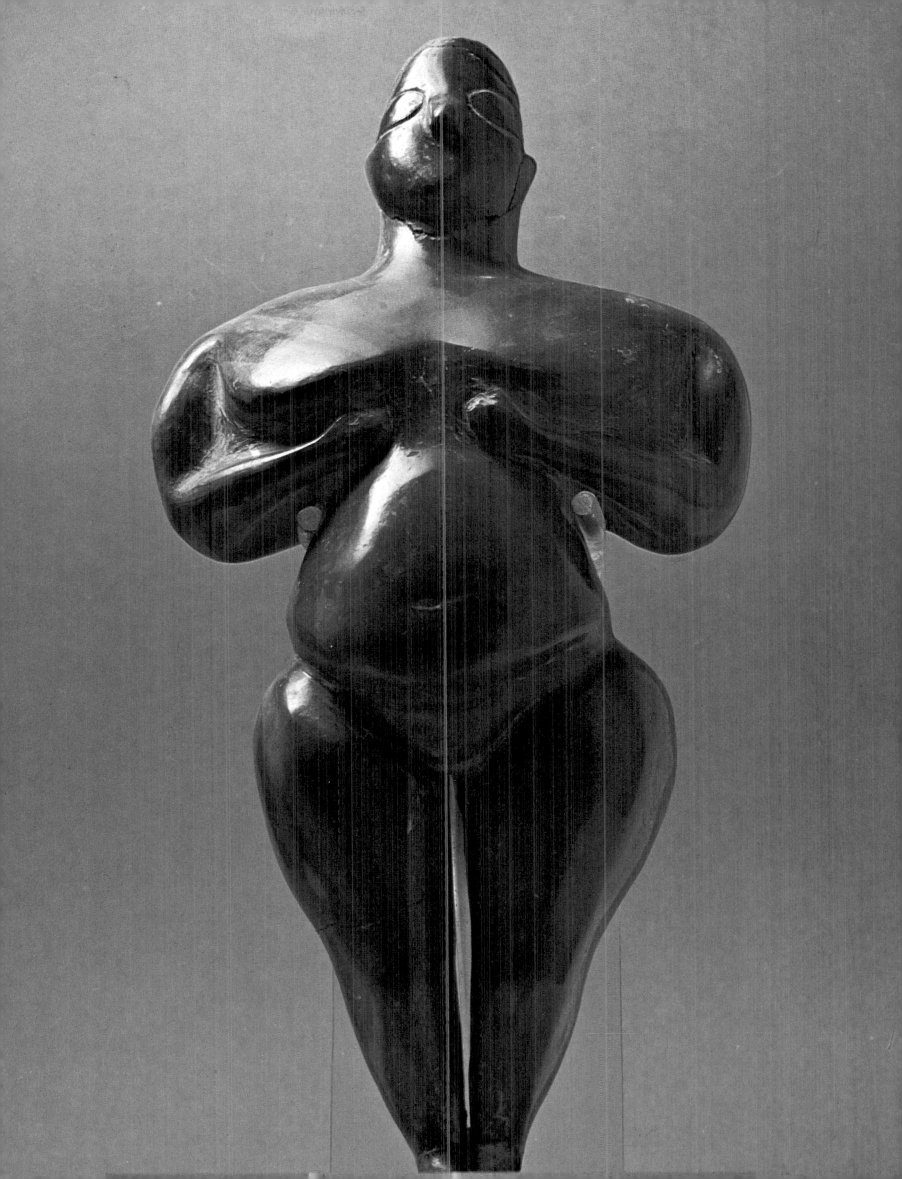

War lords surviving
the bloody chaos
of ancient times
found mighty empires,
while their artists
narrate the heroic deeds
in carved stone reliefs

below: The *Stele of the Vultures,* the earliest of its kind to survive from Mesopotamia, is a major artistic monument as well as a historic document of inestimable value. It was erected by Eannatum, king of Lagash, to commemorate his victory over the neighboring city of Umma and to solemnize the treaty that ended the conflict. Of the six fragments that survive, all arranged in horizontal registers, that of the military victors is the most interesting, since the piece not only invites stylistic analysis of its qualities as two-dimensional sculpture, but also permits us to measure the degree of military sophistication then attained by the Sumerians. At the head of the soldiery marches the armed and helmeted king, his body covered by a skin worn on the bias. Behind the leader, trampling ground paved with the enemy dead, which vultures have begun to dismember, the fighting men of Lagash advance behind lances and copper shields. To create the impression of numbers, of power and discipline, the sculptor made a timid attempt at perspective, overlapping the lances and stacking them in tiers of six each. Thus, the whole story comes through with all the rigorous order that the Sumerians liked to cultivate.

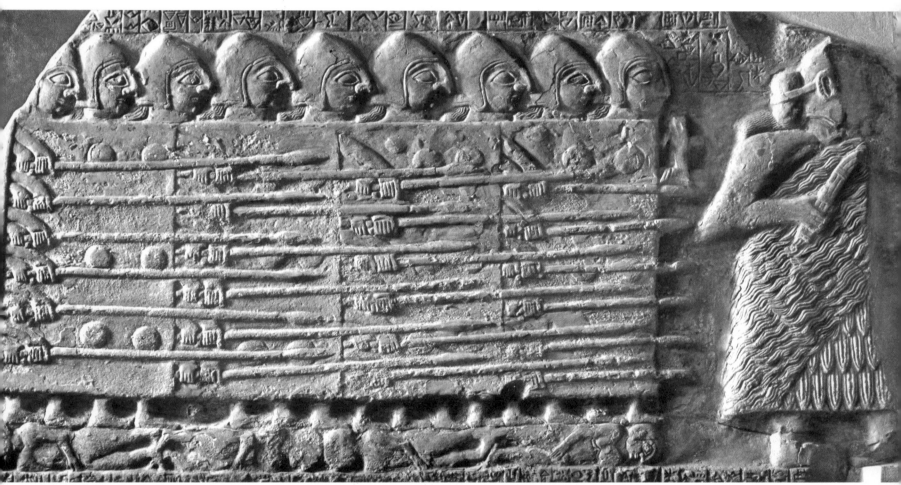

Stele of the Vultures (detail). 3000–2500 B.C. Tello, Mesopotamia. Limestone, height 1.88m/6'2".

right: The *Stele of Naram-Sin* celebrates the victory of the King whose name it bears. Erected originally in the city of the god Shamash, it was found at Susa, where it had been transported some thousand years later as a trophy of war. The martial figure of the sovereign dominates the scene both by his size and by his position. Naram-Sin has arrived at the foot of a boldly schematized mountain above which shine rayed stars, symbolic of divine favor. By the very imperiousness of his look, he petrifies the enemy army, while a double column of his warriors climb implacably toward an assault upon the bastion. About a century and a half later than the *Stele of the Vultures* (above), the *Stele of Naram-Sin* manifests a much greater freedom in technique as well as in composition. The tiered arrangement of the figures produces an effect of remarkable equilibrium. It also corresponds to objective reality since the battle unfolds in mountainous terrain.

far right: The *Knife of Jebel El-Arak* is one of the oldest works in the Louvre. The motifs carved on the sleeve evoke a struggle between warriors with shaved heads and others with long, plaited hair. Also represented are two fleets of boats. Those with curved bottoms (below) are Egyptian, while those with raised, hornlike ends (at center) belong to the aggressors. A work of rare perfection, the *Knife of Jebel El-Arak* reveals how early the art of bas-relief, which had its original development in ivory, produced real masters, whose achievement would spread to other media and expand to vast scale. The piece also proves that the ancient Egyptians had already become the peerless craftsmen that they would remain throughout their history.

Stele of Naram-Sin. 2500–2000 B.C.
Susa, Mesopotamia. Pink sandstone, height 2m/6'6¾".

18

below: *War Lord*, an impressive figure 10 centimeters tall, attests to the fact that the artists of Mari, who were great stone carvers, had no less power in small pieces than in large ones. Finely worked in shell, the warrior is represented according to convention, his torso in frontal stance and his head, right arm, and feet in profile. He wears a neck-shield helmet, a skirt in the archaic style, and, over his nude torso, a skin with long tassles that recalls the battle dress of Eannatum in the *Stele of the Vultures* (left).

War Lord. c. 2500 B.C. Mari, Mesopotamia. Shell, height 0.099m/4″.

Knife of Jebel El-Arak. Predynastic era (4000–3000 B.C.). Egypt. Ivory and flint, total length 0.253m/10″.

right: The *Stele of the Serpent King* was found in the actual tomb of a king of the 1st Dynasty (Thinite). Another, identical stele, on which the hieroglyphics were carved in reverse, no doubt functioned as a pendant work at the entrance to the court. The plaque here bears the name of King Ouadji, represented by the serpent relief-carved within an enclosure whose portals and setbacks are realized with great precision. Surmounting the enclosure is a falcon, symbolic of the god Horus, protector of the Egyptian kingdom. The bird is treated in accordance with the principles of Egyptian design, with one foot forward, so as to be visible, and the tail seen as frontal.

Stele of the Serpent King. c. 3000 B.C. Abydos, Egypt. Limestone, height 1.45m/4′9″.

At the same time that
the Pharaohs have themselves
portrayed as sphinxes,
the ateliers of the Nile
display their virtuosity
by developing a potently
realistic style,
thus making the funerary
statue all the more a
double too holy to profane

left: *The Sphinx of Tanis* joins to a lion's body a head carved in the likeness of the sovereign, thus symbolizing the majesty of the Pharaohs. Here the monarch wears the royal headdress—*nemsit*—ornamented with *ureus*, or sacred cobra, but free of the frontal band. Three kings—Apophis, Mineptah, the son of Ramses II, and Osorkon—would subsequently inscribe their names (an act the Egyptians called "usurpation") upon the rose granite of the sphinx, whose nobility and power incontestably mark it as a work of the Old Kingdom.

right: *Seated Scribe,* the most famous masterpiece to survive in Egyptian art, was discovered in 1850 by the French archaeologist Mariette in a tomb at Saqqarah. In the middle of the debris lay five broken statues, but a pair of concealed niches sheltered two other statues. The first, a seated figure, represented an administrator of the province called Kaï. An image that bears no inscription and thus was dubbed the *Seated Scribe* is probably a second portrait of the same Kaï. During the Old Kingdom, sculpture had to conform to certain conventions requiring that men be represented in only three or four established poses and always in the prime of life. The strict geometry to which the artist subjected the *Seated Scribe* accounts for the sense of acute tension that emanates from the personage. In a face animated by a faint, enigmatic smile, the stone-encrusted eyes offer a look of prodigious intensity, made even more pronounced by the slight squint. The figure's right hand, which holds a reed pen, appears ready to write, but the whole statue evokes great intellectual concentration.

The Sphinx of Tanis. Old Kingdom (2720–2260 B.C.). Egypt. Rose granite; height 2.06m, length 4.79m/6'9"x15'8½".

Seated Scribe. c. 2500 B.C. Saqqarah, Egypt. Polychromed limestone, height 0.53m/1'8¾".

Paros. Marble, 0.27m/10¾".

A figure seems ready to come forward from the remote past, then freezes in midstep, implacably claimed by the block it was carved from

Chancellor Nakht. 18th Dynasty (2000–1785 B.C.). Egypt. Wood painted red, height 1.75m/5'9".

left: *Chancellor Nakht* is the jewel of all the monumental wood sculpture to survive from Egypt's Middle Kingdom. It was in 1903 that Chassinat discovered the work in an unviolated tomb at the necropolis of Assiout. The sculpture rested next to another statue of Nakht, but with the subject wearing a wig and a short robe. Following the Assiout find, Capart hypothesized that Egyptian tombs should, in principle, contain at least two effigies for each of the dead. Originally, the image of Nakht no doubt possessed full polychromy, reduced by time to the red underpaint. Thus, the head, which would have been painted, now assumes the pure form of a sphere. Such geometry continues in the long, stiff, trapezoid of the skirt, which is a deliberate evocation of the architectural lines of an obelisk. This stylization, however, does not preclude the almost casual thrust made by the right thumb into a section of the skirt that the hand has brought down from the hip. Even though the pose is in strict accordance with the laws of frontality, it still allows some genuine sense of movement. This makes the figure seem like a man striding forward from the far reaches of another civilization, his extraordinary "presence" emanating from every side.

Inner Chest of the Coffin of Chancellor Nakht (detail). 12th Dynasty (2000–1785 B.C.). Wood, total length 2.14m/7'1¼".

right: Two "mystical eyes," splendidly drawn, ornament the outer wall of the *Coffin of Chancellor Nakht,* found in the course of excavations carried out in the early 20th century in the necropolis of the old principality of Assiout by the French Institute of Oriental Archaeology in Cairo. The hieroglyphics covering the unpainted wood are intaglio-carved and filled with a blue color obtained, no doubt, from crushed lapis. Surrounded by makeup lines, "mystical eyes" frequently appear on the casing of sarcaphogi and on funerary steles. They had a twofold purpose—to allow the deceased to see the offerings left in his tomb and also, by their magical power, to protect the body of the dead from profanation.

Manual dexterity
endows votive figurines
with the spontaneity
of life,
while eternalizing
the image of everyday
as well as
religious experience

right above: *Women Doing Laundry* evinces the close
relations that developed in the late 3rd millennium
B.C. between Cyprus and continental Europe. Until
then under the influence of Anatolia, insular ceramics gradually began to diversify. Terra-cottas
proliferated, for the most part representing scenes
of daily life, as in the laundry with its bevy of chatter-
ing women. Pieces of funerary furniture, such works
were apparently meant to remind the deceased in
the world beyond of domestic events once experienced in the world here below. On the extreme left,
note the image of a woman holding a child in her
arms: it is a figure typical of Cypriot iconography.

right: This *Votive Chariot* of the 2nd millennium B.C.
was found in scattered pieces by the Schaeffer team,
which one by one assembled the two bearded men in
long Syrian tunics, a fragment of the chariot's body
and a wheel, then an axle and two wheels, and finally
the extraordinary horse's head. Phoenician ceramics
yielded a whole series of statuettes on the same order, mostly funerary offerings. Certain of the pieces
are effigies of domestic gods, others temple offerings
made by those unable to afford more costly images
made of stone.

left: This *Female Nude,* modeled by hand, was probably an expiatory figure intended to assure life and
fertility. Representations of the female nude survive
from prehistoric times. At first sketched out in a
summary manner, they progressively reproduced
feminine anatomy with greater fidelity. The huge
eyes, the heavy hair that frames the face and spreads
over the shoulders as it falls, the globelike breasts,
the double necklace encircling the neck—all are
pieces of clay realized by the so-called *pastillage* technique. As in most of the "primitive Venuses," the triangle symbolizes the figure's sexual attributes, but
the curious belt across the hips defies explanation,
even though it often appears on this type of figurine.
Rare for this time is the placement of the image on a
pedestal.

Female Nude. 2500–2000 B.C. Susa, Mesopotamia.
Terra-cotta, height 0.17m/6¾".

Women Doing Laundry. c. 2200 B.C. Vounous, Cyprus. Terra-cotta, height 0.17m/6¾".

Votive Chariot (reconstruction). 3rd century B.C. Ras Shamra, Phoenicia. Yellow and gray frit.

Cast in bronze
or carved
in obdurate dolerite,
the governors of Sumer
perpetuate themselves
in a state of prayer

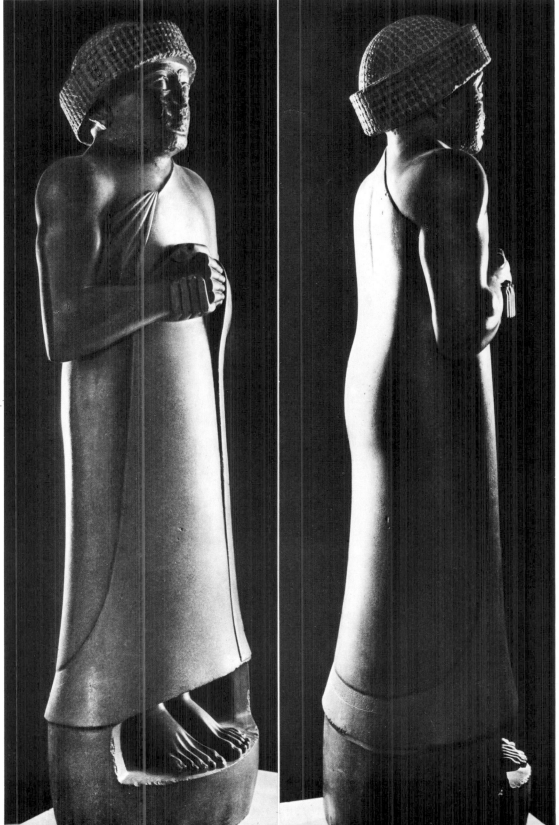

right: *Gudea,* governor of Lagash, is without doubt the person in antiquity who was the most obsessive about having himself portrayed. Of the thirty known statues of Gudea, half are in the Louvre. The one here presents the dignitary standing, in an attitude of humility and devotion. His feet are bare because the sanctuary was a holy place that could not be desecrated by dust from the streets. The arms crossed over the chest seem to contain the form, to close it with the seal of hands strongly clasped in prayer. Leaving one shoulder exposed, the garment falls vertically. Quite apart from the sensitive treatment of the flesh, four folds at the armpits and four at the figure's left elbow suffice to suggest that a man's body inhabits this rigid vestment. In the lightest way possible, the sculptor succeeded in rendering the volume of a muscle, the contour of a shoulder, the smoothness of skin. As for the face, it is that of a great lord, who preferred the durable glory of a Maecenas to the hazards of war. Rubbed and polished to the ultimate perfection, the stone simply implores light to flow over its forms. No material other than dolerite could be so suitable to the expression of human compactness, of tension felt toward the ineffable, of victory over time.

left: *The Worshiper of Larsa,* despite its small size, displays a quality of workmanship that endows the piece with great artistic value. The figure is shown in an attitude of extreme modesty, making a suppliant gesture to the divinity. The space left between the finger tips and the mouth seems to hold all the fervor of prayer. And the plating of gold over the face and hands does not so much reflect a concern for ornament as assume the character of purification brought by precious metal to the human being's most noble parts. At the socle or base, we find, at the front, a small depression intended no doubt to contain incense, on one side a sleeping ram, and on the other a pious figure kneeling before his god.

Human forms
animate inert matter,
which, however,
asserts its density and hardness,
like a symbol of life
in the Ancient Near East

Head of a Youth. 21st century B.C. Tello, Mesopotamia. Diorite, height 0.158m/6¼".

left: This *Neo-Sumerian Statue,* impressive in its power and density despite small dimensions, formed part of the De Clercq collection before it entered the Louvre in 1967 by gift of Comte Boisgelin. What is most immediately striking about Neo-Sumerian statues is the extremely short proportions adopted by their creators, reflecting a choice that may have been originally determined by the nature of the material itself. Lower Mesopotamia held no stone quarries, and the diorite used here had to be imported from Arabia, in large blocks whose length rarely proved sufficient for carving the human figure on a large scale. The fact remains, however, that the physical limitations imposed by the material well served artists whose purpose was not to imitate nature but rather to transcend it, to make visible in their pious effigies the very idea of eternity. It is by this tendency towards abstraction that Neo-Sumerian statues reach across the ages and touch us profoundly.

Neo-Sumerian Statue. 22nd century B.C.
Tello, Mesopotamia. Diorite, height 0.35m/1'1¾".

above: The *Head of a Youth,* probably Ur-Ningirsu, son of Gudea (see page 29), is carved in diorite with all the prodigious mastery possessed by Mesopotamian artists in their work with hard stone. An ovoid form of remarkable purity, the head has the serene and irrefutable power of mineral, as well as the obsessed and secret presence characteristic of Sumerian masterpieces. "The reference to the immemorial, the process that relates the head of a worshiper to a boulder and Gudea to a menhir," explained André Malraux, "is evidently a means of identifying with eternity." This reduction of human forms to the essential, this analogy with the elementary curvature of an egg—but subtly reinvented by the hand of man—evoke directly, across the centuries, one of the great sculptors of our own era—Brancusi. "Sumerian art," Malraux noted further, "moves us by its denial of illusionism, by its free, schematic qualities, all of which are at one with the spirit of modernism."

31

Lion-headed Demon. 22nd–21st century B.C.
Tello, Mesopotamia. Terra-cotta, height 0.13m/5".

An ancient,
royal melancholy
finds release
in the sovereign perfection
of an ovoid shape
and polished pink granite

The *Head of Amenophis III*, whose proportions remain splendid despite the mutilations wrought by the millennia, gives witness to the artistic transformations initiated during the reign of this Pharaoh of the 18th Dynasty (1408–1372 B.C.). The gravity, the serenity, the imperious attitude that artists once attributed to the deified sovereigns now gave way to a subtle charm, to a new idealism tending toward a meditative expression. This more intimate spirituality freely manifests itself even in the royal colossi where abstraction still prevails over naturalism. In the work at left, a rhythmic pattern governs the play of grand planes over the face, with its elongated chin, its drawn-out almond eyes, its lips lightly curled in a dreamy half-smile. Amenophis III wears the "white crown" assumed by the kings of Upper Egypt before the reunification of the realm during the 1st Dynasty. The tall mitre transforms the royal head into a gigantic ovoid form, brought to ultimate perfection by the sweetness and polish of rose granite. The outrages of time, which have reduced the whole of the left half to a leprous state, add a very moving dimension to this work. The contrast simply emphasizes the purity of the part remaining intact, as if, under our very eyes, there surged up from the depths of the past the intimacy of a human countenance.

Head of Amenophis III. 18th Dynasty (1580–1314 B.C.).
Egypt. Rose granite, height 1.70m, 5'7".

Curves and countercurves
animate angular profiles,
linking a pair of objects
to their cultural origins

Ritual Vase. c. 1100 B.C. Amlash, Iran. Glazed terra-cotta, height 0.21m/8¼".

Female Head. c. 1370–1360 B.C. Tel El Amarna, Egypt. Wood, 0.20m/7¾".

left: This *Ritual Vase* in the form of a hump-backed bull, with great horns and plow-like snout, was acquired by the Louvre in 1960. It no doubt originated in the Amlash region as a funerary item, a supposition borne out by Iranian excavations undertaken in 1962 in the same area. Whether in terra-cotta or in metal, the rhytons—vases shaped like animals—are characteristic of Iranian civilization and reveal its artists to have possessed an extraordinary sense of animal reality.

above: This *Female Head,* which surely served as the pinnacle on a harp, exudes, partly by virtue of the empty eye sockets, an air of high aesthetic tension. Could it be that the jut-jawed visage is the portrait of none other than Queen Nefertiti, wife of Amenophis IV (Akhenaton)? Certainly the elongated neck, the cut of the hair, the attenuated lines of chin, nose, and eyebrows conform to a canon of beauty peculiar to the Amarna school.

Bust of an Amarna Princess. c. 1350 B.C. Amarna, Egypt. Painted limestone, height 0.15m/6″.

above: The *Bust of an Amarna Princess,* one of Amenhophis IV's six daughters, expresses with infinite distinction the aristocratic slenderness of an adolescent graced by a disdainful and pouting mouth. The wig consists of a brief cap with stiff, uniform tassles contrasted with heavy tresses tied toward the top with a ribbon. Altogether, three different types of tassle make up a long, thick mass that counterbalances against the juvenile volumes of a bust clothed in a fine bodice of pleated linen.

right: *Amenemes and His Wife* have been portrayed in a bas-relief of extreme linear elegance by an artist undoubtedly contemporary with the Amarna school. But the highly linear style also places the work in the Theban ateliers that, parallel to the Akhenaton revolution, continued a manner more or less true to the classic tradition. Under rigorously applied conventions received from the Old or Middle Kingdom, the originality of the sculptor appears in the firmness of the drawing, the care of the intaglio carving, and the soft play of light.

44

During the reign
of the heretical Akhenaton,
an inner radiance humanizes
royal portraiture
of a more intimate and personal nature

Amenemes and His Wife. Late 18th Dynasty. Egypt. Limestone, height 0.55m/1′9¾″.

Funerary Mask. 1st millennium B.C. Phoenicia. Gold, 0.20m/7¾".

This *Funerary Mask,* made of beaten gold, is of a type sometimes used in ancient Phoenicia to cover the face of the dead, its purpose being to reproduce the deceased's features. But the work seen here, with its poignant intensity, proves that the artist did not content himself merely to reproduce his subject's physiognomy. The Phoenicians borrowed the custom of mortuary masks from Mycenaean civilization. And borrowing constituted one of the dominant characteristics of Phoenician art. Indeed, to know the history of this art is to trace the numerous influences that nourished it, mainly by way of continuous foreign contacts made in the course of a vigorous commercial life. Paradoxically, this constant submission to imported experience did not preclude the development of a native style of genuine splendor. Excellent goldsmiths, the Phoenicians knew how to ally a surprisingly free attitude toward the model with an incomparable mastery of material and technique.

Death freezes
the expression of
both face and figure
in those condemned to die

The *Libyan Captive* provides a marvelous illustration of the perfection attained by the bronze casters of Egypt. Originally the figure formed part of a group in which it was shown kneeling before the Pharaoh, ready for immolation. The silver-inlay phallus shield held by the belt designates the subject as Libyan. He would have also worn another Libyan accoutrement—a headpiece of two ostrich plumes. His left arm was no doubt raised in a gesture of supplication toward the sovereign, who stood behind the kneeling victim seizing him by the hair. The dramatic character of the scene and the respective positions of the two actors allowed the artist to give the lines of his work an extraordinary tension.

Libyan Captive. 2nd Theban period. Egypt. Bronze and silver, 0.09m/3½".

Immense and bizarre,
their decorative elements
as regular as
their forms are disparate,
the winged bulls
of Khorsabad
stand guard at the gates
to the Assyrian palace

A *Winged Bull* of gigantic size is one of the terrible guardians placed by Sargon II at the entrance to his palace at Khorsabad as protection against all enemy intrusion. One hardly knows what surprises the most here—the technical skill, the freedom of the animal's composition, or the impression of dominating power that the whole exudes. The colossus is an audacious and highly evocative synthesis of the strange, phantasmagoric world of the Assyrians. The head represents a nobleman crowned with a horned, cylindrical tiara; the ears, the body, the legs and feet are those of a bull; the chest could be a lion's; while the wings come from an eagle. The arriving visitor first saw the bull head on, then in profile; thus, the artist gave his monster five legs so as to preserve the integrity of its form from every angle.

Winged Bull. 7th century B.C. Assyria, Khorsabad. Alabaster, height 4.20m/13'9¼".

right: The wooden steles of Egypt, like the *Stele of Lady Tent Chenat,* are generally covered with scenes and texts on the theme of rebirth after death, symbolized by Osiris or by Ra-Horkouti and Toum. The latter two gods represent, respectively, the rising sun and the setting sun, whose regular alternation assures the continuity of light and heat, therefore of life itself, in the kingdom of the dead as well as on earth. Wooden steles served for persons of modest means in lieu of the stone forms preferred by the wealthy. Certain of the wooden steles, however, are dedicated for the benefit of high-ranking individuals, in which case they display decorative programs finely worked in rich colors, as in this memorial to Lady Chenat.

below: The cat, symbol of the goddess Bastet, was particularly venerated in the city of Bubastis, which held the sanctuary of that Egyptian deity. There a special necropolis was reserved for the sacred animals, mummified and enclosed in wooden coffins or in stone sarcophagi. Their entombment was carried out in a rite corresponding at every point to that for human beings. Originally, only the sacred animals, which in their lives were adored as protectors of the community, were buried in the necropolises. However, it seems that later the Egyptians came to include all members of the species. Cats are almost always represented in a seated posture, and with a realism that does not exclude a sense of mystery, expressed in a haughty and meditative mien.

Coffin of a Cat,
placed under the protection of the goddess Bastet.
c. 1000 B.C. Egypt.
Paint and stucco on wood, height 0.645m/2'1¼".

Stele of Lady Tent Chenat. 9th century B.C. Egypt. Paint and stucco on wood, height 0.315m/1'.

In the solemn necropolises of Egypt, household animals attain sanctity

below: The *Ichneumon Worshiper* discloses an innovative aspect of Egyptian art at the outset of the first millennium B.C.—a glorious flowering of aesthetically refined and technically sophisticated bronze sculpture. The number of effigies of both divinities and mortals increased, sometimes in combination with one another as here, and all were intended for temples. The ichneumon, also called the "rat of the Pharaoh," is a small mongoose whose natural prey are rodents, snakes, and crocodile eggs. This made the creature important, causing the Egyptians of the Old Kingdom to domesticate it. Quickly, the ichneumon became a cult object, most often portrayed seated on its hind quarters, with the front paws raised. In the version here the deified animal rests upon a lotus capital. The discrepancy in scale between the monumental ichneumon and the tiny adorer is a phenomenon frequently found in the iconography of Egypt, where many works show outsized sacred animals protecting a fragile person, even when this is the Pharaoh himself.

Ichneumon Worshiper. c. 1000 B.C. Egypt.
Bronze, height 0.257m/10″.

From the Flowering of Greece to the Fall of Rome
7th Century B.C. – 1st Century A.D.

During the 7th century B.C., the Mediterranean world underwent a profound change. The Greek nation was born, the child of migrant peoples invading from the north and the east. In Asia Minor, meanwhile, the Persians achieved hegemony over the remnants of the old Assyrian empire. On the southern shore of the Mediterranean, Egypt entered its 16th Dynasty, the so-called Saitic period, whose artistic impulse was to revive the heroic past. In the course of a long rivalry, the Greeks won over the Persians and succeeded in imposing their art upon the whole Mediterranean basin. No one accepted Greek culture more fully than the Romans, who synthesized it with many other influences drawn from the remote reaches of their imperial conquest.

Greece

The Greek people evolved out of the melting pot mixed from a great many migrations. In the 12th century B.C. came the Dorians, who, while destroying the brilliant Aegean civilization, brought new blood and a vigorous new inspiration. Other intruders appeared from Asian Ionia, where sailors based in the Greek archipelago had long before established strong links. Towards the 8th century B.C. the various alien elements began to fuse and take form as the Hellenic people, arising from the long night that the Dorian invasion had caused to fall upon the land of Greece. From 621 B.C. date the famous Draconian laws, those symbols of a stable peace and organized, urban society.

Greek civilization opened into full flower in the 6th century B.C., despite the threat to its liberty and development posed by the Persians. But this too passed when the Greeks won a decisive victory at Plataea in 479. Now the influence of Greek art would become enormous, thanks to the very personalities who would enslave the nation that created it: Alexander of Macedon and the Roman imperialists of Italy.

The arrival of Greek art marked a major turning point in human history. Breaking the mystical bonds that subjected him to oppressive forces, man achieved sufficient distance from the world to develop knowledge and philosophy. He created an art governed by both reason and reality, an art whose central concern would be the beauty of the human form and face. No longer would the artist attempt to cast a spell over a god or nature, to propitiate obscure powers, but rather to elevate man above the universe in order that he might better understand its laws. In the Greek pantheon each of the deities represents one of humanity's essential faculties, such as intelligence and feeling.

Ancient Greece produced an analytical art, an art of rigor in which the Dorian spirit continued to make itself felt. The need to simplify and purify form is clearly evident in the works of the Geometric period (page 59). From this era date the large Attic vases called Dipylon (for a cemetery situated at one of the gates to Athens), with their arabesques, geometric configurations, "Greek" meanders, and stylizations that inscribe the human torso within a triangle.

Greek architecture, even if it failed to develop vault construction, does not lack revolutionary qualities. When earlier builders had wanted to create an effect of monumentality, they could do little more than pile up larger and larger masses of stone. The Greeks, however, being urbanites, began to build on a scale appropriate to cities and thus acquired the craft of wood carpentry, which permitted a light, cagelike system of modular units, made up of posts and lintels enclosed by nonload-bearing surfaces. Working in such a system, they learned to distinguish among the various elements and to manipulate their relative dimensions until these assumed aesthetic and expressive proportions. In this way Greek architects achieved something altogether new—a rhythm that had an absolutely joyous effect upon the spectator. It came from the strictest kind of mathematical calculation, whose immense success proves that harmony can indeed be the product of intelligence.

Having embraced reality, Greek art completely abandoned all interest in the fantastic and the imaginative. As the terrifying bestiaries of old disappeared, the human being became the center of the universe. Artists devoted themselves totally to a new task that took precedence over all others: the discovery and celebration of the human body, that of men in the 6th and 5th centuries B.C., followed by that of women in the 4th century. It is the male body in all its physical reality that sculptors represented in the frontal and immobile figures known as *kouroi* (pages 67, 68). Then, under the influence of the highly developed art of bas-relief, where several figures had to be grouped in varying attitudes, sculptors began to break the law of frontality and allow movement to be expressed in the form of a smile (pages 69, 70). A new charm emerged from these works of stone, reflecting the Ionian spirit, which arrived from Oriental shores bringing Greece a tender sweetness. Decorated with scenes of everyday existence, vases seemed to overflow with life. There, images were no longer mere outline silhouettes but figures fleshed out with internal modeling (page 71). Occasionally polychromed, statues approached the idea of *mimesis*—"imitation"—expounded by Greek philosophers as the essential objective of art. As Jean Charbonneaux writes: "In Greece, with few rather special exceptions, statuary followed its own path and liberated itself from bondage to architecture. It wanted to 'live its own life,' independent of all monumental decoration. This constituted a true revolution, the effects of which are felt even now, since they determined the development of modern sculpture from the Renaissance onward."

Persia

Adversaries of the Assyrians since the 9th century B.C., the Persians had settled near Elam, where they were subject to Nineveh and Media. After the ruin and dismemberment of Assyria, they seized upper Mesopotamia and contributed to the destruction of Nineveh. In the 6th century B.C., Achaemenes came to power, founding a mighty empire that, under Cyrus, Cambyses, and Darius, gradually extended as far as India. It was this nation that would engage Greece in the endless conflict known as the Medic Wars. Repulsed at Plataea, Achaeminid Persia was finally shattered in 331 B.C. by Alexander the Great, who, the same year, made his incursion into Babylonia.

Achaeminid art, the last art to emerge in the Ancient Near East, achieved a high period that endured two centuries, from c. 550 to c. 350 B.C. The direct heir to Assyrian culture, this was a royal art, intended primarily to glorify the sovereigns of the greatest empire to evolve in antiquity before Rome. Persian art developed as a form of decoration for the gigantic palaces built by the reigning potentates: Cyrus at Pasargadae, Darius and Xerxes at Persepolis, and Ataxerxes at Susa. In all these establishments the *apadanas,* or "throne rooms," were sumptuous in the extreme, supported by tall, fluted columns with capitals shaped in the Assyrian manner—that is, like bulls paired back to back (page 75).

The art of the Achaeminids was secular and made, above all else, to enhance civic life. The Persian religion, whose rites consisted merely of fire worship on open-air

55

That is why funerary art, with special emphasis on the sarcophagus, held such an important place in Etruscan culture. Etruscans rendered their attitudes timeless in portraits of the dead, the faces fixed in expressions of smiling serenity (pages 76, 77). They also gave effect to them in a remarkable technique of bronze casting, the perfection of which amazed even the Renaissance (pages 64, 66). Finally, the Etruscans were splendid builders who would transmit their architectural science to Italy's Roman conquerors.

Rome

Exhausted from internal strife, Greece became a province of Rome in the 2nd century B.C. By then, however, it had already contributed generously to the formation of Roman art, mainly through the connection between Etruria and Greece.

A civilization of architects and organizers, Rome realized its greatest achievements in monumental ensembles of incomparable power and amplitude: baths, circuses, pantheons, and triumphal arches. But in the realm of painting and sculpture, Rome took its nourishment entirely from Greece, grafting this source onto the old Etruscan stock.

The cultural exchange between Rome and Greece never ceased. While Roman artists traveled to Greece to work with its masters, Hellenistic artists were invited to the altars (pyres), forbade the construction of temples. Only tombs provided an occasion for the artistic expression of piety, and this was limited to decorating the façades of underground chambers conceived after the fashion of Egypt, as in the Naqsh-i-Roustan tombs.

On the glazed bas-reliefs of the great halls and stairways appears nothing but long processions of soldiery and vanquished peoples, who seem to walk right along with the modern visitor (page 74). But having felt the influence of neighboring Greece, Persian art no longer evinced the violence of its Assyrian prototypes. Winged bulls and griffins now took on a heraldic quality the elegance of which had a purely decorative purpose (page 79).

Following reunification in 663 B.C., Egypt attempted to revive art by returning directly to its own origins. Choosing models from among the heroic masterpieces of the Old Kingdom, Egyptian sculptors hoped to endow their works with the power of former times. However, they could neither escape from their own age nor forget what the intervening centuries had given them: a taste for the pretty and the pleasing. Thus, their productions would never possess the vigor of the Old Kingdom. With its suave lines and highly purified forms, Saitic art always remained somewhat cold and artificial.

The sculptors of Saitic Egypt often used the hardest stones, very fine in grain, and then polished the surfaces to

Greek beauty
first asserts itself
in smooth spherical
or bell-like volumes

Bell-Idol. c. 700 B.C. Boeotia, Greece. Terra-cotta, height 0.395m/1'3½".

The *Bell-Idol* is a rare and precious piece, belonging to Hellenism's formative period when the figure of a divinity was almost never represented. A hole perforated through the head suggests that the *Bell-Idol* was attached to the wall of a tomb. Molded separately, the legs are suspended with copper wires from the interior of the conical garment, perhaps to endow the sacred image with life. The decoration on the apron echoes such pre-Hellenic themes as swastikas and aquatic birds holding serpents in their beaks. On the arms, the swastikas, like the circles around the breasts, seem to correspond to actual ta-

Bird Vase. 7th century B.C. Cyprus. Painted terra-cotta, height 0.22m/8¾".

The *Bird Vase* offers a remarkable example of Cypriot pottery from the geometric period. The decoration is strictly subordinated to the host form whose profile it accentuates, but the various combinations of broken lines no doubt relate to circles and spirals inherited from ancient Aegean civilization. While providing an occasion for subtle plastic manipulations, the theme of the stylized bird also served as a conjuration against the "evil eye," which the winged creature attacks with its beak. On the body of the vessel, arrows and swastikas seem to have the same purpose. Then, as reinforcement for the efficacy of the exorcism, symbolic eyes were added here and there on the vase's lip. Belief in the magical powers of imagery is a trait common to many peoples of the ancient Mediterranean world, but for the idea of ornamenting utilitarian objects, Cypress and later Greece were probably indebted to Syria, by means of its textiles.

59

Attenuated figures
and cavorting clowns
form a strange company
on the fringes
of emerging classicism

Dancing Satyr. c. 450 B.C. Sicily.
Bronze, height 0.078m/3″.

Dancing Silenus. 6th century B.C.
Greece. Bronze, height 0.092m/3½″.

left: These *Votive Figurines,* as attenuated as taut wire, inevitably demand, for modern eyes, comparison with the wasted images of Alberto Giacometti. Ironically, they derive from the prosaic concern of pure economy. Once an Etruscan sought to obtain the protection of a god, he made a solemn promise to dedicate to his sacred guardian a statuette whose height was fixed by that of the devout himself. But as concerned to minimize the expense of this propitiatory enterprise as to respect the height promised, the dedicator ordered that only the head be modeled in the round, while allowing the rest of the body to be reduced to the simplest form of expression. One can imagine, however, that artists, far from resisting the dictates of this pecuniary strategem, perceived it as an occasion to give effect to a deep, native predilection for the strange and the supernatural, inherited, probably, from the race's Oriental ancestors.

above and right: Silenuses and Satyrs formed, along with the Maenads and the Bacchantes, the riotous retinue of Dionysos, the god of wine, inebriation, and generation. They are not divinities but rather mythical beings of household familiarity whom the Greeks regarded as hooligans, drunkards, and willful wantons. They enjoyed abundant representation in the Archaic period, which endowed them with caricatural attributes: fanlike beards or bulbous bellies. Treated with verve and high humor, dancing Silenuses and Satyrs reveal a less well-known aspect of Greek art than that associated with the ideas of classical beauty. And in the evolution of this art, bronze casters played an important role. Not so enslaved as the stone carvers to the exigencies of their material, they became the first to break with the laws of frontality and to give their images greater vivacity and freedom.

Votive Figurines. 5th–6th century B.C. Etruria.
Bronze, height 0.50 and 0.33m/1′7¾″ × 1′1″.

Silenus. 6th century B.C. Greece.
Bronze, height 0.082m/3¼″.

As ancient Mediterranean humanism finds its proper image, proportions emerge that would entrance the Renaissance

right: The *Goddess Turan* is one of the works, among the many owned by the Louvre, that best represents the skill of the Etruscans in the fabrication of bronze figurines and reliefs. The statuette of Turan, a goddess analogous to the Greeks' Aphrodite, displays the Etruscan conception of the female canon. The breast is clearly articulated under a long, clinging chiton that accentuates the thinness of the body and the fragility of the waist. Simple curved lines indicate the draping of the garment, especially in the skirt, which is lifted in a movement of exquisite elegance. Fine workmanship is evident throughout the bodice and sleeves. The tutulus, or embroidery-banded cap of Oriental origin, almost forms a lozenge with the face, distinguished by slit eyes and prominent cheekbones. More than the art of Greece, for which the Etruscans had great admiration, the delicate charm of this statuette evokes the mannerism of Ionia.

left: The *Apollo of Piombino* was found in the sea and owes its name to the small Italian town near the recovery site. The left foot bears a three-line silver inscription making the work an offering to the goddess Athena. Written in the Dorian dialect, the inscription allowed scholars to attribute the statue to the ateliers of the Peloponnessus, probably the one in Sicyone, the main center of Dorian sculpture. This magnificent bronze should represent Apollo, an identity that seems to be indicated by the gesture of the left hand, which could grasp a bow, while the right hand might hold an object. Copper inlays form the eyebrows, lips, and nipples. Especially striking is the work's somewhat archaizing quality, its frontality and symmetry, which are only slightly relieved by a timid urge toward torsion. Still, the modeling has softened, reflecting a more direct observation of reality.

Apollo of Piombino. c. 500 B.C. Greece.
Bronze, height 3'9¼".

Turan, Etruscan Deity. c. 520–510 B.C. Etruria.
Bronze, height 0.202m/8″.

below: The *Javelin Thrower* relates to the greatest of ancient Greek works through its solid structure as well as through its harmonious musculature, where archaic stylizations still linger. The very perfection of their technique made the Etruscan bronze casters famous everywhere in the Mediterranean world. The repertoire they favored reflected an attachment to local traditions as much as it did a respect for Hellenic models. Next to figurines like that representing the goddess Turan (left), which evinces native Italic tendencies, the *Javelin Thrower* reveals the full power of Greek influence upon Etruria. Here, as in the kouroi, the subject is given a frontal stance, with the left foot forward. Originally the raised hand held a sling for launching the javelin, but nothing in this athlete suggests actual movement.

Javelin Thrower. Early 5th century B.C. Etruria.
Bronze, height 0.458m/1′6″.

An expression of human tenderness transcends the archaic rigidity of Etruscan statuary

This sarcophagus, one of the masterpieces of Etruscan terra-cotta sculpture, was recovered from the necropolis of Caere, the most brilliant of ancient Etruria's cultural centers. Keenly preoccupied with the hereafter, the Etruscans sought to save the deceased from all sense of exile by giving their effigies a familiar setting. The image of the dead, alone or in the company of his wife, appeared on the lid of the sarcophagus, and every effort was made to endow it with the warmth of everyday life. Thus, it is the atmosphere of a banquet that the artist has re-created here. The figures are half reclining, propped upon their elbows in the manner of Oriental or Greek diners, their hands extended to hold cups. The protective gesture of the man and the woman's trusting surrender to his shoulder illustrate the tenderness that united Etruscan couples and that so amazed the Greeks. Extreme care governed the execution of this group, a fact evident in the precision of the attitudes, as well as in the expressive physiognomy of the faces, all of which renders the scene strikingly real and immediate. Despite the archaic stylization that attenuates the legs, the work reflects an affinity for the "psychological portrait" and the evolution of Etruscan art toward a secular realism that anticipated the sculpture of Rome.

The Sarcophagus of Caere. c. 500 B.C. Etruria. Painted terra-cotta, 1.17 × 1.98m/3'10" × 6'6".

Rampin Head. c. 450–425 B.C. Athenian Acropolis. Parian marble, height 0.29m/11½".

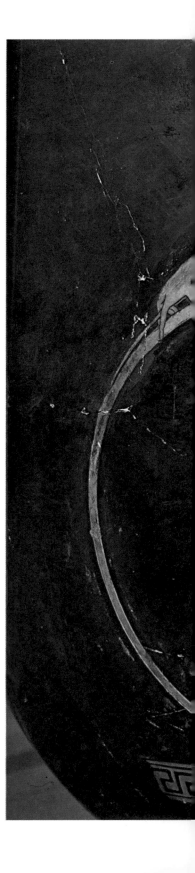

above: The *Rampin Head*, so-called for its first owner, was found in 1935 to be part of an equestrian statue whose other fragments belong to the Acropolis Museum in Athens. The figure, therefore, represents a member of the "golden youth" in the time of Pysistratos, probably a victor in a horse race, since he wears a crown of oak leaves. The sculpture reflects a considerable aesthetic shift in the history of Greek sculpture or, more particularly, of Attic sculpture. The head, for instance, inclines and turns slightly to one side, thereby abandoning the principle of frontality. This principle, which had governed the statuary of both Egypt and the Ancient Near East, required that an absolute symmetry be maintained from part to part on either side of the main vertical axis. Instead of reproducing the features of an individual person, the *Rampin Head* expresses a certain type of human ideal, an ideal that is in no way compromised either by the somewhat mannered smile or by the patterned treatment of the beard and hair, which echo conventions originating as far back as Achaemenid Persia and Mesopotamia.

First the ghost of a smile,
then little by little
attitudes relax
as Athens discovers humanism
and gives it classical form

below: This *Attic Krater* must be counted among the most beautiful examples of its kind ever to have left the studios of the Athenian potters at the outset of the 5th century B.C. "At a moment when architecture was undergoing a crisis, which left few monuments to decorate," writes Pierre Devambez, "the artists of Athens had no recourse other than to work for the potteries, there bringing to modest assignments the whole of their talent and creative power." The motifs with which they ornamented cups and kraters most often evoke the "symposion" where pretty women and graceful youths played and danced. The decoration on this krater shows the mythological hero Ganeymede driving a hoop with his left hand and, with the right hand, holding a cock, symbol of love and friendship. On the other side of the vessel, Zeus pursues another youth whose amused nonchalance suggests that the intentions of the lord of Olympus are not altogether hostile. Clearly the painter knew how to fill the human figure with a sense of life. The composition, the elegance of which is brought out by the pure geometry of the hoop, evinces a firm grasp of structure, a taste for monumentality that would find its complete realization in the Age of Pericles.

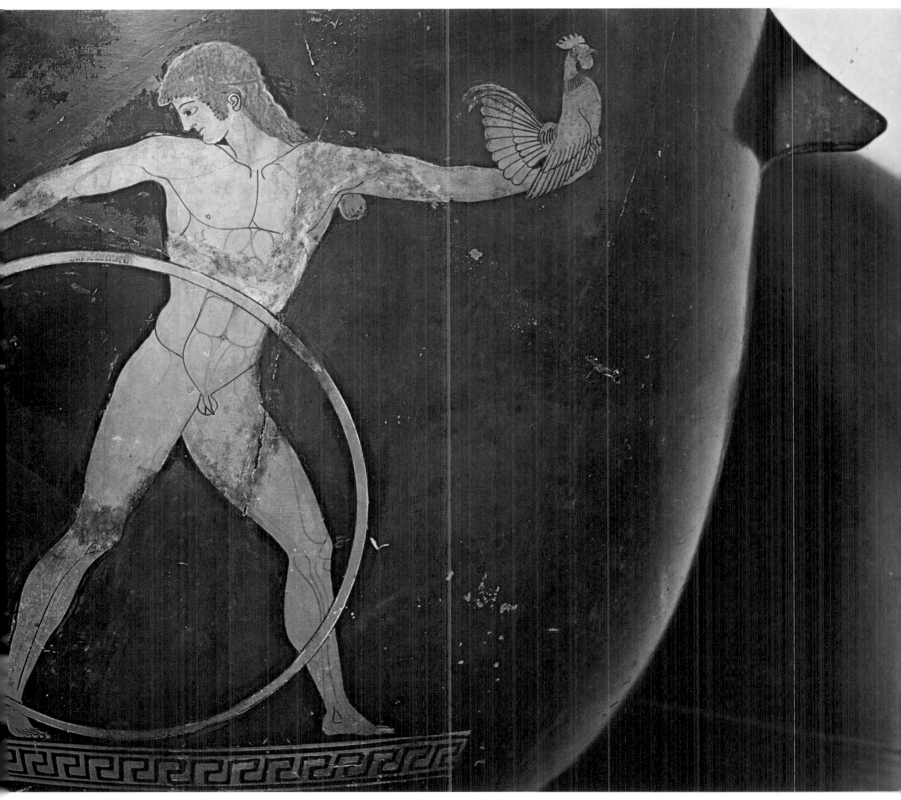

Attic Krater. c. 480 B.C. Greece. Height 0.33m/1'.

71

In colossal masterworks,
Achaeminid artists fix
a grandiose setting
for imperial pomps

left: The *Archers of the Persian Guard,* famous "Immortals" interminably on the march across the friezes of the royal palace at Susa, were supposed to assure magical protection in the event of defection by the real guard. But without their lances, bows, and quivers, these hieratic images would be difficult to identify as representations of warriors who conquered one of the largest empires known in the ancient world. Everything implies order, ritual, solemnity, but without reference to either time or place. Altogether impersonal are the dark profiles set with frontal eyes. Meanwhile, the same figures are repeated again and again, with only the slightest differentiation in the motifs ornamenting the tunics. A real mastery of color adds to the impression that here the ancient Mesopotamian tradition of enamel relief has received one of its highest expressions. "With the defiles of archers, lions, griffins, and winged bulls, with the friezes of marguerites, zigzags, and palmettes," wrote André Parrot, "the glazed-brick panels are like tapestries hung simply to delight the eye. It is in this setting that we should reread Esther, made Queen of Persia by favor of Ahasuerus. A legendary account certainly, but one that merits being evoked whenever we wish to recover the atmosphere of an Iranian palace."

above and right: This *Colossal Capital* came originally from the palace at Susa, where a forest of columns, 20 meters high and all crowned by the same capital, supported the ceiling of the apadana, an immense reception hall encompassing more than 2 acres of ground space. Bulls paired back to back stand upon the summit of a fluted shaft ornamented with regular volutes. Feet tucked under, heads lowered, chests covered with golden fleece, the beasts are dressed in a sumptuous harness. Such works are characteristic of an entire civilization and reflect the taste of the Achaemenids for a monumental art, for a grandiose architecture suitable to the pomps and feasts of their brilliant court.

Colossal Capital. 5th–6th centuries B.C.
Susa, Achaemenid Persia. Gray marble, height 5.80m/19'1¼".

Archer Frieze. 5th century B.C. Susa, Achaemenid Persia. Glazed brick, height of each figure 1.47m/4'9¾".

Stele of Phyllis (detail). c. 430 B.C. Greece. Marble, total height 1.35m/4'5¼".

The more
Greek sculptors
gain control
of their chisels,
the more
the marble yields
nuances of
individual character,
thereby heralding
the advent of
psychological art

left: The *Stele of Phyllis* witnesses a revival of funerary art around 430 B.C. The completion of the sculptural program for the Parthenon liberated the team assembled by Phidias, and in the absence of further state commissions, the sculptors turned to private clients, devoting themselves to the execution of decorative tombstones of a sort that had been proscribed by sumptuary laws at the beginning of the century. The funerary steles, like the period's portrait sculptures, evince a growing concern with individualization, an ever greater desire to make the face "the mirror of the soul." On the upper molding of this stele the artist took care to engrave the name of the youthful deceased: Phyllis, daughter of Cleomedes. The hair is caught up in a *cecryphale*, from which a lock escapes in the Thracian fashion. Carefully dressed curls crown the melancholy face, enhancing the pure line of its profile. A sense of introspection, of private feeling, emerges from this relief, which has more than one trait in common with those of the Acropolis figures.

right: The *Head of Apollo*, moving in its sensitivity, is an antique replica of a work attributed to Calamis, the Athenian sculptor whose maturity coincided with the youth of Phidias. Two other copies exist of the same original, which proves the fame early acquired by an artist characterized as "the maker of gods." However, the pensive nobility of the face, the short locks that frame the brow, the veiled sweetness of the eyes relate the Head of Apollo to a genre that just then was being born in Greece: the portrait. Until that time nothing had motivated the Greeks to do portraits. Unlike the Egyptians, they did not believe in the survival of a "double" perpetuating itself in an effigy made to resemble the deceased. Moreover, the deepest urge of Hellenism was to suppress the ephemeral and the singular in favor of humanity's most typical or general aspect. But in the middle of the 5th century B.C. the advent of democracy brought a new awareness of the individual, a sentiment that, of course, had its effect upon art. By then sculptors had solved all their technical problems, which left them free to concentrate on rendering subtle feelings with the greatest delicacy, or, as Aristotle put it, "on representing moral expression." A product of this conjunction of factors, the art of portraiture would enjoy enormous popularity throughout the Greco-Roman world.

Head of Apollo. 5th century B.C.
Attica, Greece. Marble, height 0.29m/11½".

The phantasms
of the
ancient mind
find expression
in grotesqueries,
both frightening
and humorous

Drinking Bowl. 550–500 B.C. Greece. Terra-cotta; height 0.133m, diameter 0.188m/5¼″ × 7½″.

Rooted in the collective unconscious, a strange universe continued to live on the margins of the reason and harmony that governed the high arts. The drinking bowl reproduced above, with its menacing decoration, was thought to possess the magical power to petrify every possible aggressor. The moment anyone held the bowl to his lips, the hideous Gorgon mask painted on the ceramic was supposed to implant itself upon the drinker's face and render him invulnerable. The Egyptians attributed the same kind of protective power to the figure of *Bes* (right). This deformed dwarf, from the mysterious lands near the sources of the Nile—where legend placed the country of the Pygmies—was not a god in the strict sense of the word, but one of the secondary deities who, like the Greek satyrs, escorted the true gods. Most often he is shown standing, as here, with his broad, grimacing face and snub nose, and with pendulous cheeks so bearded as to make the image seem coiffed in an extravagant arrangement of feathers and palms. Such an irresistible ugliness explains the double role played by Bes in Egyptian mythology. Because laughable, the figure was associated with joyous ideas and interests, such as dance, music, and fine attire. But since it was also frightful to behold, the Egyptians believed the statue capable, solely by its appearance, of putting to flight all the enemies and phantoms that assailed and tormented humankind, waking or sleeping. Perhaps it was the desire to disarm accusors either by terror or by laughter that so often caused Bes to be represented with his tongue stuck out.

Large Statue of Bes. 30th Dynasty (378–341 B.C.). Egypt.
Limestone, height 1m/3′3¼″.

Stroked by an ardent hand,
the Greek ideal
of feminine beauty
comes to life

Venus de Milo (detail). Late 2nd century B.C. Greece. Marble, height 2.04m/6'8¼".

left: The *Venus de Milo,* one of the highest achievements of antique sculpture, was accidentally discovered by a farmer some 500 feet from the theatre in the city that gave the figure its name. The French Ambassador bought the work in the early 19th century and offered it to Louis XVIII for the Louvre. For a long time the *Venus de Milo* was dated in the 4th century B.C., mainly because the serenity of the face and the imposing nobility of the pose seemed to place the statue in a direct line with the works of Phidias. But it was carved at the end of the 2nd century B.C., a fact that affirms a return made by Hellenistic artists to classical sources in the aftermath of the explosive baroque style developed at Pergamon. But if the sculptor sought his inspiration in the great creations of the past, he also endowed these models with renewed expression. The moving quality of the sculpture's lines, the studied antithesis between the soft plenitude of the breast and the mannerism of the drapery dropped about the hips evinces a very personal sensibility. Moreover, the figure's turning movement attests to a perfect mastery of three-dimensional form.

right: The *Aphrodite of Cnidos* constituted one of the most popular works in all of Greek art. Few statues inspired such a quantity of replicas and copies, among which the version in the Louvre is one of the best. Possibly the *Cnidian Aphrodite* owed some part of its popularity to the scandal the work caused among the pious. Praxiteles presented the goddess ready for her ritual ablutions, thus entirely nude. The female nude, already treated in Hellenic sculpture, was not anything to shock the modesty of the Greeks. But never before had a female deity been shown in a simple condition thought suitable only for mortals. The statue had been commissioned from Praxiteles, an Athenian, by the inhabitants of Cnidos, and tradition held that the artist offer them the choice of an Aphrodite draped or an Aphrodite undraped. The preference of the Cnidians accorded with a persistent belief in Asia Minor, a belief just then renewed, which held that divine nudity was not only linked to the concept of fertility, but that it also exercised a magical influence upon the prosperity of both human beings and their land. The copyist in this instance understood how to preserve the essence of Praxiteles' genius, which reveals itself in the purity of the composition, the fullness of the contours, the subtle and imperceptible tremor that animates the softly modeled forms.

Aphrodite of Cnidos,
antique replica of the Greek original by Praxiteles.
c. 364–354 B.C. Marble, height 1.20m/3'11¼".

Honor
to virile power
under the Roman Empire

Pugilist of Autun. Gallo-Roman period.
Bronze, height 0.275m/10¾".

Wrestler Group. Hellenistic period.
Bronze, height 0.179m/7".

Warriors, athletes, and gladiators multiplied from one end of the Roman Empire to the other. But each of the colonized nations gave the art we call Hellenistic a different interpretation—brutal, almost barbaric in Gaul with the *Pugilist of Autun* (above left), but naturalistic and tortured in the *Wrestler Group* from Egypt (above). The *Wounded Gaul* (left), an excellent Roman copy, recalls one of the gravest invasions suffered by Greece and Asia Minor during the 3rd century B.C. The invaders' ethnic type, with its powerful build and thick hair, captured the imagination, especially that of the artists of Pergamon. The rippling muscles of the stocky warrior, his pathetic and theatrical expression are true to the spirit of the Pergamene school. A more sober image is the *Borghese Gladiator* (right), despite the minuteness with which the musculature has been detailed, almost as if the figure were *écorché* ("flayed"). The movement of the left arm extends along a great diagonal the pure lines the Ephesian sculptor gave this masterwork from the closing moments of the Hellenistic era.

Wounded Gaul, replica of an original
from the beginning of the 2nd century B.C.
Italy. Marble, height 0.86m/2'9¾".

Borghese Gladiator. 1st century B.C. Italy.
Marble, height 1.99m/6'6¼".

Along with naturalism, an anecdotal art emerges and spreads, the perfect accompaniment to Roman pragmatism

right: The *Borghese Vase,* recovered from the gardens of Sallust in Rome, is in all likelihood the work of a Greek. After the Roman conquest, neo-Attic art remained essentially traditionalist. Now, for instance, there existed "model books" from which artists could take subjects for their compositions, even allowing themselves to mix several at a time. Their vases, amphoras, and kraters, all beautifully decorative, served as embellishments for the promenades and peristyles of Roman villas. So successful were these works that they gave rise to a quasi-industrial production. By the conventionality of its themes, the *Borghese Vase* belongs to this line of development. But the rapid rhythm of the dance, the realism of detail that places new demands upon marble, and the congenial integration of the figures combine to make this a highly original piece of work. Another unifying factor is the dedication of the whole to the god of the vine. A joyous cortege illustrates the general inebriation brought by Dionysos' invention of wine and the individual ecstasy of the participants in the orgy. Among them can be recognized the habitués of the Bacchic scene: the elegant dancer with castanets, the satyr, and the double-flute player.

left: The *Hunting Satyr* belongs to a series of reliefs called "picturesque," whose style, which undoubtedly originated in Alexandria, spread throughout the Greco-Roman world in the course of the 2nd century B.C. By the nuanced shading of the eyes and by the sheer variety of the planes, these works succeeded in rivalling painting and granted to landscape an importance never allowed by the Greeks. Abundantly imitated and copied during the reign of Augustus, the picturesque bas-reliefs reflect the Romans' taste for nature, which simultaneously expressed itself in the verses of such poets as Virgil. But despite the multiple bucolic touches surrounding the Hunting Satyr, this relief was not exclusively a decorative work, since the scene occurs in a grotto dedicated to the god Pan and the youth was originally accompanied by a Dionysiac panther, whose head has been erroneously restored as that of a dog. In the tension that fills the interval between this animal and its prey, a rabbit, the sculptor had the genius to create a sense of living space. Meanwhile, the half-pleased, half-cruel expression on the face of the hunter adds a certain ambiguity to a charming "genre scene."

Hunting Satyr (detail)
replica of Hellenistic relief. 2nd century B.C.
Marble, total height 1.88m/6′2″.

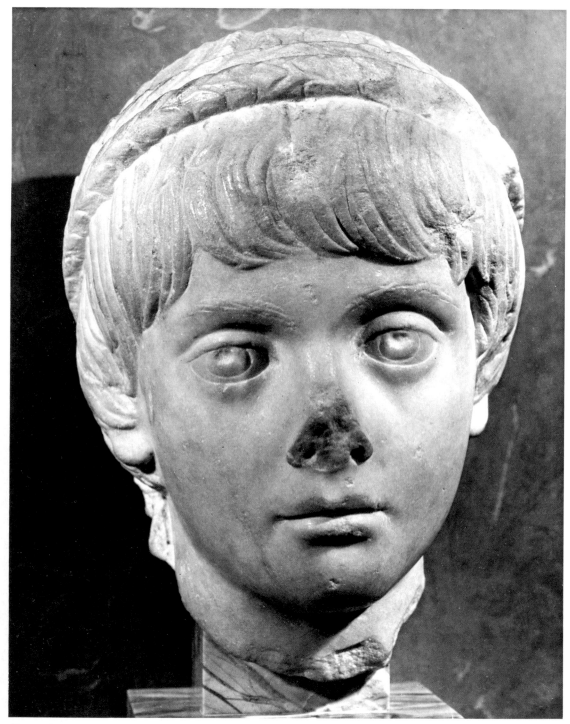

Portrait of Annius Verus. A.D. c. 160. Marble, height 0.21m/8¼".

above: The *Portrait of Annius Verus,* son of Marcus Aurelius, would have been the work of an Athenian sculptor. In the 2nd century A.D., under the influence of the Emperor Hadrian and his friend, the luxury-loving Maecenas, Herod Atticus, Athens experienced a veritable artistic renaissance. It would continue under Antoninus and Marcus Aurelius, producing one of the era's most beautiful works in the portrait of Annius Verus. The image probably represents the boy, who died at the age of seven, in the last year of his life. The double crown of laurel indicates that he had been elevated to the rank of Caesar. The conscious disorder of the hair emphasizes by contrast the delicate modeling of the face, which is heavy with melancholy. The practice, frequent at the time, of incising a half-circle upon the pupils results in the somewhat strange expression, suggesting a kind of disquiet, as if the subject were expecting to enter a new spiritual state, to experience a profound shock. What it reflects is the entrance into Greco-Roman life of the preoccupations and sentiments of nascent Christianity.

right: The *Altar of the Twelve Gods,* a Roman monument of the eclectic sort, belongs to the neo-Attic style that, beginning in the 1st century B.C., departed from the models of the classical period while also mixing them with more recent types. On the periphery of a round table appear the twelve signs of the zodiac alternating with the heads and attributes of the twelve corresponding deities: Jupiter, Minerva, Apollo, Juno, Neptune, Vulcan, Mercury, Ceres, Proserpine, Diana, Mars, and Venus. The almost surreal strangeness of this altar has never failed to intrigue lovers of the bizarre. Some have even wanted to see affinities between the Roman visages disposed around a mysterious "table" and the severed heads of the late-19th-century Symbolist painter Gustave Moreau.

94

At the very heart
of triumphant Rome,
the unexpected face
of melancholy

Christian Art from Its First Dawning to the Decline of Gothic

2nd–15th Centuries

In the Roman-Egyptian portraits of Fayum (pages 100, 101), which date from the 2nd century A.D., can be felt the first symptoms of the new man proclaimed by Christianity. Instead of the haughty or amiable serenity seen in antique busts, the faces of Fayum express a profound inner struggle, the anxiety of people on the threshold of eternity.

In 476, Rome collapsed under the impact of repeated Barbarian invasions. This brutally interrupted the slow evolution that the Empire had been experiencing under the influence of its Oriental dominions. Henceforth, the Mediterranean world would be cut in two.

The Eastern Empire, born of Rome, progressively expanded throughout the Mediterranean for the next ten centuries. Its capital, Byzantium, the capital created by Constantine, would attract the best artists and the most prestigious ateliers, from Antioch, Syria, Palestine, Alexandria, and Ephesus. Rivaling one another in virtuosity and invention, this throng of architects, mosaicists, painters, engravers, enamel workers, and ivory carvers brought about the flowering of a brilliant new art.

In Western Europe, the Visigoths of Spain, the Lombards of northern Italy, the Franks in Gaul, and the Saxons in Britain all came from such migratory traditions that their art tended to be light and portable, consisting mainly of a few decorative themes, geometric or animal in nature, worked in fabrics, jewelry, weapons, and riding equipment. For these Barbarian groups to be capable of anything more, they had to wait until a settled life could encourage greater artistic activity and until conversion to Christianity brought them all the expressive resources of sacred art.

Soon, however, the more gifted of the tribes learned to imitate the precious objects that arrived from the eastern Mediterranean through such intermediaries as itinerant merchants and monks. In certain types of art, especially manuscript illumination and fine metal work, the Westerners went beyond slavish copying and devised new formulas. But not until the beginning of the 9th century would the Occident, under the impulse of Charlemagne, experience a true artistic "renaissance." Tightly integrated in the style forged by the Carolingians were influences from Hellenistic, Oriental, and Barbarian sources.

Early Christian Art

A specifically Christian iconography emerged at the beginning of the 3rd century A.D., working its way free of the great profusion of themes used to decorate the walls and sarcophagi of the Roman catacombs. This imagery would come into the open and spread widely after the new religion gained toleration under Constantine. The dissemination was made possible by the Edict of Milan (313), which in effect assured the triumph of the Church of Rome. Of course, it would be several centuries before Christian art could develop the full potential offered by the Old Testament, the Life of Christ, and the stories of the saints. But here already were the subjects that, all the way to the Renaissance, would inspire the artistic production of the Christian world.

The Early Christian period also saw the formulation of church architecture, especially that of the Christian basilica. It would rise in marked contrast to pagan and Jewish temples, which did not admit congregations. As the Christian sepulcher dedicated to martyrs evolved, it provided the occasion for an extraordinary array of frescoes and bas-reliefs, all realized in an eminently religious style. And while taking their themes from the Old and New Testaments, the artists of this age felt no hesitation about Christianizing the old and familiar pagan subjects and thus endowing them with new significance. Here the Copts would prove especially adept.

The vision of the physical world propounded by Christian art grew out of the feelings that Christianity inspired. Henceforth, all literal reference to terrestrial reality would be banished from the language of art. Freestanding sculpture, the glory of Classical art, entered into a long period of decline, the victim of its closeness to the world of appearances. What counted now was the expressive power of the composition, which scaled and arranged form according to the instructional value of the subjects represented. Landscape simply disappeared, leaving figures and objects disposed across a flat, uniform ground. It was as if the events depicted occurred in neither time nor space, but rather in some abstract, ideal realm. The material order gave way to a spiritual hierarchy.

Byzantine Art

Byzantium early produced two of its most characteristic types of art: the triumphal and the monastic.

Triumphal art developed primarily in the great metropolitan centers. It aimed not only to propagate the Christian gospel, but also to imbue the masses with respect for temporal authority. This dual concern explains how, often, the same work (as on page 107) can contain two fundamentally antagonistic styles, one linked to the realism of Classical antiquity, and the other to the expressionist tradition of the Orient. Such compromises occurred often enough during Byzantium's golden age (526–565) but they began to proliferate at the end of the "iconoclastic" crisis.

It was in the first half of the 8th century that iconoclasm erupted and shattered the old equilibrium between the real and the ideal in art. The fervent love shown by some of the faithful toward holy images came to appear idolatrous in the eyes of those who were equally passionate in their pure spirituality. The latter brought about a violent reaction, causing the Emperors and the clergy to forbid the veneration of icons. For more than a century, iconoclasm would tear at the Byzantine world. Coming as it did in the wake of Arabic conquests in the Mediterranean, the crisis made Christian nations susceptible to penetration by the aniconic principles of Islam. As a consequence, Christian artists could produce little but profane decorations. Of all the great Christian symbols, only the Cross was tolerated. However, after years of struggle between the Western Papacy, which remained attached to images, and certain of the Emperors in the East, who banned them, the iconoclasts were defeated. In the middle of the 9th century, Empress Theodora officially restored the devotion to icons. Soon thereafter Christian art experienced an unprecedented efflorescence.

At the very moment when the military power of the Eastern Empire began to wane, the triumphal style reached its climax. The very finest of Byzantine artists gathered around the Doges in Venice and the Norman kings at Palermo in Sicily. During the 11th and 12th centuries, these schools conceived and executed works of stunning luxury and perfection. Even after the occupation of Constantinople (early 13th century), Byzantine art lost none of its vitality and went on to produce one last "renaissance," a humanizing manifestation that occurred under the Paleologue Emperors. This burst of creativity ceased only with the fall of Constantinople to the Turks in 1453.

Monastic art—essentially a popular art—was meant to arouse emotions and to fill the faithful with compassion. Using moralistic subject matter, it emphasized the dramatic side of Christian history. The style adopted was, relative to that of triumphal art, primitive; it was also purely Oriental in character. As the name would imply, monastic art had its origin in the monasteries, developing there from the first centuries of the Christian era, at remote reaches of the interior, far from the coastal metropolises. The arid lands of both Syria and Egypt favored the growth of religious communities, producing two quite different and independent modes of expression.

Syria cultivated an art of images designed not to please but rather to evoke, with maximum concision, an event or a person from religious history (page 111).

Thus, Christian antiquity inaugurated a new consciousness based neither on the instinct of primitive cultures nor on the reason of Greek civilization. Instead, Christian consciousness derived from intuition founded upon feeling. It would have its culminating fulfillment in Romanesque art.

Egypt, on the other hand, developed a deep and sensitive art. The Copts, who accepted Christianity at a very early date, expressed their faith in extraordinary sculptures, textiles, and tapestries (pages 104, 105, 108, 109).

Romanesque Art

Medieval art is didactic. It seeks to lead the faithful, through the simple contemplation of its images, to grasp the multiple aspects of belief. Artists took their inspiration from the age's great theological works, the *summae*, which, in their commentaries on Scripture, asserted four different meanings for each chapter and verse: literal, moral, mystical, and allegorical. And however complex the representations produced by this approach, medieval viewers did not find them confusing, since the art was nothing more than the visual equivalent of the sermons heard throughout the era.

In order to communicate its message, the educational art of the Middle Ages had recourse either to symbolic themes or to decorative forms borrowed from nature. The extraordinary spread of sculptural embellishments over stone façades has caused the great 13th-century cathedrals to be compared with the *summae* themselves—those veritable encyclopedias of religious and social learning that reflected the medieval West's immense and characteristic thirst for knowledge.

Medieval art is also an act of monastic faith, since the most beautiful churches produced by the High Middle Ages belonged for the most part to the convents established throughout Europe by the powerful Cluniac and Cistercian orders. The development of Western monasticism came about in reaction against the dark period of anarchy that followed the dismemberment of the Carolingian empire and the Barbarian invasions. For almost two hundred years, feudal war, religious persecution, famine, and epidemic reigned. The calamities subsided only with the onset of the 11th century, when the Church finally succeeded in imbuing the feudal lords with some respect for moral principle—such as the *trêve de Dieu* ("truce of God")—which tended to moderate what had become chronic and universal brutality. As it spread, organized religion constituted Romanesque Europe's main force for order and stability.

Romanesque art developed simultaneously in all areas not under the direct influence of Byzantium, but it proved especially strong in France, Spain, and England. It aimed primarily to glorify God, doing so by means of numerous symbolic forms absorbed pell-mell from every conceivable culture and tradition: pagan mythology, Christian history, Classical antiquity, Barbarian ornamentation, Byzantium, and Sassanian Persia. The mélange can be seen in Mosan enamels or in the Hildesheim candlestick (page 118). Although drawn mostly from the past, Romanesque style and iconography nonetheless achieved genuine originality, thanks to its prodigious energy and verve.

The Romanesque age achieved its greatest works in sculpture and architecture. Essentially decorative, the sculpture was conceived of as a function of architecture, with which it was closely integrated. This relationship brought the technique of relief carving to a high point (page 115), while limiting the use of sculpture-in-the-round. One of the chief innovations effected by the artists of the Middle Ages was the representation, in bas-relief, of the human form, not for itself as in antiquity, but rather for purposes of ornamentation. According to the specific need, the human image could be shrunk (page 116), stretched (page 114), or otherwise distorted (page 118). Most of the forms represented in Romanesque sculpture had their origin in works generally classified among the minor arts, which themselves played an important role at this time. On numerous tympana, capitals, and voussoirs appear figures and compositions borrowed from pieces realized in metal, ivory, or miniature painting.

Toward the end of the 12th century, medieval society began to organize itself politically and to attain a certain unity and equilibrium. No longer could the austerity, rigidity, and heaviness of the Romanesque style serve to express the soaring ardor of the human spirit. Romanesque art would not survive beyond the 12th century.

Gothic Art

Other than the art of ancient Greece, Gothic art is the only instance in the West of a completely integrated aesthetic renewal. Of course, in the early, gestation period of the 12th century, Gothic offers a number of striking analogies with Romanesque art. Moreover, its first manifestations were often limited to ogival, or pointed-arch, vaults raised upon Romanesque structures. But once matured, Gothic departed so radically from anything ever seen before that it becomes difficult to establish the lines of the style's genesis and development. Quite simply, Gothic constituted a revolution that would affect every aspect of creative life.

Gothic art was born in the Ile-de-France around 1125. Its appearance in France coincided with the consolidation of French royal power and the establishment of the French national state. Soon Gothic would conquer England and then, in the 13th and 14th centuries, spread across the whole of Europe. If, like Romanesque, Gothic sought to glorify God and to instruct, it also wanted, above all else, to move the faithful and to arouse their religious fervor.

Gothic architecture is immediately identifiable by the verticality and lightness of structures in which voids prevail over solids. The art of stained glass developed progressively as massive walls gave way to huge, spacious windows. Decoration in cathedrals became more abundant than in Romanesque churches, but lost much of the earlier style's imaginative character. A new principle required that nature be respected by reproducing its appearance with fidelity. Ornamental compositions, still admirably inventive, were realized less for themselves than as a framework for human figures that, during the 13th century, attained a marvelous perfection.

Gothic sculpture, along with the cathedrals, is one of the most moving and beautiful achievements of the Western Middle Ages. In the words of Pierre Pradel, the Louvre's chief curator of sculpture: "Corresponding to the revolution in the art of building is another, less daring but more profound, revolution — that of sculpture. After a half-century, in the course of which Romanesque stone carvers, enthusiastically engaged with a reviving process, had used bas-reliefs as occasions for indulging their imagination and their love of strongly rhythmic compositions and conventional figures, there appeared a great aspiration toward a less rigid style, a style more related to human reality, a style that found its true expression in the perfected form of the statue."

The minor arts also bore remarkable fruits in the 13th century. Paris, with its university, was a city of libraries, which encouraged the development of numerous ateliers of illuminators specializing in psalters, breviaries, books of hours, all filled with minute and richly colored designs (page 124). The French capital also saw the establishment of the most accomplished ivory carvers (pages 122, 123), whose finely wrought works were exported throughout the known world.

But the Hundred Years War, during which the greater part of France was occupied by English armies, brought the nation political ruin in the 14th century and put an end to its cultural ascendancy in Europe.

Italy, which lay outside the conflict, undertook important artistic experiments and with them succeeded in liberating painting from domination by Byzantine art. The new spirit brought by Saint Francis of Assisi reinforced the realist and humanistic current in art, which had early manifested itself in Cimabue's *Madonna with Angels* (page 127) and, even more, in the work of Giotto (page 126). This opened a direct route to the Renaissance.

The fascinated eyes of Fayum mirror the decadence of Rome and the dawning of a new age

The *Portraits of Fayum* are the only examples of easel painting that have survived from antiquity, and they disclose the profound mutation that occurred in the Roman Empire during the 2nd century after Christ. Provincial and popular arts grew tremendously in importance, a phenomenon explicable, on the one hand, by the decadence of the traditions practiced in metropolitan ateliers and, on the other, by the loosening of Imperial authority over its distant possessions. Orientalism, long suppressed by Western illusionism, experienced a new flowering, which often expressed itself through a spirit obviously troubled by the unstable times. The so-called "Fayum Portraits" take their name from the Egyptian oasis where the works were discovered, held in the wrappings that bound the mummies the paintings represent. In a style of naive, expressionistic realism, the artists worked from life, using natural colors mixed with hot beeswax. For the broad surface—as in the background and the clothing—they employed a brush, but, for the faces, replaced it with a kind of spatula. The enlarged eyes, the intense expression, which seems almost hallucinated in the man and rather melancholy in the woman, announced even at this early date the dominant characteristic of Byzantine painting.

Portrait of a Woman.
2nd century A.D. Antinoë, Egypt.
Encaustic on wood, 0.42 × 0.24m/1′4½″ × 9½″.

Portrait of a Man, indigenous type.
1st century. Thebes (?). Egypt.
Distemper on wood, 0.29 × 0.18m/11½″ × 7″.

below: This Egyptian relief belongs to the Coptic period, long regarded as an artistic desert lying between the Egypt of the Pharaohs and that of the Moslems, but now found to possess a vigorous and interesting personality. "One of the great benefits bestowed by modern art will have been to modify our vision of things and to help us perceive the value of forms and styles different from the Greco-Roman ideal" observes Père du Bourguet, curator in charge of the Louvre's Christian antiquities. In the beginning the word "Copt" designated the entire population of the Nile Valley that, during the first centuries after Christ, passed progressively from paganism to Christianity. Legitimate heirs to the Hellenistic repertoire of motifs, the Copts radically modified the treatment and meaning of this legacy. The pagan Victory would become a Christian subject—an angel raising to heaven a portrait medallion bearing an image of the dead.

With the crumbling of authority, hybrid gods suddenly appear along the frontiers of a disintegrating Empire

Dionysiac Figure. 4th century. Egypt. Limestone, 0.61 × 0.60m/1'11½".

Bas-relief decorating a Panel Enframement (detail). 6th century. Egypt. Limestone; height 0.34, total length 0.89m/1'1½" × 2'11".

Horus on Horseback. 4th century. Egypt. Sandstone, 0.49 × 0.32m/1'7¼" × 1'½".

right: *Horus on Horseback* provides a perfect illustration of the syncretism that operated in early Coptic art between the Hellenistic themes introduced by Egypt's foreign occupants and the Pharaonic traditions preserved in popular memory. Protector of Egyptian royalty since the earliest times, the god Horus is here represented in the hybrid form given him by the sculptors of ancient Egypt: the body of a man and the head of a falcon (see page 63). With his lance he pierces a crocodile, symbol of evil in Nilotic mythology. But as a result of the iconographical mingling, Horus becomes a Roman cavalryman, an image that inevitably recalls the "victorious imperators" on the ivories of Byzantium (see page 107).

far right: This *Dionysiac Figure,* surrounded by vines, stands forth in high relief within the cavity of a carved stone. The style remains naturalistic—proving the persistence of Hellenistic influence—but already characteristics that are distinctively Copt have begun to appear: disproportion and disequilibrium, swollen forms, stylization. Without threatening the harmony of the figure, the artist has made an assault upon the Greco-Roman canons. The short legs with their massive thighs are in marked contrast to the elongated waist and the fullness of the bust. With musculature suppressed, the transition from one part of the body to the other has become smooth and almost imperceptible. The face, set with prominent, hypnotically fixed pupils, has lost all individuality in favor of an expressive intensity that, more and more, would reject the imitation of nature.

In the simplification
of its forms
and the brilliance
of its colors,
Coptic art seems
not only timeless
but distinctively modern

Textile with Bucolic Subjects. Late 5th century. Egypt. Tapestry, full height 1.47m/4′9¾″.

Fragment with the Head of a Dancer. 5th century. Egypt. Tapestry, 0.42 × 0.32m/1'4½" × 1'½"

Textiles and tapestries undoubtedly constitute the most brilliant creations of Coptic art. Thanks to the dry climate of Egypt, clothing, cushion covers, and wall hangings have survived in quantity, sufficient to reveal the complete evolution of style in this genre. The works, although secular by definition, borrow their decorative themes from pagan mythology, often mixing geometric or biomorphic patterns with Dionysiac scenes. The *Strip with Bucolic Subjects* (far left), for instance, offers a succession of rectangular boxes, enclosing Bacchic dancers whose modeled forms derived from earlier Greco-Roman sculpture. But around the boxes unfurls an ornamental border whose flowers—shown spread out or in profile—are stylized in a way that reveals more concern for the total effect than for the individual detail. Such stylization exists even in the magnificent *Fragment with a Dancer's Head* (left). Here, a face whose features have, in general, been given the most summary treatment seems overwhelmed by immense, almost square-shaped eyes. Animating the image is a play of flat, violent colors bounded by thick contours. Despite its modest dimensions, this masterpiece affirms that the art of Coptic weavers equaled the monumental elegance of Byzantine mosaics.

In the rich and elaborate harnesses
created for their horses,
the Byzantines and Sassanians
reinvent the decorative brilliance
of Ancient Near Eastern art

left: This *Head of a Horse* reflects the magnificence of the Sassanian dynasty that reigned in Iran from the 3rd to the 7th centuries. Silver, an abundant resource intensively exploited, fostered the fashioning of luxurious objects: plates, cups, bottles, and reliefs, all finely worked. Rarely, however, did this art produce sculpture-in-the-round, which makes the Louvre's piece especially precious, apart from the fact that it belonged to an ornamental ensemble on the throne of the Great King. Heirs worthy of the civilizations that preceded them in Asia Minor, the Sassanian Persians registered a marked predilection for animal subjects and for sumptuous harnesses decorated with geometric motifs. Horses figure frequently in scenes of combat and royal investiture, but, most of all, in hunting episodes.

right: The *Barberini Ivory* is one of the most important artistic creations of Byzantium's first Golden Age. It represents a powerful compromise between the Hellenistic tradition and the plastic conceptions of the Orient. The "Emperor Triumphant"—possibly Zeno—is treated in the antique manner: pronounced relief, the three-quarter angle of the rearing horse, relative observance of perspective. On the other hand, the angel or winged Victory, the consul standing on the left (who would be Theodoric), and, under the horse's hooves, the vanquished people bearing trophies—all display the direct influence of the Orient, which gave the artist the freedom to deploy the resources of his imagination. Responding to expressive needs, he varied the disposition and scale of his figures, since what really counted, in Asian eyes, was the work's narrative force.

Barberini Ivory (detail). c. 500.
Byzantium. 0.342 × 0.268m/1'1½" × 10½".

Head of a Horse. 4th–5th century. Sassanian Persia.
Silver and gold, height 0.14 × 0.20m/5½" × 7¾".

Transcending
their Greco-Roman heritage,
the ateliers of the Nile
grope toward
a new image of humanity
that would haunt
the high period
of European civilization

right: *The Annunciation,* fragment of a decorative panel possibly made for a church, is one of the most arresting monuments of Coptic sculpture in wood. It is also one of the oldest representations of the Virgin now preserved in France. Seated, with a basket of wool on her knees, Mary extends her hand toward the angel, a figure for which only a foot and part of a leg survive. The work is related to other Annunciations made in Syria and Palestine. But the frontal orientation of the face combined with the profile presentation of the rest of the figure, the stylized eyes, the nose, and the pointed chin, like the proportional relationship of the head to the other members, are all typical of the "rude" manner of the Copts.

left: This *Portrait of a Woman,* discovered at Antinoë in Egypt, was painted directly upon the shroud in which the deceased was buried. The realism of the face evokes the style of the best Fayum portraits, of which this work constitutes a late manifestation. It is characteristic of a period in which works of pagan inspiration coexisted with those of nascent Christianity. The "looped" cross that the subject holds in her hand is, for instance, an ambivalent emblem, reproducing the *ankh* sign that designated "life" for the ancient Egyptians. It could therefore represent a revival of old local beliefs, or it could be an adaptation of a pagan sign to Christian usage, signifying the adherence of the subject to the new religion.

Female Portrait on a Shroud (detail).
4th century. Egypt. Encaustic on canvas;
total height 2m, width 0.84m/6'6¾" × 2'9".

The Annunciation. 5th–6th century. Egypt. Wood, 0.285 × 0.145m/11¼" × 5¾".

Inspired by a new faith, curious abstractions shatter the old realism but yield deeply moving works

left and below: These abstract *Paintings on Stucco* decorated the walls of a convent at Baouit in Middle Egypt. Monasticism—that great movement destined to spread throughout Christianity—had its birth on Egyptian soil, where the monasteries quickly multiplied, forming an almost unbroken chain along both banks of the Nile. Since the country remained a province of the Byzantine Empire, these monasteries, which dominated Christian life in Egypt, would impress their relentless search for the absolute upon the artistic production of their time. When the Arab conquerors came in the 7th century, the iconoclasm they brought could only stimulate an extreme development of a tendency—stylization—in which the Copts, or Christian Egyptians, were already past masters. Whatever remained of naturalism in their art soon gave way to geometric motifs. In this way, remarked Père du Bourguet, "Coptic art integrated all its own aesthetic preoccupations. Not content to transform the appearance of a subject in favor of the total effect, it succeeded in eliminating the subject altogether."

Painting on Stucco. c. 6th–7th century. Egypt. 1.72 × 1.87m/5′7¾″ × 6′1½″.

Painting on Stucco. c. 6th–7th century. Egypt. 1.72 × 1.87m/5′7¾″ × 6′1½″.

right: This cast-iron *Crucifix* reflects the ardent and austere faith of the Christian communities in Syria. Its almost abstract form must be understood in the light of the scorn felt by Orientals toward realism and illusionism. "For the Oriental," writes Etienne Coche de La Ferté, "the true reality is that of the spirit, and for him the Platonic equilibrium of body and soul is tipped in favor of the soul." Perhaps, suggests Père du Bourguet, "This is the true reason why the naturalistic representation of the Crucifixion, so common in our time, is absent from Early Christian art. And not, as has long been thought, because the agony of the Cross, reserved for slaves and serious criminals, would have gone against the sensibilities of the first Christians."

Crucifix. Early Middle Ages. Syria. Cast iron, 0.085 × 0.053m/3¼″ × 2″.

As a new empire-builder appears in Europe, a royal imagery develops, creating individualized portraits of the medieval monarchs

right: The *Statuette of Charlemagne* shows the extent to which the Carolingian age remained faithful to the antiquarian spirit that found particularly strong expression in the metal arts. The taste for equestrian statues—fostered no doubt by the heroic likeness of Marcus Aurelius still standing in Rome—reveals itself in certain facts of history: Charlemagne brought back from Ravenna an equestrian statue of Theodoric and decided to have his own image, mounted on horseback, cast in bronze. For a long time experts hesitated to identify the subject of the Louvre's statue as "the emperor with the white flowing beard." However, the round visage crossed by heavy mustaches recalls the face of Charlemagne in the mosaics of the Lateran. Moreover, the imperial costume corresponds closely to the minute description left by Einhard: "On fast days he wore a garment woven of gold, shoes embellished with gems, a gold fibula to pin his mantle, a diadem of the same metal and it too ornamented with stones." The treatment of the horse, infinitely freer than that of the rider, suggests that it derived from an antique bronze reused in the 9th century. In any event, the work is representative of Carolingian art—an art glowing with the last embers of classical culture, yet pregnant with a new formal synthesis that would give birth to Romanesque art.

left and below: These magnificent *Chess Pieces* withhold the secret of their origin. Because of the abstract floral decoration, they were once attributed to islamicized countries. But the motifs, which spread widely in the 6th to the 8th centuries, were as prevalent in the iconographic vocabulary of northern Europe as in the aniconic repertoire of Islam. Whether Arabic, Norwegian, or German, the pieces are carved in ivory with a remarkable sense of volume. It is their ruggedness and their compactness that for us constitute the little works' singularity and value. The details of material, like the king's sword, or those of psychology, as in the face, seem to emerge slowly from the mass, all the while retaining the density of the substance out of which they were born.

Chess Pieces. 12th–13th century. Scandinavia(?). Walrus ivory, 0.087 × 0.055m/3½" × 2¼".

Statuette of Charlemagne. 9th century. France. Bronze, height 0.24m/9½".

left: This Christ figure no doubt once formed part of a group representing the Descent from the Cross, a probability suggested by the position of the right arm. While such Descents are fairly numerous in Italy and Spain, they scarcely exist in France. Thus, the theme, by its extreme rarity, suffices to place the Crucifix among the greatest masterpieces of Romanesque art. The elongated silhouette and the emaciation of the torso are of a notable refinement, but Romanesque convention governs the closed eyes and the overall sweetness of the expression. In the stylization of its face, the figure evokes the Christ in the narthex of Vézelay. At Vézelay, however, the rhythm of the drapery endows the figure with a movement meant to induce sorrow, while in this Crucifixion the loincloth's sober elegance helps to emphasize the work's tragic serenity.

Christ of the Descent from the Cross.
12th century. France.
Painted and gilded wood, 1.55 × 1.68m/5′1″ × 5′6¼″.

Cain and Abel (detail). 11th century. Salerno, Italy. Ivory, 0.109 × 0.120m/4¼″ ×4 ¾″.

above: *Cain and Abel* is a fragment from a larger and aesthetically more important work by the Romanesque ivory carvers: the front panel for the altar of the cathedral at Salerno. "The 11th century," writes Pierre Héliot, "was the century of the caesura that would separate an old world attached to antiquity by tradition, habit, and nostalgia, from a new world, forged in trial and endeavoring to organize and define itself." This detail displays not only a naïve expressiveness meant to move us, but also the triangular composition dear to Romanesque artists. According to Pierre Francastel, the stability of the triangle stood for a universe conceived of as powerfully hierarchic and dominated by the idea of God.

right: *Daniel in the Lion's Den* is one of the first appearances made by the human figure in the décor of Romanesque capitals. Bound to architecture, Romanesque sculpture was required to dramatize the dominant structure's forms and volumes, which meant that a preestablished framework dictated the proportions and attitudes of the subjects represented in sculpture. This, in turn, accounts for the disconcerting figural deformations that the Renaissance and its classical aftermath failed to understand and thus condemned as a whole, even though the "defects" had in no way troubled the sensibilities of the 11th century. Little did it bother this age that verisimilitude was not respected, that the human image might be caricatured, as long as the artist achieved his goal, which was to *suggest*. Architectural imperatives, moreover, obliged sculptors to exercise ingenuity and derive advantage from each situation. As a consequence, they gained a power of expression that could be deployed throughout a repertoire of prodigious variety. While taking themes from Scripture and the lives of the saints, Romanesque carvers also sought inspiration in Oriental flora and in the fabulous bestiaries created by the civilizations of the Ancient Near East.

Daniel in the Lion's Den. Late 11th century.
Paris. Marble capital, height 0.50m/1′7¾″.

A burgeoning population,
both secular and sacred,
appears in
the sculptural embellishments
of Romanesque Europe,
all dominated
by the idea of God
and the fate of human souls

Saint Michael Slaying the Dragon exhibits one of the traditional themes of medieval sculpture. It symbolizes the triumph of the divine cause over the rebellion fomented by Lucifer. That the demon has assumed the form of a dragon in Romanesque iconography is once again explained by the fascination that medieval Europe felt for the bestiaries of the Orient. Monks and merchants alike returned from their voyages to the Holy Land bearing textiles and objects that made the West familiar with this wild menagerie, whose exotism and expressiveness appealed to Europeans even more than its original value as imagery endowed with magical powers. The Louvre's *Saint Michael* can be compared with a relief treating the same subject on the portal of the priory of Anzy-le-Duc in Burgundy. The sense of movement, the twisting of the monster, the drapery style, and the tense expression of the Archangel, his eyes inlaid with metallic pupils, make it possible to attribute the work to the atelier of Burgundy and to give it a date of 1130, close to that of the Anzy-le-Duc relief.

Saint Michael Slaying the Dragon. c. 1125–50. Burgundy. Stone, height 0.85m/2'9½".

Funerary Mask. 13th century. Limoges, France.
Gilded copper, height 0.37m/1'2½".

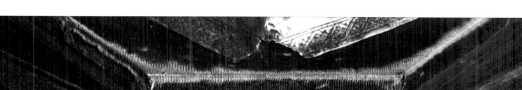

Ethereally
elongated statues
emerge from stone columns
to evince
the radiant purity
of faith in the time
of the great cathedrals

King Solomon and the Queen of Sheba, both figures from
the Old Testament, ornamented the central portal
of Notre-Dame de Corbeil, erected around 1150. Although they date from the end of the 12th century,
these "column-statues" are characteristic of the royal
portal art introduced at Chartres from 1145 to 1170.
In such figures a genuine Revolution—the Gothic—
occurred. Here sculpture began to free itself from
the architectural enframement that had claimed it
for so long. In their stiffness, in their straight and
attenuated forms, in the shallow, parallel fluting of
their drapery folds, these two works still embody the
spirit of the Romanesque. But by standing forward
of the columns, there defining a volume independent of the structural members, they anticipate the
rebirth of a kind of monumental statuary not created
in the West since classical times. A gentle humanism
would supplant the visionary art of the Romanesque
sculptors. Even a note of luxury appears in the
Queen's brooch and long plaits (left), adding to the
nobility of a face that already reflects the naturalism
of the approaching Renaissance.

King Solomon and the Queen of Sheba.
1175–1200. Ile-de-France.
Stone; height of the King 2.38m,
height of the Queen 2.28m/7′9¾″ and 7′5¾″.

121

Descent from the Cross. 1250–75. Paris. Ivory, height 0.29m/11¼".

Virgin and Child. 1330–70.
Paris. Ivory, height 0.195m/7¾".

above: This *Virgin and Child* possesses all the elegance and refinement that, throughout Christianity, would bring glory to the "tailors of images" in the Paris ateliers. A majestic figure nobly draped in a mantle of wide folds, this standing Virgin exemplifies the aristocratic quality of the "courtly art" that emerged in the 14th century. Still, the artist succeeded in endowing his grand lady with human warmth, evident in the smiling looks exchanged between Mother and Child, linking the pair in mutual love and confidence.

left: The *Descent from the Cross,* one of the most moving of Gothic ivories, evokes the sculptural reliefs on the tympana of Senlis, Chartres, and Paris' Notre-Dame. The work must have formed part of an ensemble—perhaps an altarpiece—narrating the life of Christ. Inspired by monumental sculpture, Parisian ivory carvers in the second half of the 13th century attained a perfection that would never be surpassed. The sense of measure, the absence of all excess, the truth of feeling expressed by this Descent lend scale and amplitude to a small and delicate art.

Ivory brings out
the delicacy and verve
of Gothic carvers,
allowing them
to endow religious art
with the expressive quality
of everyday life

Flagellant of Christ. 1300–30.
Paris. Ivory, height 0.20m/7¾".

The Taking of Christ. 1300–50. Paris. Ivory, 0.186 × 0.100m/7¼" × 4".

above: This *Flagellant of Christ,* to which the ivory carver strove to give a fierce look, constitutes an early manifestation of the mannerism that would flourish during the 14th century, reaching a fevered climax in the Flamboyant style. The work here once belonged to a group representing an episode in Christ's passion. Despite its torsions, the figure seems capable of not even the slightest violence, and only with difficulty could one imagine that such a preciously tormented figure actually brandishes a whip for the purpose of beating Christ.

left: *The Taking of Christ,* by its tight, closed composition, attests to the influence of manuscript illumination on ivory carving. The scene is realized with a rare economy of means that nonetheless allows for an element of spontaneity. Thus, to show all the protagonists and their sudden acts, the artist "foreshortened" the actors in the foreground, where Saint Peter severs the ear of Malchus, the high priest's servant. With a gesture of his hand, Jesus orders Peter to return his sword to its sheath. As Judas embraces the Savior and prepares to give the traitor's kiss, two soldiers—who no doubt once brandished arms—approach to make the arrest.

123

At the dawn
of the humanistic Renaissance,
painting makes
the stories
of the saints
a present reality
and demystifies
the images of kings

Jean Fouquet (1420–1480?). *Saint Martin,* from the *Book of Hours of Etienne Chevalier* (detail). France. 15th century.
Illumination of vellum, total height 0.16m/6¼".

above: This manuscript illuminated by Jean Fouquet represents Saint Martin cutting his cloak in half so as to share it with a beggar. The painting belonged to the *Book of Hours of Etienne Chevalier,* a masterpiece from which only forty-two leaves survive, preserved in the Louvre and at Chantilly. It was in illumination that the essentials of a pictorial tradition were developed in France. Indeed, the pages of manuscripts gave artists the opportunity to discover all the problems that would have to be resolved later in panel painting: the representation of the human image and open nature, the suggestion of bodily volume on a flat surface, linear perspective, the suggestion of light. Beginning in the 13th century, the ateliers of Paris dominated the artistic production of Europe. In the 14th century the Parisian artists adopted a more descriptive style, a style more responsive to visual reality. The miniature became a veritable painting, although executed in a book, and took inspiration from scrupulously observed facts of everyday life. The art of Jean Fouquet marks the apogee of this movement. Here the master places the scene of Saint Martin's charity in Paris—on the Pont-au-Change it would seem—thus leaving us a rare view of the city at the end of the Gothic age.

right: The *Portrait of Jean le Bon* is both a powerful work of art and a historical document of inestimable value, being the first known portrait in Western medieval art. No doubt executed by the *peintre du roi* Girard d'Orléans, it witnesses the transition that art made from unrealistic conventions to closely observed reality. Nothing could be less "official" than this work, in which neither insignia nor crown suggests the rank of the sitter. Only a simple inscription discloses his identity. "Jean II desires to be as he is, not the King, but a man," remarked Galienne Francastel. "The artist, taking account of this desire, which in 1360 was something wholly new, learned how to forfeit a full-length image in order to concentrate on the head. With this planted squarely on powerful shoulders, the secular portrait is born, dedicated to the pursuit of an inexhaustible career."

Portrait of John the Good. c. 1360. France.
Panel, 0.55 × 0.34m/1'9¾" × 1'1½".

125

In monumental
compositions,
Cimabue and Giotto
begin to open up
the closed space
of the Middle Ages,
a radical, daring departure
that lays
the foundations of
Renaissance perspective

right: The *Madonna with Angels* dates from late in the career of Cimabue, whose existence can be documented from 1240 to 1302. Dante cited the painter as the most famous artist of the generation just before Giotto. Pioneer of Italian painting, Cimabue was the first Western artist who made an effort to throw off the yoke of Byzantine influence. If the figures remain like neatly contoured cutouts, the urge to suggest volume can nonetheless be felt. The curving folds that fall about the Madonna's face, hips, and knees tend to create the illusion of a real body underneath. And despite the two-dimensionality of the throne, we feel an eagerness on the part of the painter to render depth. For instance, he slips the Virgin's aureole between the head and the back of the throne. On either side of the central group he places three angels upon a sequence of rising tiers and so arranges them that they animate the pictorial field. No longer is the gold ground an impenetrable screen, for Cimabue's brush has filled it with air and lightened it as if to evoke the limitless, immeasurable space of celestial splendor. Avoiding both rigidity and tortured vehemence—the two poles of Byzantine figural art—the Florentine master achieved a restrained, harmonious lyricism in which he affirmed the serene depths of his faith.

left: *Saint Francis Receiving the Stigmata* reveals a revolutionary conception of reality. Here the genial pupil of Cimabue gave effect to movement and space; he humanized the saints. Of Giotto, his contemporaries enthusiastically asserted: "He translated the art of painting from Greek into Latin and made it modern." No more for Giotto the frontality and hieratism of Byzantine figures. The discovery of the three-dimensional world placed man at the center of things. Thus, bodies became solid and substantial—almost "sculptural"—in space. Giotto focused the whole of his composition upon Saint Francis kneeling before a crucified angel borne aloft, as the legend stated, by three pairs of wings, one of which is as long as the legs. Calculated to have a psychological impact, the Saint's gestures are striking by virtue of the inner truth they convey. But in addition to religious feeling, the crossed diagonals linking the palms and feet of the two figures betray a concern for structure, for the intellectual clarity that is so fundamental to Giotto's modernity. "A century later," writes Charles Sterling, "he would inspire Masaccio and revive Florentine painting. His sense of the essential was recognized as 'classical,' for one finds it again in Raphael. His 'cubist' simplification of volume and his dramatic sobriety, typical of the Italian 'primitive,' never ceases to amaze the artists of our time."

Cimabue (1240–1302). *Madonna with Angels.*
Florence, Italy. Late 13th century.
Panel, height 4.24 × 2.76m/13′11″ × 9′¾″.

Giotto (1266–1337).
Saint Francis Receiving the Stigmata.
1300–35. Florence, Italy.
Panel, 3.14 × 1.62m/10′3½″ × 5′3¾″.

127

Late Gothic and Early Renaissance
15th Century

The 15th century was a period of transition that saw the final, twilight masterpieces of the Late Gothic and, simultaneously, the dawning of a new spring-fresh period — the Early Renaissance.

The Hundred Years War and the Great Schism in the West had profoundly shaken Europe's political equilibrium and the authority of the Church. In general, the period proved to be one of the most eventful in all of history. In France, the insanity of Charles VI, having created a power vacuum, encouraged the recrudescence of bitter feudal rivalry. On top of this internecine struggle came the war with England, whose Henry V inflicted the terrible defeat of Agincourt upon the armies of France. The consequences would be disastrous: fourteen years of occupation, resistance, and violence. Only in 1429, when Joan of Arc broke the siege of Orleans, did France begin the reconquest of its territory. This would not be completed until 1453, with the liberation of Guyenne (Aquitaine), which the English had held for almost a century. Louis XI, who mounted the throne of France in 1461, became an able and persevering statesman, tirelessly devoting the whole of his reign to eradicating the last of feudal independence and to the process of national reunification.

The Duchy of Burgundy, a powerful vassal state of France, would pose a redoubtable danger throughout the 15th century. Remaining loyal to the French monarchy until the death of Duke Philippe le Hardi in 1404, Burgundy allied thereafter with England in order to protect its dominant interests in the industrious and wealthy Low Countries. After a long conflict — sometimes devious, sometimes overt, always pitiless — France finally won out over its ambitious rival. In 1482, defeated and dismembered, the Burgundian state was divided between the House of Austria, which took possession of Flanders and Franche-Comté, and the House of France, which annexed the original duchy.

By the time Charles VIII died in 1498, French national unity had almost been realized, with all the great feudal fiefs firmly attached to the crown, with the exception of Venaissin.

The Germanic Empire, by contrast, was a mosaic of principalities and kingdoms, the governing of which required a combination of diplomacy and strength that proved beyond the capacity of a succession of 15th-century sovereigns. Hostility among the Prince-Electors, insurrection, and incessant conspiracy made the task of a German monarch even more arduous. When Frederick III of Hapsburg died in 1493, "the union of Flanders and Austria might appear like a resurrection of the Holy Roman Empire," wrote Cécile Goldscheider, "but the imperial idea that had so profoundly influenced the evolution of the medieval world lost its initial significance."

Quattrocento Italy was torn by conflict among its constituent states. The successive waves of *condottieri,* whose opportunism hardly permitted ideological rigor, contributed considerably to the instability of the region's political chess game. The most powerful principalities were the Papal States, the Duchy of Milan, the republics of Florence and Venice, and the Kingdom of Naples and Sicily, whose interrelationships were dominated by ceaseless intrigues, alliances, coalitions, and armed conflict. The paradox is that chronic military disorder in no way impeded the flowering of a brilliant civilization.

At the end of the Middle Ages, European art was essentially characterized by the coexistence of two, absolutely distinct styles: the Gothic, which reigned supreme in the North; and, in Italy, the first blooming of the Renaissance.

Late Gothic

Gothic art progressed gradually toward decadence with a grandiose "swan song," its commitment to universality giving way to an ever-more pronounced nationalism. In its final form—the Flamboyant style—Gothic enjoyed great favor in 15th-century Germany. Italy, however, escaped its influence almost entirely.

Sculpture liberated itself definitively from architecture to become a wholly independent art form. Because of sculpture's deep involvement with reality, it also broke free of Byzantine symbolism. No longer would the image be an ideogram; it became a faithful reproduction of some visible form. Like Greco-Roman sculpture, Western statuary took on a palpable realism, but with spiritual accents rarely seen in antique works. Gothic visages show neither Classical serenity nor the rude moral tensions of Romanesque faces. Their features, all refinement and elegance, were meant to inspire tenderness and feeling. Gothic sculptors, who needed new themes in which to exercise their talents, did much to enrich Christian iconography, finding characters from the Old and New Testaments and from among the saints and ordinary priests and prelates more interesting to represent than allegorical figures. Woman, the subject favored by the literature of courtly love, became the object of an admiration and a respect absolutely unprecedented in the history of civilization, reflecting a sentimental turn of mind that gave rise to the cult of the Virgin, Mother of Christ. Thus, more than ever, emphasis fell upon the Annunciation (page 163), Mary's maternal love, and the nursing of the Infant Jesus (page 162). The attitudes given to feminine figures relaxed, as a supple and slowly spiraling S-curve replaced the stiff frontality of the older forms (page 165).

The evolution of the minor arts lost momentum. Despite substantial improvements in techniques, artisans failed to recover the rigor and purity of their Gothic predecessors.

But in the pictorial arts, a prodigious technical development began to occur in the 14th century. Painting now assumed an international style that affected regions already dominated by the Renaissance as much as countries still bound to the Gothic aesthetic.

In northern Europe two different schools held sway: Flemish painting, with its Gothic spirit, and French painting, which more and more turned toward Italy.

Flemish painting resulted from a synthesis of the precise, linear manner of the Parisian miniaturists, the delicacy of Lombard color, and Gothic naturalism. All these characteristics can be seen in the work of the van Eycks—especially in the *Virgin of Autun* (pages 142, 143), painted by Jan, the younger of the two brothers.

From the 16th century until our time a multitude of researchers have dedicated themselves to the recovery of the processes by which the van Eycks obtained the extraordinary luminosity and incomparable finesse that are so characteristic of their art. The oldest explanation is one given in 1550 by the Florentine, Giorgio Vasari, called the father of art history. According to him, that miraculous virtuosity came from the use of oil painting, which was the invention of Jan. In 1951, after a chemical analysis of this master's colors, certain specialists confirmed Vasari's assertion. The scientific results indicate that the technique originated by the founders of the Flemish school was an elaborate and painstaking one in which many extremely thin, translucent glazes of oil-based colors were applied over a wood panel coated with a white preparation. Other experts, however, have officially contested these findings and insisted that the van Eycks merely followed established procedures and used color powders bound in both the white and the yolk of egg. This means that the jewellike brilliance of the colors comes from a varnish applied to the surface after the painting was finished. Such an interpretation reduces the van Eycks' secret to an ingenious exploitation of all the resources proper to the painting of their time. But whatever the precise nature of the technique involved, there is no denying that with the van Eycks the art of painting had come into its own, breaking entirely with drawing. Bounding contour lines disappear as colors and their infinitely subtle nuancing assume the full burden of defining form, texture, and volume. Through the careful gradations of tones, Flemish masters succeeded in creating upon a flat surface a powerful and convincing effect of solid forms located in deep space.

Power, vigor, and realism distinguish the Flemish school until the end of the 15th century, when Memling added his own special note of serenity (pages 144, 145). But the Flemish personality and the Gothic spirit would continue even beyond the century, especially in the work of two very great masters: Hieronymus Bosch (page 169) and Pieter Bruegel the Elder (page 168).

French painting, meanwhile, detached itself bit by bit from the Gothic tradition. In Burgundy, artists like Bellechose and Malouel adopted the Flemish style and even made it more mordant. In Avignon, where French and Italian influences converged, an art both mystical and monumental developed. One of its finest expressions, and a very great work of art, is the *Pietà* reproduced on page 157. Later, as Italy became an ever-more irresistible model,

a new harmonious beauty (page 166) raised French painting to a level attained only by the very greatest masterpieces of the Quattrocento.

In Germany, the Renaissance encountered stiff resistance from the Gothic sensibility. A master like Albrecht Dürer (pages 171, 173), richly nourished as he may have been by his Venetian experience, would retain throughout his life an essentially medievalizing attitude, a mind-set that would revive in full force with the agony and troubles brought by the Reformation. Thus, the spiritual space separating the two ages seems scarcely to have been penetrated by the "Red Knight" of Hans Baldung Grien (page 170).

The Early Renaissance in Italy

The revolution that Italians undertook in thought and art was carried out under inspiration from Classical antiquity. Prepared by an effort made throughout the Middle Ages, the movement took on distinctive form in the 15th century. After 1453, the year that Constantinople fell to the Turks, many scholars and men of letters arrived in the West from the eastern Mediterranean, where Byzantium had carefully preserved its Greek heritage as a living tradition. These learned classicists brought a new vitality to Western research in ancient texts, thereby encouraging the rapidly developing taste for the Greco-Roman past. The invention and practical application of printing toward the middle of the century made possible a broad diffusion of the old texts, which contributed further to the general curiosity about the ancients' conception of man and his place in the world.

Reason reclaimed its rights. Italian artists emancipated themselves from the imperatives of medieval faith and submitted to a subtle game of numbers and proportions by means of which they hoped to discover, beyond surface

15th Century

appearances, the laws of the ideal world.

The dominating idea in sculpture was to restore the beauty and power of the human body. Sculptors hoped to produce a replica of reality. Donatello, a great master in both stone and bronze, created portraits whose perfection could be compared only with the finest of Roman works.

But it was, above all, through the prodigious burst of genius among the various schools of painting that Italy gained an incontestable supremacy in the history of Quattrocento art.

The Florentine school was the first to develop. "Under the Medici, Florence became a new Athens," writes Jean Babelon, "proudly proclaiming its assimilation of the ancient city par excellence, which made the [Italian] 'city of the lily' the center of arts and letters, all united in a development that involved economics and politics as well." Florentine artists proved especially remarkable in their plastic genius and in their insatiable appetite for experimentation. From both these qualities flowed a decisive innovation that would determine the next five centuries of pictorial language: linear perspective.

Three painters fixed the main characteristics of the Florentine school. After Masaccio completely defined the formal, humanist ideal of the Renaissance, Uccello systematically applied the laws of perspective in pictures like the *Battle of San Romano* (pages 136–137). Simultaneously, Fra Angelico gave feeling a privileged place, but in this world of lingering Gothicism he integrated all the new discoveries in the depiction of form and movement (pages 132–35, 141, 142). At the end of the 15th century, the mannerism of Botticelli announced the decline of the Florentine school.

The Sienese school, at the opening of the Quattrocento, still excelled in the refinement, elegance, and charm first achieved by its founder, Duccio di Buoninsegna. This loyalty to a 14th-century ideal is particularly evident in the works of Sassetta (page 138), whose style would influence Sano di Pietro (pages 138, 139).

The Lombard school is exemplified by one of the greatest painters of the Quattrocento: Andrea Mantegna of Padua (pages 152–155). "Before anyone else in the Renaissance," writes Charles Sterling, "he conceived the heroic scheme of making an exact reconstruction of the world of the ancients....But such were his enthusiasm and his imaginative powers that he created a marvelous antique theatre."

The school of Verona found its strongest representative in Pisanello, who exhaustively investigated human and animal forms. A draftsman of genius (page 146), he invented a genre of art — the medal — which enjoyed immense popularity. Pisanello's astonishing virtuosity shines brilliantly in the *Portrait of a Princess* reproduced on page 147.

The Venetian school began to develop strength only with the arrival of Jacopo Bellini at the beginning of the 15th century. His son Giovanni (page 148) then proved an apt pupil. Interested in innovation, Giovanni transformed his technique under the influence of Antonello da Messina, who had learned to reconcile the sculptural vision of Italy with the pictorial vision of Flanders (page 149). Somewhat on the margin of the period's great experiments, the sensitive and delicate Vittore Carpaccio painted one of the first of the Venetian chronicles. A cosmopolitan city open to the Turkish Orient, Venice served as the backdrop against which to stage the lives of the saints. Thus was inaugurated a tradition in the art of a *la Serenissima* that two centuries later would climax in the work of Guardi.

Northern Europe resisted Italy for two hundred years. As a consequence, the declining Gothic and the ascendant Renaissance create a striking disequilibrium. In the 16th century, Italy would break through all barriers, as its Renaissance invaded the whole of Europe.

Mary receives glorification in the subtly new and radical art of Early Renaissance Florence

The Coronation of the Virgin by Fra Angelico extended medieval mysticism into the very midst of the Early Italian Renaissance. All the while that, in the bosom of the Florentine school, the realist current rose and spread the full length of the 15th century, Fra Angelico so saturated his painting with angelic piety that it gave the artist his name. It was the luminous musicality of celestial rites that he attempted to re-create. A palette of sweet tones, sometimes mingled with old-fashioned gold, endows the painting with the delicacy of an illumination—a technique practiced by Fra Angelico during the years of his apprenticeship. By disposing the choir of angels on either side of the Gothic dias, and by placing the saints at the foot of the throne, the artist built up a strong structural pyramid. Even so, the rhythm of the aureoles involves the figures in a girating movement that inevitably draws the viewer's attention to the central group: Christ crowning the Queen of Heaven.

Fra Angelico (1387–1455). *The Coronation of the Virgin.* c. 1435. Florence. Panel, 2.11 × 2.11m/6′11″ × 6′11″.

An inspired monk
finds the perfect analogy
of divine love
in colors and a perspective
of miraculous clarity

"Such a pure masterpiece," wrote Vasari concerning the *Coronation of the Virgin*, "could have been painted only by a saint." But if for Fra Angelico art was above all else the language of faith, it would do little justice to the actual scope of his work simply to look at its pious imagery, or to see the paintings as nothing but the projection of a serene mysticism. "Fra Angelico possessed a marvelous genius for giving plastic expression to his feelings," notes Pierre Francastel. "He was an authentic form giver." Even more than the overall composition of the *Coronation,* the details disclose pictorial preoccupations that were closely related to the most advanced painting of 15th-century Florence. Fra Angelico learned to harmonize the discoveries of his era—when a new conception of the visual world emerged—with his own personal vision, which remained faithful to the spirit of the Middle Ages. The faces of his saints, moving as they are, also evince a concern for giving a more persuasive definition to volume (left). For instance, the geometric configurations of the paving and the steps of the throne organize the space in accord with the principles of linear perspective (right), which became the greatest artistic triumph of the 15th century, and continued to govern painting until the very end of the 19th century.

Fra Angelico. *Coronation of the Virgin* (details).

A new spatial order forms
in the apparent chaos
of a forest of lances

The Battle of San Romano is one of the three panels executed by Uccello to commemorate the victory of the Florentines over the Sienese in 1432. Painted a dozen years after the event, the work hung in the Palazzo Medici, where it decorated the bedchamber of Lorenzo the Magnificent. It admirably summarizes the driving passion of Uccello's life: the application to painting of the laws of perspective, derived from Euclidean geometry, so as to create the perfect illusion of what the Renaissance considered to be "true" reality. Thus, his *Battle* obeys a rigorous mathematics, for in the inextricable tangle of warriors and horses nothing is left to chance. Lances, halberds, banners, rumps, and harnesses all exist solely to indicate the lines of recession, to suggest the retiring sequence of volumes in deep space. "From an art avid to reconstitute nature, and yet so unnatural," remarked Charles Sterling "Uccello extracted genuine poetry. The gestures seem suspended in air as if enchanted. The terrible melee is immobile and silent; its petrified intensity has the halluminating magic of a dream."

Sassetta (1392–1451). *The Blessed Ranieri
Delivering the Poor from the Prisons of Florence.*
c. 1440. Siena.
Canvas over wood, 0.45 × 0.65m/1'5¾" × 2'1½".

For the sake of pictorial truth,
Renaissance painters cultivate
the art of optical deception

Sano di Pietro (1406–81). *The Dream of Saint Jerome.* 15th century. Siena. Panel, 0.23 × 0.35m/9" × 1'1¾".

above left: *The Blessed Ranieri Delivering the Poor from the Prisons of Florence,* given to the museum in 1965 by the Friends of the Louvre, is a work by the delightful Sienese painter Sassetta. Originally the painting formed part of the predella to a polyptych commissioned from Sassetta for the high altar in the cathedral at Borgo San Sepolcro. Since the altar rose directly over the tomb of the Blessed Ranieri Rasini, the predella was made to recount the miracles attributed to this local saint. Here, dressed in Franciscan homespun and his head nimbed in gold, the holyman comes down from heaven to work the miracle of liberating the poor wretches incarcerated in Florentine prisons. Sassetta is one of the most representative masters of that marvelous artistic flowering known as Sienese painting. Poets and mystics, the Sienese conceived of art as a profession of faith. Toward that end every means of expression was brought into service, old plastic formulas as well as new flights of pictorial experimentation. With a mood positively saturated with religiosity, Sassetta mingles a knowing naïveté, a sense of the fabulous that reminds us of Douanier Rousseau (see pp. 310–11).

above right: *The Dream of Saint Jerome* attests to the concern the Sienese had for the Florentines' radical departures in matters of spatial organization. The episodes of the Passion and the lives of the saints now unfold in marble palaces whose architecture is controlled by a new kind of linear grid. Sano di Pietro, the most productive of the Sienese masters, took over much of the Sassetta manner and quickly discovered the persuasive formulas that would become the basis of his atelier's fame. But the charm, the astonishing suppleness of the drawing, and, above all, the exquisite freshness of the color save his oeuvre from the banalities of overproduction. Here Sano di Pietro illustrates the well-known dream of Saint Jerome, in which the holy man appears, on summons, before the tribunal of God, to be judged for his excessive love of reading the pagan authors of classical antiquity. As two angels flail the Saint, God—seated under a portico and flanked by four female figures personifying the Virtues, or possibly the Gospels—points an accusatory finger symbolizing censure: "Thou art the disciple of Cicero, not the disciple of Christ."

138

Saint Jerome and the Lion, once formed part of the same predella to which the *Dream of Saint Jerome* belonged (opposite page). And it displays the same poetic imagination, the same religious feeling. Undoubtedly the monastery portico and the paving appealed to Sano di Pietro for the opportunity they provided to experiment with illusionistic perspective. Still, the painter's interest remained concentrated on the foreground, where a scene from the life of Saint Jerome unfolds. In the presence of two terrified monks, the Saint kneels before a lion—more cublike than frightening—and with the greatest solicitude extracts a thorn from the creature's paw. According to legend, the lion would then remain at the side of his benefactor. When the beast suffered the unfair accusation of having devoured the convent's ass, it went after the thieves actually responsible for the donkey's disappearance and returned in triumph, bringing not only the lost animal but also two camels belonging to the now-fled malefactors.

Sano di Pietro (1406–81). *Saint Jerome and the Lion* (detail). 15th century. Siena, Italy. Panel, 0.23 × 0.78m(total)/9" × 2'6¾".

Painted poems endow barbaric scenes
of Christian martyrdom
with a surreal strangeness

below: To modern eyes the predella of Fra Angelico's *Coronation of the Virgin* possesses some of the strangely poetic juxtapositions that we now associate with 20th-century Surrealism. A horse in a jeweled harness charges into a marble colonnade and fixes us with a fascinating eye, while blood spurts from a man trampled by the beast. It is a sumptuously barbaric image with the timelessness and enigmatic precision of a dream. The purpose of the painting, however, is to illustrate a scene from the life of Saint Dominic founder of the Order of Preachers to which Fra Angelico belonged. One day when Saint Dominic, with Cardinal Stefano di Fossa Nova, was at a convent he had established, the pair learned of the death of the prelate's nephew. The adolescent had fallen from his mount and fractured his skull. Moved by his friend's grief, Saint Dominic had the body brought in, began to pray, and then approached the deceased. "In the name of Our Savior Jesus Christ, I say to thee: Arise!" By endowing this little picture with a dreamlike quality, Fra Angelico leads the viewer into the "climate" of miracle.

Fra Angelico. *The Coronation of the Virgin* (predella detail). c. 1435. Florence. Panel, 0.22 × 0.31m (total)/8¾″ × 11¼″.

Fra Angelico (1387–1455).
The Martyrdom of Saints Cosmas and Damian.
c. 1400. Florence.
Panel, 0.38 × 0.47m/1′3″ × 1′6½″.

above: *The Martyrdom of Saints Cosmas and Damian* belongs to the predella of a retable painted for the high altar at the San Marco convent in Florence. The Middle Ages had given this subject abundant treatment, and Fra Angelico may have revived it in honor of "the father of the nation," Cosimo de' Medici, whose generosity permitted the Dominican monks in 1440 to restore and decorate their priory. The Cosmas and Damian legend held that the pair, who were twins, had lived in Asia Minor during the 3rd century. There they practiced medicine without asking payment from their patients, which disinterestedness earned them the title of *anagyres* ("enemies of money").

But when the persecution of Christians set in, Cosmas and Damian were put to death, along with three of their brothers. Fra Angelico depicts the decapitation scene with deliberate precision. His purpose, however, is not to arouse the faithful to ecstasy but rather to induce reflection. Thus, the painter's natural gentleness prevails, and, to mitigate the cruelty of the spectacle, he shows the people pained by the martyrdom of their benefactors, spangles the meadow with small flowers, and, over a landscape of exquisite sweetness, hoists the spires of five cypress trees symbolizing the flight of the sainted souls toward heaven.

Jan van Eyck (c. 1380–1441). *Virgin of Autun*. c. 1435. Flanders. Panel, 0.66 × 0.62m/2'2" × 2'.

Seeing the earth
and all its beauties
as luminous with
divine presence,
Flemish painters make
a minute inventory
and magisterially
take possession of
their own environment

The Virgin of Autun is surely, despite its modest dimensions, the masterwork of Jan van Eyck—a revolutionary painting that definitively consummated the break already made by pictorial art with its medieval antecedents. This can be seen first in the panel's audacious iconography, where Our Lady, instead of occupying the central position always reserved for her in Adoration or Presentation scenes, has here withdrawn to one side, "sharing the pictorial field equally with the donor" (G. Francastel). Moreover—and also without precedent—van Eyck has given the sacred figure of Christ's Mother the same scale as that of a mere mortal, a praying figure traditionally identified as that of Nicolas Rolin, Bishop of Autun and Chancellor of the sovereign Duchy of Burgundy. Although kneeling before the Madonna, the Chancellor displays neither the humility nor the ecstasy normally present in such scenes. The gulf separating the divine and the human has been spanned. Thus, van Eyck confronts his subjects, not in some abstract, unearthly realm, but *hic et nunc* in a landscape whose decidedly terrestrial qualities reveal a fresh and avid curiosity before the richness of a world the artist has just discovered. It is a landscape constructed of a succession of planes receding into depth. But the eye pauses along with the two figures seen from the rear as they peer over the crenelations of a rampart. According to Jean Lejeune, the pair represent Jan van Eyck and his brother, Hubert. From that point beyond the meandering river leads the viewer into distance and on to the mountains on the horizon. The bridges, the turreted houses—all of which suggest the town of Liège—constitute a "microcosm aswarm with life." At no point, however, does this exhaustive inventory of the visible world degenerate into chaos. The compositional simplicity, the coloristic warmth, the "tissue" of light control and unify the abundance, extracting from it a magisterial synthesis.

Jan van Eyck. *Virgin of Autun* (detail)

143

In paintings
of great silence,
Memling portrays
solidly structured faces
in which
the industrious bourgeoisie
of Flanders
recognize their
own meditative reserve

The portraits of Memling developed the discovery of humanity made by Jan van Eyck. As the religious pretext weakened, the figure of the donor often succeeded in occupying an entire wing of an altarpiece. When separated, the wing becomes an independent portrait. The obsessive, psychological acuity of an observation devoid of compromise and flattery characterizes the style of Memling. His oeuvre reflects the rigor, the austerity, the severe faith of the bourgeoisie of Bruges among whom the artist found his patronage. Rather than vehement mysticism, these impassively dignified faces reveal a reluctance to unleash the movements of their inner lives. This simplicity is reinforced by the unified background in the *Study of a Head* (right), then softened in the *Portrait of an Elderly Woman* (left), where Memling has placed his subject in front of an open window. The formula seen here expands the sitter's space by incorporating the natural world, without however becoming lost in descriptive detail or otherwise threatening the "presence" of the person portrayed.

Hans Memling (c. 1433–94). *Portrait of an Elderly Woman.* c. 1470–75. Flanders. Panel, 0.35 × 0.29m/1'1¾" × 11½".

Hans Memling.
Study of a Head. c. 1470.
Paper, 0.221 × 0.168m/
8¾" × 6½".

145

Pisanello. *Head of a Young Woman.* 1400–50. Ink drawing, 0.245 × 0.182m/9¾" × 7¼".

above: This *Head of a Young Woman* forms part of a group of 318 drawings that the Milanese dealer Vallardi sold to the Louvre in 1856, claiming they were from the hand of Leonardo da Vinci. Subsequently most of the sheets in the Vallardi album have been reattributed to Pisanello. The Louvre therefore finds itself the owner of a unique collection of work by the great master of Verona. While showing what a passionate observer of life Pisanello was, the drawings also reveal his qualities as a gifted designer of medals. It was he moreover who created this new art—the medal—which could be regarded as the Renaissance's most distinctive form of expression. Alternately utilizing the precision of silverpoint or the pen's freedom of accent (as here), the artist immediately seized the essence of his subject and expressed it with the concision and economy of means required by the genre he invented.

right: The *Head of the Virgin Inclining to the Right,* executed in silverpoint on paper prepared with a gray ground, is a rare drawing by Rogier van der Weyden. Spare, delicate, linear—these are the distinctive qualities of the art of a master who may be the most representative exponent of the Flemish school after Jan van Eyck. The sobriety of his style allows him to achieve a dramatic intensity purified of every excess, while his sensibility endows women with a grave charm in which ardent spirituality blends with the everyday realities of the age. Van der Weyden's drawing, with its rich and precise modeling, traces the contours of the face but without the kind of hardness that would prevent the expression of tenderness. This artist, writes Charles Sterling, "brings to climax all the religious feelings of Gothic society, in everything that these contained of the bourgeois, the serious, and the concrete, in what they retained of feudalism's softened, courtly Romanesque."

Drawing with incisive purity, a great artist seizes the quintessence of a human image

right: The *Portrait of a Princess* has given rise to numerous controversies concerning the identity of Pisanello's sitter. The device embroidered on the sleeve—symbolizing the house of Este—has directed research toward two princesses of that family. The sprig of juniper stitched into the piping of the armhole suggests that here may be Ginevra (meaning "juniper") d'Este, the ill-fated spouse of Sigismondo Malatesta, the cruel condottiere who tyrannized Romagna, carried on tumultuous love affairs, and rid himself of his twenty-two-year-old wife by having her poisoned. But whatever its subject, the portrait is a masterpiece of the mature Pisanello, whose incisive drawing brings out the purity of the profile, the elegance of the neck, and the convexity of a brow that is made all the more prominent by the severe hairdo. The young woman stands against a background sprinkled with carnations, bluebells, and multicolored butterflies—altogether making a rather contrived landscape that owes more to dream than to reality.

Rogier van der Weyden (c. 1400–64).
Head of the Virgin Inclining to the Right.
15th century. Flanders.
Drawing, 0.128 × 0.109m/5" × 4¼".

Pisanello (c. 1395–1455). *Portrait of a Princess of the House of Este*. c. 1436–38. Verona. Panel, 0.43 × 0.30m/1′5″ × 11¾″.

Elegaic or brutal, soft or compact,
the portraits of the Renaissance
affirm the triumph of a new god:
l'uomo singolare ("individual man")

left: The *Portrait of a Man* comes from an artist who would carry Venetian painting to one of its summits and become the most remarkable master of his generation in the city of the Doges: Giovanni Bellini. With a spirit open to every experience, he submitted humbly to what his peers had to teach, without however denying himself the possibility of reinterpreting their lessons so as to integrate them with his own genius. From Antonella da Messina, who worked for a while in Venice, Bellini acquired the techniques of northern painting, but, endowed with a keen sense of religion, he expressed in his portraits of young men a dreamlike poetry unknown to the author of the *Condottiere* (right). Here, the face with its fine features, for which Bellini employed a whole range of warm tones, seems enshrined under a somber dome formed by the hair and cap. As if to relieve that severity, the artist bathed his subject in the soft light from a Venetian sky traversed by clouds, which themselves convey the nuances of human feeling.

right: *The Condottiere*—such is the title acquired by this portrait of an unknown subject, a work that places Antonello da Messina in the front rank of the very best Italian portraitists. For Germain Bazin, former chief curator of the Louvre's department of paintings, "few panels give such powerful expression to the overriding sense of pride that was the human attitude of the Early Renaissance. Those contracted jaws, that stern look, which conveys a will of iron, supported by a lucid intelligence, and the scar on the upper lip—all make one think the subject must have been an army commander." It was at the court of Naples, where he remained for some time, that Antonello encountered the Flemish painters who initiated the use of oil. But if the modeling and the translucency of the fleshtones affirm the artist's assimilation of the techniques and spirit of Jan van Eyck, the sculptural solidity, the monumentality, and the dense structure of the face show his complete mastery of the Italian tradition.

Giovanni Bellini (c. 1430–1516).
Portait of a Man. 15th century. Venice.
Panel, 0.32 × 0.26m/1′½″ × 10¼″.

Antonello da Messina (c. 1430–79).
The Condottiere. 1475. Sicily.
Panel, 0.35 × 0.28m/1′1¾″ × 11″.

Carpaccio. *Sermon of Saint Stephen.* 1511–15. Venice. Canvas, 1.52 × 1.95 m/4′11¾″ × 6′4¾″.

Carpaccio expresses the troubling splendor of Venice, doing so in fantastic piles of architecture teeming with Europe's most cosmopolitan society

The *Sermon of Saint Stephen,* a delicate and sensitive work characteristic of Carpaccio, illustrates one of the Venetian school's most original genres: the chronicle. Undoubtedly it is Jerusalem that has been represented—a Jerusalem that seems to have been confused with Constantinople. But while the strange buildings presented here derive in large part from the artist's imagination, such architecture was not totally foreign to Venice, or even to Italy in general. To the right of Stephen, scholars have identified Trajan's arch in Ancona (right), which would later serve as Palladio's model for the *arco delle Scalette* in Vicenza. Like his master Gentile Bellini (the father of Giovanni), Carpaccio succumbed to the picturesqueness of the Christian East, which had fallen to the Turks only in 1453. Thus, he populated his fresco with tiny people dressed in exotic costumes—the models for which could have been found on the quays of Venice, a port traditionally oriented toward Asia Minor. However, under the complex turnings of the turbans, one can recognize faces that are purely Venetian (left). But even more than the orientalizing fantasies and the chronicling of life, what appealed to Carpaccio was the quality—the blondness—of the light playing on these dense piles of fictional architecture. "Color as a space-generating principle," writes Jean Babelon, "would come from Venice whose moist light had the effect of encouraging that dislocation of contours which brought about modern art."

Carpaccio. *Sermon of Saint Stephen* (details).

151

Andrea Mantegna. *Calvary* (detail).

At the foot of the Cross, a tragic chorus of women, their faces wasted with grief

The *Calvary* of Mantegna formed the central composition of the predella to a large altarpiece commissioned when the painter was only twenty-six, for the church of San Zeno in Verona. Brought to France in 1798, following Napoleon's Italian campaigns, the altarpiece was restored to the Veneto after the fall of the Empire. But the museum in Tours and the Louvre each retained one part of the predella. In his love of the antique, in his feeling for nature, and in his sense of structure solidly nourished by the exact sciences, Mantegna is completely a man of the Renaissance. The whole arrangement of the *Calvary* is calculated in order to "hollow out" space. Thus, on either side of the axis defined by Christ's Cross, figures dispose themselves along two converging orthogonals that extend the road leading to the fortifications of a distant city. Even the receding squares of the paving underline the essential structure of the space. But in his most daring stroke, Mantegna arbitrarily "frames" the two soldiers in the foreground, thereby reinforcing the perspectival effect. The figures—both as solid as sculpture—reflect the example of Donatello whose presence in Padua had a profound effect upon Mantegna. The group of Holy Women (left), seemingly carved from a block of stone, are like a monument to sorrow, transformed by the restrained power of the artist's style into evangelical grandeur.

Andrea Mantegna (1431–1506). *Calvary* 1456–60.
Padua, Italy. Panel, 0.67 × 0.93m/2'2½" × 3'¾".

153

With archaeological precision
and an implacable line,
Mantegna fixes
the stark tragedy of Golgotha
in an antique setting

Andrea Mantegna (1431–1506). *Calvary* (details). 1456–60. Padua. Panel, 0.67 × 0.93m/2′2½″ × 3′½″.

Every detail of the *Calvary* reveals the incisive draftsmanship of Mantegna, who developed his art through a rigorous study of antique Roman gems, sarcophagi, and bas-reliefs. Not one anachronism is to be found in this scrupulous reconstitution of the drama of Golgotha. The meticulously described armor and weaponry of the legionnaires confirms a knowledge of antiquity and a concern for archaeological exactitude that are exceedingly rare for this period. But the love of nature—so typical of the Renaissance—shines through in the precision with which Mantegna depicts the seamed rocks, ramparts, and buildings of Jerusalem. Raised at the heart of the picture, the agonized figure of Christ reminds us that the science of anatomy was also one of the great conquests of the Renaissance. But neither the historical authenticity nor the quasi-experimental study of the human body deterred an artist called "the old pagan" from imparting to his work a bruising sense of the tragedy of Golgotha.

155

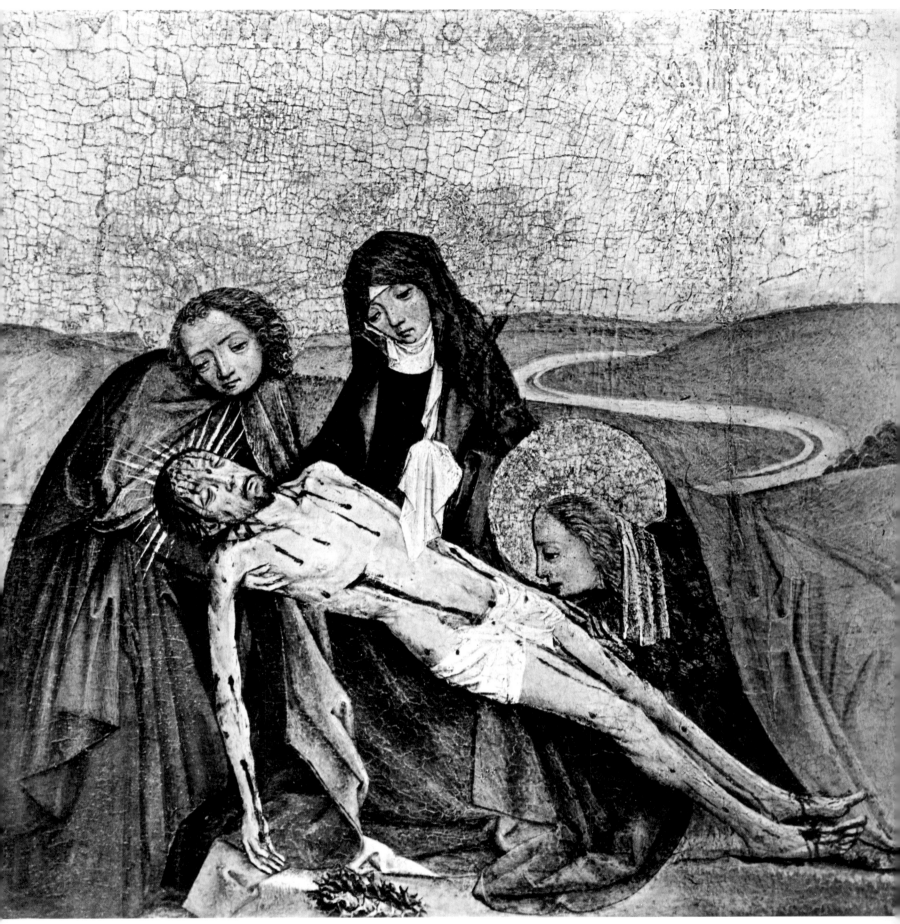

Rhenish master working in Provence. *Pietà.* c. 1480. Panel, 0.325 × 0.315m/1'¾" × 1'½".

above: This *Pietà*, attributed to a Rhenish master working in Provence, does not have the finish or the imposing grandeur of the *Villeneuve Pietà* (right). But it possesses a raw strength and a brutal directness that 20th-century art has prepared us to appreciate. In the very awkwardness of the forms, eyes liberated from the canons of classicism can recognize a disarming sincerity of feeling. The similarities of the two pietàs—the figural grouping, the fall of the draperies, the synthetic landscape, the gilded sky—simply underline the very profound differences in vision and treatment: in the one painting, vehement emotions and crude brushwork; in the other, complete mastery and sophisticated drawing.

right: The *Villeneuve Pietà*, the most famous masterpiece of the French 15th century and a climactic work of Christian art, probably came from the hand of the Provençal master Enguerrand Quarton. Drawn with almost sculptural precision, the figures detach themselves from a gold background invested with the intense luminosity of a Mediterranean twilight. The flow of the draperies, the attitudes struck by the Virgin, Saint John, and the Magdalene, the stiff arch of the dead Christ's body, and, above all, the tapering of the hands—all partake of the refinement that give this Lamentation its moving lyricism. "The tears are real," observes Charles Stirling, "but the accompanying gestures . . . they retain their reserve and express an unerring dignity."

Medieval fervor lingers long
in the pietàs of Avignon,
with their disturbing images of Christ
lost in desolate spaces

Enguerran Quarton(?). *Villeneuve Pietà*. c. 1450. Provence. Panel, 1.62 × 2.18m/5'3¾" × 7'1¾".

right: The *Statue of Saint John* illustrates the vitality of the wood sculpture ateliers in Touraine around the middle of the 15th century. The work once formed part of a Calvary made for the Cistercian abbey of Baugerais; eventually, however, it came to rest in the small neighboring church of Loché. Sold to a dealer at the end of the last century, the figure entered the Louvre in 1904. The disappearance of the original polychromy serves to reveal not only the quality of the wood the piece is made from but also the vigor of the handling. The touch is robust, candidly realistic in impulse, and the construction of the head set off powerfully by the grooved lines of the hair. The artist who carved this wooden statue was no doubt a contemporary of Jean Fouquet. Indeed, the treatment of the face evokes the Saint Stephen of that Touraine master.

below: These *gisants,* which must be counted among the greatest of all achievements in medieval funerary sculptures, are striking for the disparity in the treatment of the two faces. Whereas the man looks wasted, cadaverous, frozen in death, the woman seems alive with the grace and freshness of youth. The first sculpture, obviously, was made from a death mask, and the second *ad vivum.* In 1411, Pierre d'Evreux-Navarre, grandson of Jean le Bon, had married a young woman of fourteen, Catherine d'Alençon. The following year he died of a wound received at the siege of Bourges. Here the hero wears a knight's armor under a tabard quartered with the arms of Evreux and Navarre (the fleur-de-lis of the latter visible on the subject's left shoulder). His spouse wears a widow's guimpe and coif, which makes it possible to date the tomb between 1412 and 1413, the year of her remarriage to the Duke of Bavaria-Ingolstadt. The masterful carving and the precision of the details ally these *gisants* to the realism of the portraiture developed at the beginning of the century.

Along with purified profiles and smooth volumes, a forthright realism emerges to nourish the exalted spirituality of the Late Middle Ages

Saint John (detail). c. 1450. Tours, France. Wood, total height 1.40m/4'7".

Pierre d'Evreux-Navarre and His Wife, Catherine d'Alençon. (detail). c. 1412–13. Paris. Marble, full height 1.88 and 1.80m/6'2" and 5'10¾".

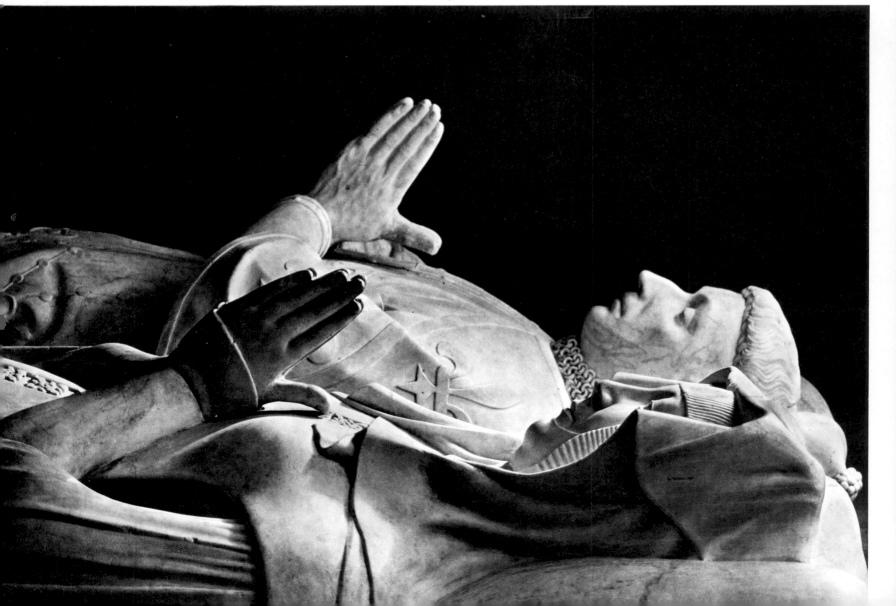

In grand-ducal Burgundy,
a procession of *pleurants* forms
to bury the fallen great
with the solemnity of epic theatre

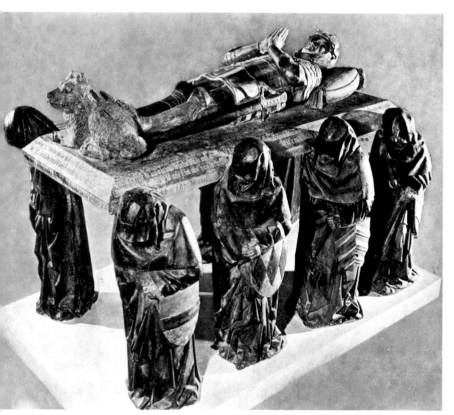

Antoine Le Moiturier(?). *Tomb of Philippe Pot.* Late 15th century.
Burgundy, France. Painted and gilded stone, 1.80 × 2.65m/5′10¾″ × 8′8¼″.

The *Tomb of Philippe Pot* marks the ultimate realization of the funerary style inaugurated by the Dutch sculptor Claus Sluter at the court of Burgundy. What Sluter bequeathed to Burgundian art is chiaroscuro—the taste for violent contrasts of light and dark, for the spectacular and the theatrical. To the *pleurants* theme, popular in Dijon since the end of the 12th century, Sluter succeeded in bringing a powerful majesty. His successors then enlarged it to a monumental scale, as in this instance, where the relatives of the dead, dressed in mourning, seem to advance in a lugubrious and slow-moving cortege, bearing on their shoulders the stone slab with the *gisant* upon it. High Bailiff of Burgundy, Knight of the Golden Fleece, Chamberlain to Louis XI and then Charles VIII, Philippe Pot had ordered the tomb built during the years 1477–83 for his burial in the abbey church at Cîteaux. The sculptor represented his patron dressed in armor from head to foot. But in contrast to the realism of this figure is the expressionism of the *pleurants* enveloped in heavy cowls and cassocks, all falling in deep and almost anguished folds. A masterpiece, the tomb is attributed to that "sovereign carver of images" Antoine Le Moiturier.

The spirit of courtly love brings an exquisite grace to Late Gothic images of Mary

right: *The Annunciation*, although a fragment from a great altarpiece of unknown origin, begs comparison with sculptural groups preserved in northern Germany. After having been separated by the vicissitudes of the art market, the two figures—the Virgin and the Annunciatory Angel—have been reunited in the Louvre. Their extreme elegance and refined charm reflect a precious moment in civilization. As an era slowly came to a close, it recalled in its final creations that Europe, for more than a century, had cultivated a courtly love, and that Germany had honored this spirit with some of its most beautiful monuments.

The Annunciation.
Late 15th century. Brabant.
Painted and gilded wood,
height of the Virgin 0.45m/1′5¾″.

left: *The Nursing Madonna*, thought to have originated in Swabia or Bavaria, is one of many works demonstrating the success that Gothic carvers had with this theme. The devotion to the milk of Mary spread widely throughout the Middle Ages. Pilgrims to the Holy Land actually returned home with white rocklike substances found in the grottoes of Bethlehem and regarded as Marian relics. In one of his "meditations" Saint Bernard recounts how the Virgin appeared to him, nursing the Christ Child, and how he himself received on his own lips a drop of the sacred milk. This story, told by the founder of the Cistercian abbey at Cîteaux, could only reinforce the special veneration of the Nursing Madonna. The theme continued to engage sculptors right up to the Renaissance, becoming more and more naturalistic as the Age of Humanism approached. In the work reproduced here Mary appears simply as a mother bending over her son with the full warmth of maternal love. As the Infant's hand touches a familiar breast, the mouth comes near in a movement of urgent, and altogether mortal, expectation.

The Nursing Madonna (detail).
Late 15th century. Germany.
Painted and gilded wood, full height 1.21m/3′11½″.

In its final stage,
the Gothic tradition expresses itself
in art both turbulent and baroque,
whose mannered and meandering forms
reflect the enduring tenacity
of the medieval spirit

right: This packed assemblage of religious entered the Louvre in 1958, along with additional works from a rich collection bequeathed to the museum by Elisabeth Mège. Forming the left shutter of an altarpiece, the group consists of two popes, a cardinal, a bishop, a canon, and several praying monks. German art offers numerous examples of altarpieces composed of the elect of paradise grouped about a Crucifixion and arranged according to the major categories of society. Here no doubt the artist wanted to achieve a representative synthesis of the clergy. Interesting in its iconography, vigorous in its style, this sculpture holds a special appeal for the 20th century by reason of the dense, all-over massing of volumes, which endows the ensemble with a strange dimension, quite unlike the spatial and compositional hierarchies of Renaissance art.

far right: *Mary Magdalene* exhibits the essential tendencies of German Gothic style at the end of the Middle Ages. Sensual and delicate, the product of an impeccable mastery of wood carving, this statue was originally surrounded by gilded rays and flying seraphims. According to legend, Mary Magdalene withdrew into a grotto and remained there for some years—clothed only in her long tresses—until one day, during her recitation of the holy office, a band of angels bore her off to heaven. But while honoring the subjects favored in medieval iconography, and while individualizing his images of the Virgin and the saints, Gregor Erhart nonetheless gave effect to a personal sense of the nude that approaches the Renaissance ideal.

Prelates and Other Religious. c. 1500. Thuringia, Germany.
Painted and gilded wood, 1.20 × 0.57m/3′11¼″ × 1′10½″.

Gregor Erhart (active 1494–1540). *Mary Magdalene.* Early 16th century.
Augsburg, Germany. Painted and gilded wood, height 1.74m/5′8½″.

As realism invades the art of 15th-century France, it anticipates the triumphs of La Tour and Le Nain in the 17th century

right: This portrait manifests a firmness and a delicacy that have no parallel in the 15th century. As grave as the Christ Child, the prayerful infant may represent Suzanne de Bourbon, daughter of Pierre I and Anne de Beaujeau. Simplicity, freshness, nobility—all the characteristics of the Master of Moulins reveal themselves in this portrait. At work here was one of the great painters of childhood, those artists who knew how to render a milky skin with softness and sensitivity, how to capture the spontaneity of gesture and expression proper to children. A peculiarly French gift, it would expand and mature through the art of Le Nain, Chardin, Fragonard, Houdon, and on to Renoir in the late 19th century.

left: The left wing of a triptych whose other panels have disappeared, *The Magdalene* was formerly attributed to Jan van Eyck. It is now thought to have come from the hand of that master of a dozen works associated with the great *Virgin in Glory* triptych in the cathedral at Moulins. The precise identity of this famous unknown has given rise to considerable research. Today art historians believe him to be one Jean Hey, a painter of Flemish origin who played an important role at the court of Charles VIII and Louis XII, after having been in service to the Duc de Bourbon. Thanks to Pierre II de Bourbon and his wife, Anne de Beaujeau, daughter of Louis XI, Moulins at the end of the 15th century became a lively center of artistic activity. Jean Hey succeeded in reconciling the Flemish manner with the French spirit. Thus, the realism of the faces is tempered by modeling that is smoother, rounder, and softer than that of the masters to the northeast of France. "Such an alliance of the real and the ideal within the natural," notes Germain Bazin, "belongs only to French art."

Master of Moulin.
The Magdalene and a Donor (detail). c. 1490.
Panel, 0.55 × 0.39m/1'9¾″ × 1'3¼″.

Peter Bruegel the Elder (c. 1525–69). *The Beggars.* 1568. Flanders. Panel, 0.18 × 0.21m/7″ × 8¼″.

above: *Beggars,* the only Bruegel in the Louvre collection, evinces the artist's fidelity to the Flemish tradition—most particularly to the precedent of Bosch. While standing in resolute opposition to the Italianism of the age, Bruegel's art also goes well beyond the painting of manners to which observers long tried to confine it. Bitter and sarcastic witness to a distressed century, Bruegel describes its miseries and suffering, usually in an allusive way, using symbols or proverbs. The headdress worn by the five beggars are carnival attributes and thus may stand for the various classes of society: monarchy (cardboard crown), bourgeoisie (beret), army (paper shako), peasantry (cap), clergy (bishop's mitre). Moreover, the foxtails attached to the figures' jackets contain political implications, being emblems of the *Geux,* or "beggar," party that opposed the Inquisition and revolted against Philip II of Spain. But it is also possible that Bruegel may have wanted merely to represent, in a time when miracles seemed to have ceased, the physical frailties and morals of humanity. Certainly the picture bears out the inscription given on its reverse side: "Here nature translated into painted images and seen in her disabilities/Is dismayed to state that Bruegel is her peer."

right: *The Ship of Fools* takes up an aspect of 15th-century literature that sought to satirize the corruption of the clergy. A nun and a monk occupy the center of this "ship of high livers" in which Hieronymus Bosch offers a startling "resumé of humanity." All the terrors, all the nightmares that troubled the dying Middle Ages are reincarnated in the oeuvre of Bosch. With the vehemence of a seer-prophet, he stigmatizes the sins of a humankind mired in filth and blind to divine light. As a Fleming, Bosch inherited a profound sense of nature, which he put at the service of his visionary genius. Thus, the universe he created of sulphur and darkness contains only what could have been observed in everyday life, but endowed by the artist with the most disquieting and knotty significance. By means of such realist intensity, reintensified with mystical content, Bosch seduced the Spain of Philip II and Theresa of Avila. Symbols of society adrift, the passengers aboard the Ship of Fools wear the distracted expressions of beings imprisoned by their own tormented inner lives. Bruegel, Goya, and Daumer would all remember Bosch and his tragic world.

At the dawn of
a new society with global awareness,
deformities and cataclysms
symbolize the ultimate riot of human anguish

right: *Lot and His Daughters*—a subject from Genesis—illustrates the destruction of the Cities of the Plain. "Then the Lord rained upon Sodom and upon Gomorrah brimstone and fire from the Lord out of heaven." Divine wrath shatters the city, burns the houses, and sinks the ships in an apocalyptic conflagration shot through with bilious lights and livid reflections. Sole survivors of the disaster, Lot and his daughters rest on a hilltop. "And the firstborn said unto the younger, Our father is old, and there is not a man in the earth to come in unto us after the manner of all the earth: Come, let us make our father drink wine, and we will lie with him, that we may preserve seed of our father." Altogether the passage allows the painter to create a scene of violent luminary effects, wherein he reveals himself to be a master of chiaroscuro so total that his art anticipates the 17th century. Some authorities date the picture to around 1509, others around 1517, but most connoisseurs agree on the attribution to Lucas van Leyden. "Whatever it may be, and even if the attribution should be controverted one day," says Michel Laclotte, "it is legitimate to see this work as one of the supreme masterpieces, after those of Hieronymus Bosch, of fantastic landscape painting and Netherlandish luminism."

Lucas van Leyden (1489/94–1533). *Lot and His Daughters.* 1509(?), 1517(?). Holland. Panel, 0.58 × 0.31m/1'10¾" × 1'¼".

Hieronymus Bosch (c. 1450–1516). *Ship of Fools* (detail). Late 15th century. Holland. Panel, 0.57 × 0.31m/1'10½" × 1'¼".

169

Hans Baldung Grien (c. 1480–1545). *The Knight, the Woman, and Death.* c. 1503–05. Germany. Panel, 0.355 × 0.295m/1′1½″ × 11½″.

Gothic allegory
continues to roll
across landscapes rendered
by the analytic eye
of the Renaissance

left: *The Knight, the Woman, and Death,* long considered to be a work by Barthélemy Beham, was not restored to Hans Baldung Grien until 1928. A close stylistic relationship with other pictures by the Strasbourg master and the presence of two of his most characteristic traits—the precise rendering of the plants in the foreground and the highlights on the tree trunks—make the attribution incontestable. Undoubtedly the painter executed this panel at the beginning of his stay in Nuremberg, where he went to work at the side of Dürer, his master and friend and the artist whose influence would prove so beneficial. The example of Dürer and contacts with the humanists explain Baldung Grien's predilection for the type of allegory shown here. It is true, Marcel Brion reminds us, that "macabre obsession is a phenomenon of the period, a continuation into the 16th century of fears that marked the end of the Middle Ages. German artists lived, literally, under the sign of death." In the art of Baldung Grien the grimacing image of a skeleton always slips in behind the most beautiful evocations of beauty, youth, or love, a *memento mori* that is both voluptuous and funereal. But such fantasy also gave rise to the most daring colorism, in which can be felt the anxious tension experienced by one of the most singular geniuses to have emerged from the German School.

below: This *Landscape* is one of the most beautiful and justly celebrated ever painted by Dürer. Executed in watercolor, with accents from a brush dipped in India ink, it represents a view over the Val d'Arco in the southern Tyrol. *Fenedier Klawsen,* the annotation made by Dürer in the upper right corner, means "the hill near the Veneto." The work appears to have been done in 1495, in the course of the artist's trip back to Germany after his first sojourn in Venice. The solid architecture of the landscape, the subtle indications of planes, the quality of the luminary effects all reveal the German master's debt to the Venetians, his grasp of the lessons taught by Giovanni Bellini, Mantegna, and Carpaccio.

Albrecht Dürer (1471–1528). *Landscape.* 1495. Nuremberg. Watercolor, 0.223m square/8¾".

As Germanic genius learns
the lessons of Venice,
a new kind of art
—narcissistic and erotic—
invades the north

Lucas Cranach the Elder (1472–1553). *Venus.* 1529. Saxony. Panel, 0.38 × 0.26m/1′3″ × 10¼″.

left: This *Venus* has all the characteristics that make her unmistakably a nude by Cranach. Whether called Venus, Eve, Diana, or Lucretia, his women all have the same slender silhouette, the same mannered gestures suggestive of an Oriental dancer, the S-curve posture typical of the Late Gothic period, the same heart-shaped face set with almond eyes under a high, broad brow. Then on the head is that signature object—the immense hat, disk-shaped like a cardinal's—which lends a strange and perverse quality to the charm of the nudity. The flowing veil, instead of preserving modesty, seems to reveal the body and make it seem more enticing. In the same way, the jeweled necklace serves to light the silken flesh with a play of warm reflections. "Few painters have, as this one, sought to realize the perfect representation of their erotic feelings," writes Pierre Descargues. "[Cranach] never tired of it, and without doubt he is at his best in this theme." Occasionally Cranach accompanied his figures with verses that, somewhat hypocritically, pronounced some moral. Much more often he surrounded the ladies with landscapes betraying a debt to Venice. But in Cranach's art the Italian *veduta* is thoroughly "germanized" by the cathedral spires reflected in the mirror surface of a lake, as well as by the fortified castles and citadels bathed in a pale northern light.

right: The *Portrait of the Artist*—"without doubt the first independent self-portrait painted in northern Europe," says Michel Laclotte, the Louvre's chief curator of painting— "has long been considered an *oeuvre de circonstance.*" This has its confirmation in the flowering sprig held by the painter—eryngium, then regarded as a symbol of conjugal fidelity. At age twenty-two Albrecht Dürer had prepared his own image as a formal offer of marriage to his fiancée. Before Rembrandt, Dürer was the only artist who so readily took himself as his own model. Anxious in spirit, with a philosophical turn of mind, he struggled unceasingly to reconcile his German genius, which governed the whole of his personal sensibility, with the formal beauty of the Renaissance, which claimed his intellect. This desperate quest for accord informs the whole of Dürer's art and endows it with an almost magical intensity. A youthful portrait, the picture here is remarkable for its authority, for the sense of deep introspection it imparts. Life itself seems concentrated in the eyes—sharp, watchful, melancholy—which focus on the artist and on a world where, at the dawn of the 16th century, civilization would undergo one of the most important mutations ever to occur in human history.

Albrecht Dürer (1471–1528).
Self-Portrait. 1493.
Nuremberg, Germany.
Parchment, 0.56 × 0.44m/1′10″ × 1′5¼″.

High Renaissance, Mannerism, and Baroque
16th–17th Centuries

The first years of the 16th century opened a new era, an era generally considered to be that of the modern world. Around 1500 there occurred a series of events that would give a definitive look and a philosophical dimension to the artistic and literary Renaissance launched, for the most part, in the preceding century.

In 1492, thirty-nine years after the collapse of Constantinople, Christopher Columbus embarked upon the voyage that would take him for the first time to American shores. Beginning in 1494, with France's first invasion of Italy, an exchange of men and ideas got under way that would cause the new values of Italy to spread in triumph throughout Europe. In 1520, the Papal bull excommunicating Martin Luther was solemnly burned in Wittemberg, an incident that signaled the Reformation. All these shocks seriously jolted European thought, thereby expanding its range. Clearly a historical era would seem to have come to an end, while another was starting. As if to prove it, the very term "Middle Ages" was coined specifically to indicate a period that no longer existed.

As these opening remarks might suggest, Renaissance art was a product of a complex and contradictory moment in human history. But despite the great diversity in its origins and patterns of development, the art can be recognized by certain common and all-important characteristics.

Individualism dominates Renaissance art, for its creators escaped both the anonymity of the old guild-controlled workshop system of the Middle Ages and the former requirement that painting and sculpture submit to the needs of architecture. Painting in particular assumed a new importance, equal to that of sculpture and even architecture. Pictorial art broke free of decoration, became autonomous, and increasingly gained a clear supremacy over all the other plastic arts. Henceforth, artists would seek to express their individual personalities, thereby destroying "school" art and ushering in the era of personally signed masterworks. Still another characteristic that links Renaissance art to its Classical prototypes is the overriding search for aesthetic quality, a search pursued by artists and patrons alike. All these things constitute a revolution against the Middle Ages, and while slow and gradual, the movement was irreversible.

Secularism returned to art, reintegrating it with daily life. The "cavalier" became an ideal social type, one that could flourish in a world whose new wealth and civility gave it a taste for gallantry, fêtes, dances, tournaments, and fine conversation. Pleasure being a chief aim of this society, artists found themselves called upon to create a proper framework. "Triumphs" in the Roman manner became the rage, providing an opportunity for artists to cultivate all their decorative abilities. None other than Leonardo da Vinci prepared the formal entry of France's Louis XII into Milan in 1507. But, above all, it was the search for an ideal form of human beauty that engaged the minds and gifts of Renaissance artists. Female beauty came to seem a reflection of Divinity itself. More and more, love for the Almighty transformed itself into love for His creatures.

The *heroic* was another trait of the Renaissance revived from the Classical past. This can be seen in the meteoric careers of the professional military men, those freebooting opportunists who by force of personal courage, energy, intelligence, and enterprise rose from nowhere to achieve fame and influence. A modern Herakles, the *condottiere* became as much an ideal of the age as the cavalier. For the frail bodies of the preceding era, the 16th century substituted vigorous, muscular, powerful physiognomies. This conception transformed traditional imagery, replacing the spent, emaciated Christ of the Middle Ages with a figure displaying the heroic qualities of a Classical god—a Prometheus.

Italy, where monumental ruins provided a constant reminder of antique glory, produced the Renaissance. But in the 16th century the capital of the new age passed from Florence to Rome, which, under the Popes, resumed the leadership role it had played in the ancient world.

The key monument of the High Renaissance is the new basilica of Saint Peter's designed and built to replace the thousand-year-old structure commissioned by Constantine. Here came to focus all the genius of Bramante, Michelangelo, and Raphael. But the Roman High Renaissance would be brief, lasting from 1499, when Bramante arrived, until 1527, the date of the great city's sack by the Lutheran armies of Emperor Charles V.

In this quarter-century emerged some of art's greatest

giants: Leonardo da Vinci, with his Florentine sweetness and *sfumato* ("smoky") modeling; Michelangelo, whose passion expressed itself in a drama of the male nude; Raphael, who created compositions even in portraiture; and Correggio, famous for a charm so great that it borders on decadence. By the middle of the 16th century, Venice had brought forth the incomparable colorism of Giorgione, Titian, Tintoretto, and Veronese.

France adopted the Renaissance, beginning in 1494, the year that Charles VIII made the first of the invasions that the post-medieval North would perpetrate against Italy. The taste for the new humanistic civilization would be reaffirmed by François I and maintained by his successors: Henri II, Charles IX, and Henri III. It expressed itself in a growing passion for Italian art. Charles VIII invited the peninsula's artists to come and decorate his residences. The first of these took charge of the Château d'Amboise, which they redid in an Italianizing manner. From Amboise to Blois, from Chaumont to Gaillon, Gothic retreated before the implacable advance of renascent Classicism.

After his victory at Marignano, which won Milan for France, François I imported still more Italian architects, who concentrated their activities on the great châteaux of the Loire Valley, adapting harmoniously to the altogether different character of the French environment. The monarch then transferred his interest to Fontainebleau near Paris, there assigning Sebastiano Serlio, Rosso Fiorentino, Primaticcio, and Benvenuto Cellini to build and decorate the first great palace of the French Renaissance. But under Henri II, François' son and successor, a French genius, Philibert Delorme, became the royal architect. In this, France's Third Renaissance (after the Loire and Fontainebleau), the French made their own, highly idiomatic interpretation of Italian ideas. For the rebuilding of the Louvre, they actually bypassed Italian models and went directly to the common sources in antiquity.

The Counter-Reformation

From 1570 to 1660, European history is dominated by three major factors: the Counter-Reformation, the development of the state, and the rise of the bourgeoisie.

The Counter-Reformation was the response of an aroused Catholicism to the Protestant threat. It began with the Council of Trent, which convened in 1542 and reflected the need felt by the Church to reform from within. By the time the final session closed in 1563, a movement had been initiated that would steadily expand in satisfaction of the unanimous desire for a new kind of religious expression more open and accessible than anything ever seen before. It would contribute mightily to the triumph of Baroque art.

The notion of the state would, in the aftermath of the Wars of Religion, take definitive hold in the countries of Western Europe. The victory of Anglicanism in England and of Catholicism in Spain and France affirmed the power of the state, which succeeded in suppressing factionalism and repelling all threats. Only Germany and Italy remained divided and, owing to the weakness this caused, became pawns in the competitive games played by the greater powers.

Simultaneously, technical advances, world-wide colonial expansion, and a new spirit of enterprise combined to produce the first industrial age and its handmaiden, the capitalist class. Favored by strong states and by the commerce and banking of free cities, this class demanded luxury and an art capable of reflecting its wealth and power.

Two broad trends shaped the development of art and vied for its control: the Baroque and Realism.

The *Baroque* constitutes both a period style and a timeless mode of expression. While not the official style of the Counter-Reformation, the Baroque is linked to this movement and satisfied its need to make religion appeal directly to the heart. The irrational, the mysterious, and the supernatural all reign supreme in the Baroque.

The Baroque had its inception in Italy shortly after the close of the Council of Trent. This can be traced to Rome, where in 1568 the architect Giacomo da Vignola built the celebrated mother church of the Jesuit Order—Il Gesù—a structure whose vast influence, literally throughout the world, eventually caused the Baroque style to be known as the "Jesuit Style." Originally considered the Counter-Reformation art par excellence, the Baroque soon seduced Europeans of every persuasion. Having ceased to be exclusively Catholic, the Baroque regained its intrinsic character, which is the expression of a certain kind of feeling—spacious, dynamic, theatrical and passionate, sensual, ecstatic, opulent and extravagant, versatile and virtuoso. Rubens (pages 192–195), Tintoretto (page 190), El Greco (page 196) are all, in certain aspects of their work, Baroque painters. France too succumbed to the style, which can be seen in the Louvre's own Colonnade façade (pages 1,2) as well as in the sculpture of Puget and the painting of Vouet (page 216).

Realism is the antithesis of the Baroque. Just recovering from terrible wars and religious strife, the enlightened public sought a calm, peaceful vision of the world, both animate and inanimate. Realism stood for prudence, and thus satisfied the need for stability. Realism also represented a return to primary sources, to an appreciation of simple things and the dignity of daily life. Whether popular or bourgeois, it seemed to induce inner silence and a reticent manner. Accompanying the attitude and reinforcing it was a spiritual revival in which sermons played the central role. Another factor encouraging realism was empirical science, which brought forth discoveries of immense and lasting importance.

Realism and the Baroque determined the course taken by Europe's great national schools of art. While the Baroque prevailed in Italy, Spain, and Germany, Realism captured Flanders and the Low Countries. In France, however, the two polar modes came together, counterbalanced one another, and fell into perfect equilibrium. Of course, such terms as Baroque and realism do little more than indicate tendencies. Thus, Italy had its great Realist in Caravaggio, and Spain its Ribera. Meanwhile, Flanders produced one of the most thoroughly Baroque of all artists —Peter Paul Rubens.

Italy. In the 17th century, Italy continued to dominate European art through the potent and rival styles of Caravaggio and the Carracci. The father of the new Realism, Caravaggio (page 204) concentrated on light, playing with it until he had achieved an infinitely varied drama of strongly contrasted highlights and shadows. Exploiting his bold chiaroscuro like a true virtuoso, Caravaggio endowed both commonplace scenes and religious compositions with a moving, and even shocking, lyrical intensity.

Whereas Caravaggio insisted upon the primacy of color, the Carracci brothers made drawing the glory of art. In this conflict was born a quarrel that would long agitate the world of 17th-century aesthetics.

The name that dominates 17th-century sculpture is inevitably that of Gianlorenzo Bernini. By the dynamism and sense of vibrant life with which he filled his statues, Bernini became the quintessential Baroque artist. His works seem literally to soar, and in this lies their grandeur and their elegance. The quality informs even the great colonnade at Saint Peter's in Rome, which proved to be one of Bernini's most original works.

Spain. Velázquez (page 199) and Zurbarán (page 197) are the preeminent masters of 17th-century Spanish painting. Clearly Baroque in their choice of subject matter and in the brilliance of their compositions, they are also Realist in their handling of faces and figures. The influence of Italy can be felt in the work of such artists as Ribera and Ribalta, both of whom were formed in the Carracci school.

Flanders and the Low Countries. Along with the lessons he learned in his Italian apprenticeship, Rubens retained in his art a good measure of the realism traditional to his native Flanders. He painted with true Baroque exuberance, but he also took his subjects directly from nature, thereby echoing the bourgeois sensibility of Flanders and its love of sensuous richness.

In the Low Countries it was the grave and severe religion of the Reformation that counterbalanced the region's marked affinity for Realism. Rembrandt understood immediately how to universalize the warmth of an ordinary gesture or a pensive face, how to transform bourgeois life into an awesome act of faith. If Rembrandt's celebrated chiaroscuro reflects the Caravaggism of the age, it was not merely a dramatic moment that the Dutch artist sought to express, but rather a more profound humanity.

Along with Rembrandt, Franz Hals played a major role in the creation of Dutch portraiture, while their younger contemporary Vermeer (page 127) endeavored to render the mystery of the human presence.

France. At the beginning of the 17th century, the conflict between the supporters of Caravaggio and those of the Carracci broke out in full force. Poussin (page 213) joined the latter, while Valentin de Boullogne, Simon Vouet, and

Georges de La Tour (page 205) identified with the former. Realism, which accorded with a native French tradition, was favored by the Jansenist religious revival and by the regional schools. Led by Louis, Antoine, and Mathieur Le Nain, Georges de La Tour, Sebastian Bourdon, and Robert Tournier, these were not negligible in the early part of the century.

The Baroque and Realism, which confronted one another in the decorative arts, would soon, after 1660, come together in harmony under the impact of Classicism.

Louis XIV, Arbiter of Europe

On March 9, 1661, Louis XIV took personal control of the French royal government, an act that affected not only France but also the whole of Europe. This occurred at the death of Cardinal Mazarin, who had governed the Kingdom during the sovereign's minority. Louis was only twenty-three when he ordered his ministers never again to effect any transaction, not even the issuance of a passport, without first consulting him.

Under Louis XIV the French gained genuine preeminence on the Continent, making their monarch the arbiter of Europe. Next to France, with its population of twenty-five million, the other European nations seemed paltry indeed. An agglomeration of peoples divided by differing points of view, the German states fell for the most part under French influence after the Treaty of Westphalia (1648). In Italy, the Pope survived as the only ruler not menaced either from within or from without. Spain, which had seen all its European ambitions fail, entered upon a long decline. In England, the restoration of Charles II, after the fall of Cromwell, almost coincided with the death of Mazarin. This encouraged Louis XIV to arrange the marriage of his brother, Philippe, to Henriette, the sister of the new English King. Then, there was the traditional rivalry between England and Holland, which, at the expense of both, served to strengthen France.

If 17th-century France appeared to be the most populous, the richest, and the most civilized country in Europe, it assumed even greater importance in the eyes of the King himself, whose hunger for glory was vast. For Louis, the institutions of the realm should serve as an example to all, with the arts singing the nation's magnificence in every corner of the globe. And indeed the Great Reign would shine with an incomparable brilliance.

Classicism. In the first half of the 17th century the Baroque and Realist modes shared Europe and often mingled their respective influences. But nowhere did these two currents so temper, control, and contain one another as they did in France. Out of this confrontation was born Classicism.

According to the conception of *le Roi-Soleil*, as Louis styled himself, the arts must, above all else, evince the grandeur and power of the state, which the monarch identified totally with his own person. The court made its influence pervasive, shaping the arts with directives and multiplying the organizations designed to train and employ artists. The nobility, the rich magistrates and bankers all modeled their style upon that of the sovereign. Throughout the Sun King's reign, armies of artists were kept busy building and embellishing the royal residences. The Gobelins factories worked exclusively for the crown, weaving tapestries, making furniture, engraving images, composing decorative panels, molding silver, and carving vases and statues.

Le Brun, "first painter to the King," functioned until his death in 1690 as a veritable minister of the visual arts. He supervised everything, but above all he directed, generated, and oversaw, often indicating the broad scheme of things without bothering with the details. The system produced a style that is also a décor in which craftsmen provided the unity. From commodes to the simplest spoon, interlacements, valances, and shells give the Louis XIV style its character, which is Classicism.

Classicism means, of course, a return to antiquity, therefore to the spirit of the Renaissance. But this new, purified antiquity also meant Italy, the Italy that was still considered the mother of the arts, the Italy that French Kings had loved so much. In 1666 Colbert, Louis' Prime Minister, founded the Académie de France in Rome, directing the twelve young painters, sculptors and architects enrolled there to study arithmetic, geometry, perspective, and anatomy, and to copy "everything beautiful in Rome." While the copies went to France to serve as a repertoire of models, the best of the artists entered royal service once they had returned home.

Leonardo plumbs the depths
of the human soul
in complex compositions
of great originality and
in figures contoured
with mysterious softness

Leonardo da Vinci (1452–1519). *Virgin of the Rocks* (detail). Late 15th century.
Florence, Italy. Panel transferred to canvas, 1.99 × 1.22m/6'6¼" × 4'.

left: *The Virgin of the Rocks,* ordered from Leonardo in 1483 by the brotherhood of San Francesco Grande in Milan, had a huge success and became the principal inspiration of the Lombard school. A second version, realized with the aid of students some twenty years later, now hangs in London's National Gallery. "However, the version in the Louvre," writes Germain Bazin, "is entirely from the hand of Leonardo and much superior to the London pictures whose execution should for the most part be attributed to the Preda brothers, working from drawings prepared by Leonardo. The style of the Louvre painting is still Florentine, which certainly makes it earlier than the London panel that it obviously inspired." A subtle atmosphere of ambiguity permeates *The Virgin of the Rocks,* emerging from the artist's power to transcend the conventions of a subject and suggest a philosophy of duality. His mind filled with knowledge of the antique world, he seems to use an edifying theme as a means of probing the mysteries of nature and the human soul.

right: *The Virgin and Child with Saint Anne,* although left unfinished in certain passages, seems to be the ultimate realization of a subject initially taken up by Leonardo around 1500. The first interruption came when the master commenced his work in mathematics and became an engineer in the service of Cesare Borgia. Around 1508 he returned to the composition seen on the right, but once again without completing it. "The paint, which is thin, transparent, and truly limpid, leaves the underdrawing visible in several places," notes Germain Bazin. Leonardo continued to work on the panel until his death. So interrelated are the figures that together they create a single form, suggesting the continuity of generations. The dynamic tension this generates revives a theme treated since the Middle Ages but always before in a purely theological and static manner.

Leonardo da Vinci. *Virgin and Child with Saint Anne* (detail).
Early 16th century. Panel, 1.68 × 1.30m/5'6¼" × 4'3¼".

On the faces of Leonardo's sitters, an enigma reflecting the inexpressibility of the inner life

below and right: The *Mona Lisa* is the most famous picture in the world. The Italians call it *La Gioconda* for Mona Lisa Gherardini del Giocondo (1479– c. 1550), who, according to Vasari, was Leonardo's model for this portrait. However, the identification has been challenged, with other candidates proposed in the persons of Isabella d'Este and Costanza d'Avalos, Duchess of Francavilla, whose portraits Leonardo is known to have painted. Stylistically, the picture seems to belong to the years 1503–06. A drawing by Raphael and other old copies indicate that the columns of a loggia, now barely evident, were once to be seen on either side of the figure. In painting this work, Leonardo revived the portrait, as much by a composition then unfamiliar in Florence as by the enigmatic radiance of the face. "The person," wrote the artist, "who looks directly at the master painting her [him] will also look directly at the viewer." Here the human being is shown to be an unfathomable mystery. None of the classic devices formulated to account for the workings of the psyche could satisfy the needs and interests of a modernist like Leonardo. It is the discovery of the unconscious, the anticipation of psychoanalysis that have made the *Mona Lisa* an irresistibly fascinating picture for millions upon millions of spectators—among whom one of the most captivated was Sigmund Freud.

Leonardo da Vinci. *Mona Lisa*. c. 1503–06.
Panel, 0.97 × 0.53m/3'2¼" × 1'8¾".

Leonardo da Vinci (1452–1519). *Head of a Young Woman*. c. 1480.
Florence, Italy. Silverpoint and graphite, 0.18 × 0.17m/7" × 6¾".

above: A work of subtle and tender melancholy, the drawing reproduced here is one of the purest to survive from the hand of Leonardo da Vinci. "If you were ugly," he wrote, "you would not be happy with beautiful faces, but would create ugly ones, as do many painters whose subjects often resemble them; thus, choose beautiful models as I indicated, and engrave them upon your spirit." The astonishing density that Leonardo achieved in silverpoint and graphite pencil has amazed artists for the last five centuries. Odilon Redon, himself a prodigious draftsman, noted in his journal for 1902: "I loved and continue to love the drawings of Leonardo. They are like the essence of life, a life expressed through contours as much as through modeling. I savor their refined, civilized, and aristocratic spirit. In them I feel a grave attraction that lifts me to the heights of intellectual delight."

Titian (1477–1576). *Young Woman at Her Toilette* (detail). c. 1515.
Venice. Canvas, 0.96 × 0.76m/3′1¾″ × 2′6″.

In their worship
of sensual woman,
Titian and Correggio
invent a new painting,
there dissolving
voluptuous contours
in soft, colored light

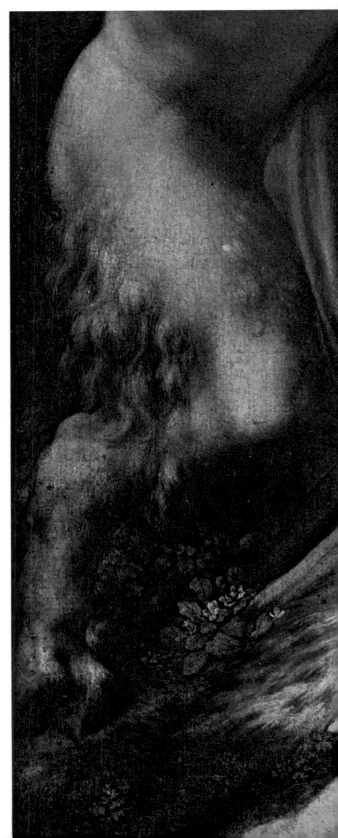

Woman—sensual, languid, available, closely attuned to the serene rhythms of nature—is the special subject of the Venetian painters. Color, with its diffuse radiance, its powers of suggestion, becomes, at the expense of line, the chief means of artistic expression. With Titian, vague outlines and the sensitive play of light replace the linear draftsmanship of Mantegna and the Florentines. The forms are bathed by a generalized atmosphere in which everything fuses—the human body and nature, vegetable and animal. Manet would copy the *Pardo Venus* (right above) and then remember it in his most scandalous work: *Olympia.* In Parma, Correggio took an approach precisely like that of Titian. Witness the *Sleeping Antiope* (right), where the subtle foreshortening, the *sfumato* ("smoky") shading, and creamy fleshtones all anticipate the powerful eroticism of Goya's *Naked Maja.* Cardinal Mazarin, that passionate collector, owned both the *Sleeping Antiope* and the *Pardo Venus,* and, if we are to believe Brienne, he bade a touching farewell to them from his deathbed: "Attired only in his squirrel-lined camelhair dressing gown and a nightcap on his head, he said: 'You see, my friend, the beautiful painting by Correggio, also this Venus of Titian . . . . Ah, my dear friend, I must leave all that! Farewell, dear pictures, which I have loved so much and that have cost me so much!' "

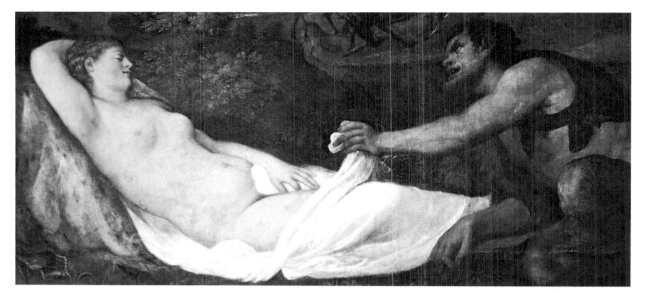

Titian. *Jupiter and Antiope*
or *The Pardo Venus* (detail_ 1576.
Canvas, 1.96 × 3.85m/6'≡4" × 12'7½".

Correggio (1494–1534). *The Sleeping Antiope* (detail). c. 1521–25. Parma. Canvas, 1.90 × 1.24m/6'2¾" × 4'¾".

At once all grace and all power,
the bound athletes of Michelangelo
sing a Promethean hymn
to the glory of man

Michelangelo's *Slaves* must be counted among the most important works owned by the Louvre. Different but complementary, the figures seem to engage in dialogue and come together as a single sculpture, with the viewer constantly referred by one to the other. Michelangelo prepared them for the tomb of Pope Julius II, a monument intended to rise at the center of Bramante's new Saint Peter's in Rome. The proud conception in which the *Slaves* would have been incorporated is now known only in its broadest outlines, but, other than the celebrated *Moses,* it was to consist mainly of male nudes generally symbolizing the arts chained by death to their great patron—Julius II. Carved around 1513 but left unfinished when the tomb project was abandoned, the two marbles in the Louvre are striking for their exceptional complexity: They seem simultaneously to be all grace and all power; they appeal, depending on the vantage point, by their rude strength or by their almost feminine delicacy. "I seek," said Michelangelo, "a type of beauty that moves and impels every sound mind to heaven." Four centuries later, like an echo, one of the 20th century's most important sculptors—Umberto Boccioni, father of Futurism—would affirm: "In [Michelangelo] anatomy becomes music. . . . the human body is a form almost uniquely architectonic. In the frescoes and the statues, the figures transcend themselves in movement, while the melodious lines of the muscles develop as if by the laws of music, rather than by those of representation."

Michelangelo (1475–1564).
Slaves. c. 1513. Italy.
Marble, height 2.15 and 2.29m/7'¾" and 7'6¼".

The Renaissance endows the monsters of old with a benign and friendly character

left: *Saint George and the Dragon* dates from 1508, when it was executed for the main chapel in the Château de Gaillon. By then the artist, having become "very old and heavy," no longer left his atelier. For M. Pradel, the Louvre's chief curator of sculpture, the subject suggests Italian prototypes: "The composition and even the silhouettes of figures can be found in certain Florentine bas-reliefs devoted to the same theme." He cites Donatello and Andrea della Robbia. At the same time, however, the work has "a kind of realism that is not typical of Italian figures." Its *douce bonhomie* ("sweet good nature") is quite French. The gentleness of the monster, with its large and friendly face, could have come only from the Touraine.

Michel Colombe (1430–1511).
Saint George and the Dragon (detail). 1508.
France. 1.75 × 2.72m/5'9" × 8'11".

Elephant Hunt (detail). c. 1530–40. Flanders. Tapestry, 2.65 × 3.82m/8'8¼" × 12'6½".

The Trojan Horse (detail). 1500–50. Limoges, France. Enamel, 0.22 × 0.19m/8¾" × 7½".

above: The *Elephant Hunt* tapestry is a precious document giving witness to the evolution of the art of jousting during the Renaissance. Stylistically, however, the medieval tapestry survives, if only in the flat, decorative disposition of the foliage and the clumps of grass and flowers, all of which are detailed with a kind of love typical of the Middle Ages. Meanwhile, every figure and animal is seen in action, as if together they represented a sequence of moments. The movement, the depth, the striving for perspective derive from new pictorial modes, which here have been combined with a Flemish mixture of exoticism, naturalism, and great luminosity of tone.

left: *The Trojan Horse* is attributed to the "Aeneid Master," a name that stands for an enameler of great talent whose exact identity has yet to be established. Working in Limoges during the first half of the 16th century, the artist took most of his subjects from a famous edition of the *Aeneid* published in 1502. The freshness of the palette adopted by this enameler is remarkable and altogether worthy of the virtuosity traditional among the artists of Limoges. The explicitness of the treatment, inherited from medieval illumination, is in marked contrast even to the subject, which reflects the new, Renaissance appreciation of Virgil. At once vital and mechanical, and radiant by virtue of both its size and its whiteness, the giant horse would not be out of place in a Surrealist work by René Magritte.

At Fontainebleau, a fascinated court mixes sophisticated eroticism with love of pagan antiquity

The *Portrait of Gabrielle d'Estrées* is an enigmatic work the meaning of which continues to be a matter of great controversy. In the opinion of most art historians, the mistress of Henri IV would seem to be represented in the company of one of her sisters, whose intimate gesture signifies the approaching maternity of the royal favorite, pregnant with the monarch's natural son, the future Duc de Vendôme. In 1968, however, Roger Trinquet published a different explanation: "If at the end of the 16th century the representation of a great lady nude and in her bath proved shocking and an affront to decency, what could be said for the presence in the same picture of two such bathers joined by the most equivocal kind of promiscuity?" This scholar finds that bathing together simply was not done in royal circles; rather, it was more likely to characterize the poorer classes and milieux of ill repute. Thus, he interprets the picture as a satire on the dissolute morals of the court of Navarre, where Henri reigned before he succeeded to the throne of. France. It represents Gabrielle d'Estrées (on the right) and the favorite who followed her in the affections of the highly susceptible Henri. After Gabrielle's death in 1599, the King appears to have been inconsolable, since he wrote: "My affliction is as incomparable as the one who caused it. Grief and regret will be with me to the end of my days. The very root of my heart has died and will never sprout again." A few days later, however, the *Vert Galant* fell into the arms of Henriette d'Entragues, and even went so far as to propose marriage. Painters of the time found inconstancy a stimulating subject, leaving us with refined allegories of a cold and sophisticated eroticism.

Primaticcio (1504–70). *Diana at Her Bath*. 1541–47. Italy–France. Brown ink heightened in white, 0.21 × 0.35m/8¼" × 1'1¾".

above: Squared for transfer, this drawing by Primaticcio was prepared as a study— *Diana at Her Bath*—for a large painting subsequently executed in the Appartement des Bains at Fontainebleu. The subject of the overall composition: Diana, while bathing with her nymphs, discovers the pregnancy of Callisto. The arrival in 1531 at Fontainebleau of the Bolognese painter Primaticcio, a pupil of Giulio Romano in Mantua, had a profound effect upon the development of French art. To Primaticcio is owed the creation of a grand style of decorative painting that took its inspiration from classical antiquity and allied a strong sense of composition to a refined attenuation of form and a febrile sensuality. During the years 1541–70 the artist, working with Nicola Dell'Abate, painted fifty-eight frescoes in the Château de Fontainebleau. This unique ensemble was destroyed in the 18th century.

right: *Diana the Huntress* is one of the most thoroughly representative paintings of the School of Fontainebleau. With its attenuated proportions, elegant Mannerism, and marked linearity, the figure reflects the nudes of Primaticcio. Undoubtedly the painting is a portrait of Diane de Poitiers, Duchesse de Valentinois and the legendary mistress of Henri II. The high forehead, the pronounced oval of the head, the long nose, the sinuous mouth—all idealize the well-known features of the royal favorite. Diane, who liked to be painted, filled the gallery at the Château d'Anet with portraits of herself, several of which show her completely in the nude—*a l'antique*. Her name, her love of hunting, and her long walks in the country quite naturally led artists to represent this great and powerful figure as Diana the Huntress. Recently it has been proposed that the work be attributed to the painter Luca Penni, a Florentine who died in Paris in 1516.

School of Fontainebleau. *Diana the Huntress*. c. 1550.
Canvas, 1.92 × 1.33m/6'3½" × 4'4¼".

Gabrielle d'Estrées and One of Her Sisters(?). France
Panel, 0.96 × 1.25m/3¼" × 4'1¼".

189

Tintoretto (1518–94). *Self-Portrait*. 1590. Venice. Canvas, 0.61 × 0.51m/2′ × 1′¾″.

above: This *Self-Portrait* provides a fascinating insight into the psychology of Tintoretto. The son of a dyer (*tintoretto* in Italian), he became an apprentice to Titian while still a child. According to Vasari, Titian soon discovered the prodigious talent of his pupil and immediately discharged him to prevent his becoming a rival. But with his determined spirit, Tintoretto could not be detained from achieving his own glory. A true son of Venice, he rarely left the Lagoon, except for a journey to Rome, where he discovered Michelangelo. In the course of a long career, Tintoretto covered his native city with powerful and tempestuous compositions, obtaining the commissions by every possible means, some of which were a bit irregular. At the Scuola San Rocco, hundreds of square meters of painting bear witness to his dramatic and grandiose manner. Remarkably dense and severe, the late *Self-Portrait* reveals the dual nature of the artist's personality, which consisted of stubborn commitment and misanthropic puritanism.

right: Veronese's *Calvary* is astonishing in the boldness of its structure, which divides the canvas in half by means of a diagonal, thereby leaving a vast space filled with a moody sky. The three crucified figures are contained within the upper left corner, where their vertical silhouettes stand in marked contrast to the compact roundness of the grieving women below. "The ingenious element that harmonizes the daring composition," explains René Huyghe, "is the high profile of the woman mantled in yellow and the unity of the light, a strange light tinted with sulfer and orange, a light for the end of the world." The group at the foot of the Cross is borrowed from the immense *Crucifixion* of Tintoretto, completed four years earlier in the Scuola San Rocco. In following his older colleague, Veronese seems to have wanted to develop greater energy and to combat—at least in this tragic theme—his natural tendency toward light and luminous decoration. "These men of the 16th century have left little for us to do," wrote Eugène Delacroix in a moment of despair as he contemplated the great Venetians. Nonetheless, it was from them, by way of Rubens, that the 19th-century Romantic would acquire the amplitude of his *Massacres at Scio* and *Crusades at Constantinople*.

190

In luxurious Venice
a new spirit arises,
harsh and tragic

Veronese (1528–88). *Calvary*. 1568. Venice. Canvas, 1.02m square/3′4¼″.

The *Disembarkment of Marie de' Medici* forms part of a series of twenty-one enormous canvases prepared for the Palais du Luxembourg and placed there in 1625. In 1621, following her reconciliation with Louis XIII, the Queen Mother had decided to have the Luxembourg's two grand galleries decorated by Rubens, one in her own honor and the other in that of Henri IV. Rubens took only three years to complete the first enterprise, which was unveiled to mark the marriage of Henriette de France, the daughter of Marie and Henri IV, to Charles I of England. There, among some rather academic figural groupings appear magnificent passages of painting, such as the one devoted to an assemblage of marine deities. Here Rubens gave effect to his favorite female type, realizing it with unparalleled tenderness and ardor. "Flesh," he said, "should be solid, firm, and white; tinted with pink, like a mixture of milk and blood, or a melange of lilies and roses." In the words of the Goncourts, who regarded Rubens as one of the great giants in the history of art, "never did a brush more furiously roll and unroll the morcels of flesh, link and unlink the clusters of bodies, all wrapped in fat and innards. The grotesque becomes epic. [In the painting of Rubens] there are necks with the finest tones, underarms where light slumbers in tints of blue, bodies highlighted like bronze. It is as if sunlight were penetrating hell; it is a palette brilliant with fleshtones; it is the grandest orgy of genius ever seen."

Through his opulent Nereids, Rubens unleashes the knowing energies of northern painting

Peter Paul Rubens (1577–1640). *Disembarkment of Mari Marie de' Medici at Marseilles* (details). 1622. Flanders. Canvas, height 3.94 and 2.95m/12'11" × 9'8¼".

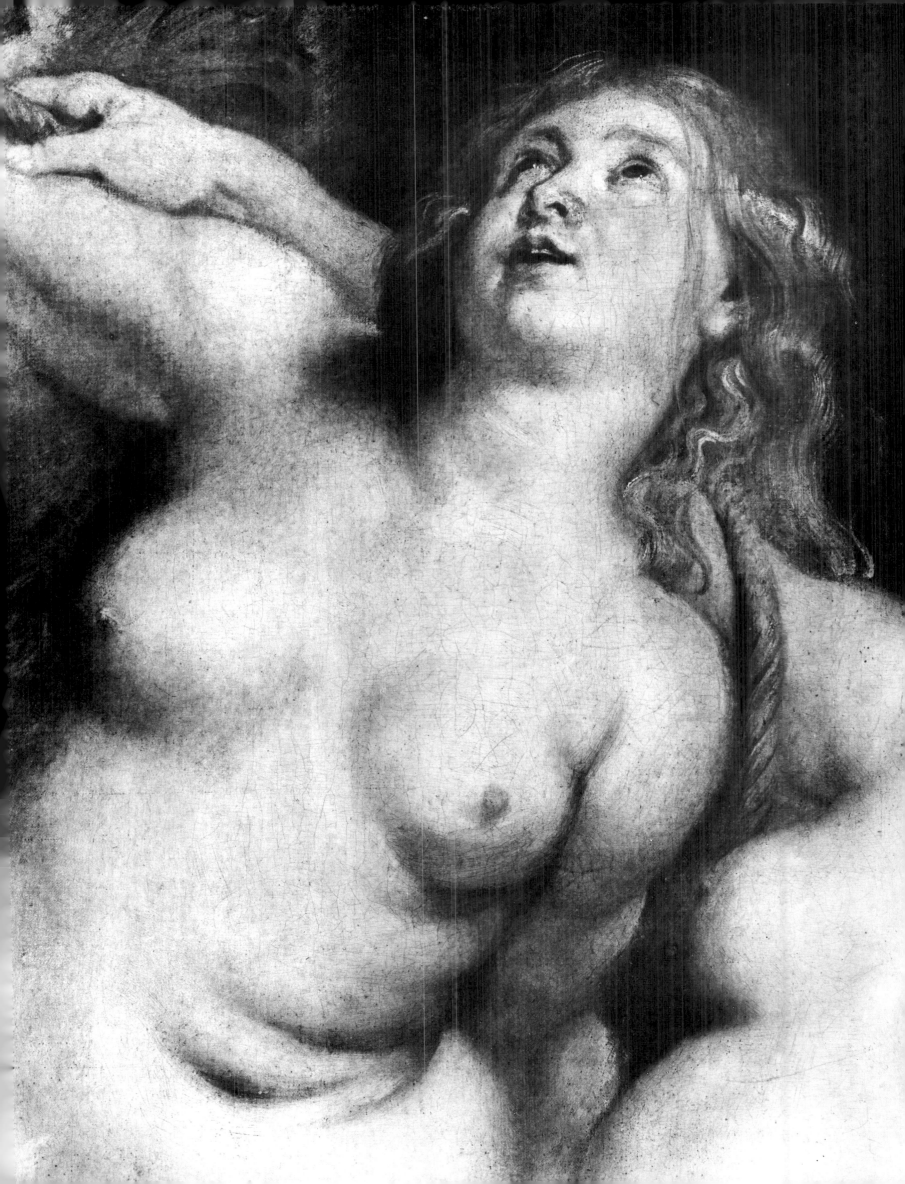

Peter Paul Rubens (1577–1640). *The Triumph of Truth*
and *The Fates Spinning the Destiny of Marie de'Medici*. 1622.
Flanders. Oil sketch, 0.50 × 0.64m/1'7¾" × 2'1¼".

Peter Paul Rubens. *The Triumph of Truth* (detail).

Out of the bounteous life of Flanders emerges the prodigious opulence and dynamism of Rubens

left above and below: *The Triumph of Truth* reveals the prodigious capacity of Rubens. Up at 4 A. M. in his studio-mansion in Antwerp, he attended Mass, then worked until 5 in the afternoon, stopping only for a light meal. The quantity and sheer size of his works have long caused art historians to see in them the hands of his assistants. But such collaboration is much exaggerated, for Rubens proved on countless occasions that he could paint several square meters in a few hours. *The Triumph of Truth,* from the series devoted to Marie de' Medici, offers the impressive spectacle of painterly vehemence tamed into art by a sure sense of pictorial order. Fully evident in the sketch is the double rotation that controls the two groups of figures. Unlike Tintoretto, whose compositions were deeply mined for this picture, Rubens likes rhythms that are self-completing. He unleashes tempests—but in a sealed vacuum. "Some would say that Poussin is dry; others that Rubens is excessive," commented Diderot. "As for myself, I am the Lilliputian who gently slaps them on the shoulder and says they are all wrong."

right: *The Kermesse,* astonishing in its flash and fury, was in fact carefully prepared by Rubens, as can be seen in two sketches owned by the British Museum. The finished work, painted around 1635–38, is characteristic of the late period, when the artist turned to old Flemish subjects like those painted by Bruegel and to turbulent compositions inspired by Italy's High and Late Renaissance. The fiery brushwork and the wild abandon of the figures express Rubens' own bounteous nature, his gifts as a colorist and his feeling for light. The acquisition of the painting by Louis XIV reflects the evolution of taste at the end of the century toward Flemish art, to which French 18th-century painting would incur a heavy debt. Watteau copied several of the groups in the Kermesse, as did Daumier in the 19th century. In the 20th century Paul Claudel found himself positively enraptured by Rubens' vital and rustic scene: "At first it is a single foot that kicks up, one arm that arches over the head and comes forward to greet a female partner, while with the other arm the male sweeps up a yielding body. Then all the couples, with accelerating passion, begin to turn about one another. His knee bent and ready to spring, the man in an irresistible grasp lifts his partner . . . . In one stroke it is a complete symphony of spirit and senses. . . . Everything moves while remaining absolutely still."

Peter Paul Rubens. *The Kermesse* (detail). c. 1635–38. Panel, 1.49 × 2.71m 4'10¾" × 3'10¾".

Fed by the arid soil of Castille, the flame of impassioned mysticism

El Greco (1541–1624). *Christ on the Cross.* c. 1580.
Spain. Canvas, 2.50 × 1.80m/8'2½" × 5'10¾".

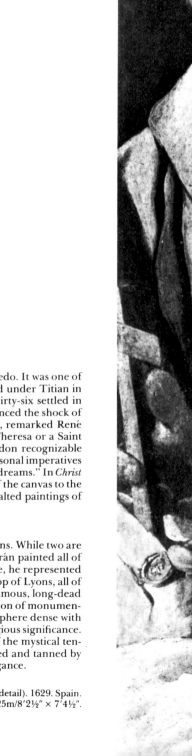

above: El Greco's *Christ on the Cross* adorned an altar in the Hieronomite church of la Reina in Toledo. It was one of the first works painted by the Greek artist after his arrival in Toledo. Born on Crete and trained under Titian in Venice, where he also worked alongside Tintoretto, Veronese, and Bassano, El Greco at age thirty-six settled in Spain in 1577, where this humanist doubling as a Mannerist in the tradition of Tintoretto experienced the shock of a city made mystical by influences from Jewish, Arabic, and Christian civilizations. His painting, remarked René Huyghe, "would in one stroke bring to life the equivalent of the spiritual transports of a Saint Theresa or a Saint John of the Cross. . . . Three centuries before modern art, he was the first who dared to abandon recognizable reality and to invent a reality modified by his own sense of things, transfigured according to his personal imperatives and desires, a reality that departs from convention with the freedom of our most fluent nocturnal dreams." In *Christ on the Cross,* where the clouds, instead of parting, form a structure of solid volumes from the top of the canvas to the bottom, the obsessed presence gives a lyric, quasi-abstract power to a work that anticipates the exalted paintings of the young Cézanne.

right: Zurbarán's *Exposition of the Body of Saint Bonaventure* forms part of a suite of four compositions. While two are in the Louvre and a third belongs to Dresden, the fourth was destroyed in Berlin in 1945. Zurbarán painted all of them in 1629 for Seville's Franciscan College of Saint Bonaventure. In the work reproduced here, he represented around the bed of the Saint, who died in 1274, Pope Gregory IX, King James I, and the Archbishop of Lyons, all of whom participated in the Council of Lyon (1629), which invoked the spiritual meditation of the famous, long-dead theologian. On the right a rather stiff group of Franciscans stand vigil over the body. This disposition of monumental figures in a constricted space is characteristic of Zurbarán, who succeeded in creating an atmosphere dense with pathos. The violently concentrated light intensifies the dramatic character of the scene and its religious significance. The painter of the convents, Zurbarán quite justly remains the most celebrated representative of the mystical tendency in Spanish 17th-century painting. His art makes him seem an Iberian Vermeer, toughened and tanned by the sun of Castille—an artist who could endow the rigidity of his compositions with restrained elegance.

Francisco de Zurbaran (1598–1664). *Exposition of the Body of Saint Bonaventure* (detail). 1629. Spain.
Canvas, 2.50 × 2.25m/8'2½" × 7'4½".

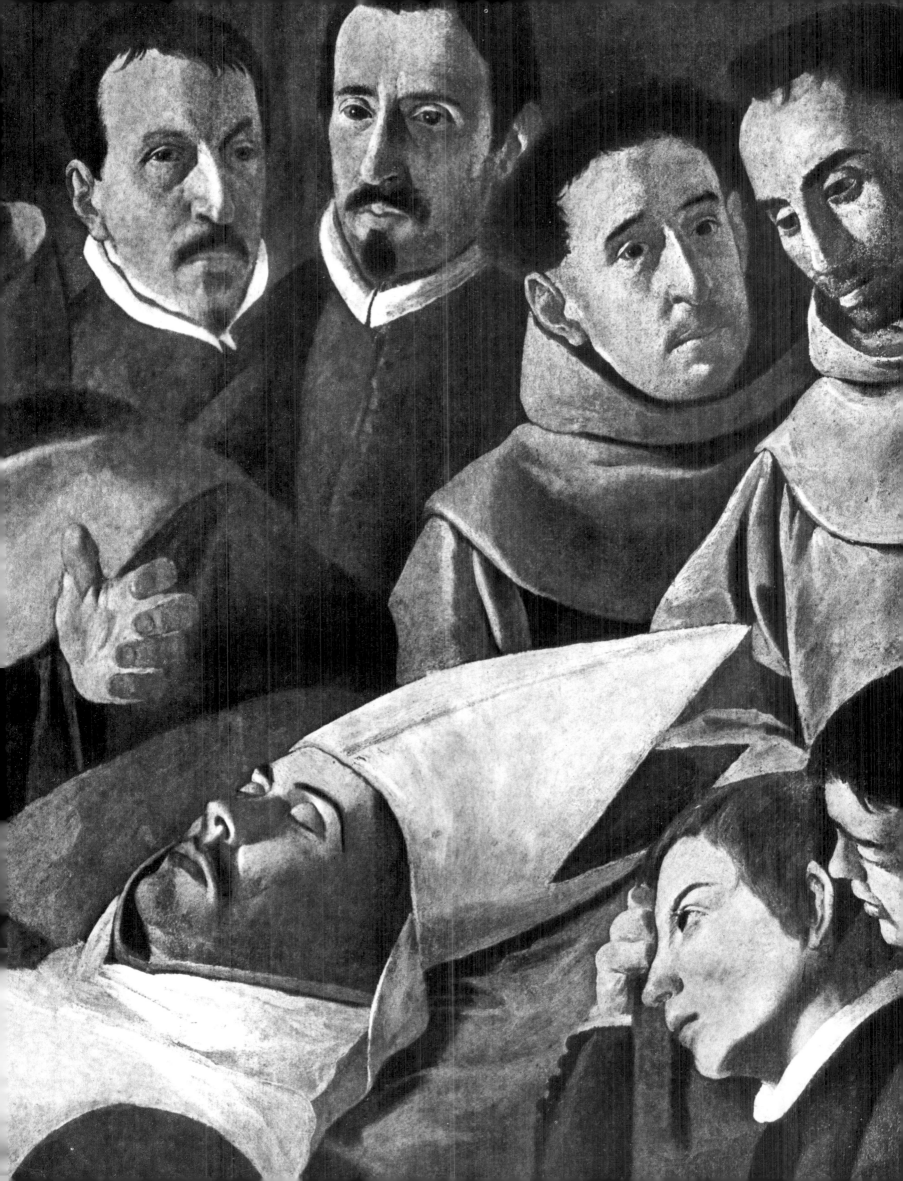

With his liberated brushwork
and blond tonality,
17th-century Velázquez
anticipates
the flickering luminosity
of Impressionism

The Infanta Marguerita portrays the daughter of
Philip IV of Spain at the age of three, a young lady
who became the favorite subject of the great Velázquez, then at the height of his power and glory. Born
in Seville, to a family of modest means, the artist had
been placed at the age of twelve in the atelier of Francisco Pacheco, a painter of no particular brilliance
but a remarkable theoretician whose daughter Velázquez was to marry. Pacheco, fascinated by the talent of his young associate, arranged to introduce him
at court, where in 1623 he was named "court
painter." The discovery of Rubens in 1628 and then
a visit to Italy in 1629–31 would liberate him from
"caravaggism" and into a light-toned, or "high-
keyed," painting now seen as prophetic of the 20th
century. "He is the only painter of his time who, in
an almost hallucinatory way, could suggest the en-
velope of atmosphere that surrounds all things," says
Louvre curator Janine Baticle. "[In the evening of
his life] his touch became more impressionistic, ever
more expressive of palpitating existence, even in the
apparent immobility of his subjects. . . Incontestably,
this is the most modern painter of the 17th century,
the closest to our own time." The close-up detail (left)
reveals the clear analogy between *The Infanta Marguerita* and the best works of Renoir or Monet.
Thanks to a stunning technique, light and vaporous,
Velázquez succeeds in capturing the ephemeral, the
transparent, the fragile. Sharp contours soften as
light and form interfuse.

Diego Velázquez (1599–1660). *The Infanta Marguerita*.
1654. Spain. Canvas, 0.70 × 0.59m/2'3½" × 1'11¼".

Rembrandt van Rijn (1606–69). *The Angel Raphael Leaving Tobias* (detail). 1637. Holland. Panel, 0.63 × 0.52m/2'¾" × 1'8½".

above: *The Angel Raphael Leaving Tobias* is one of the many pictures in which Rembrandt took inspiration from the Apocryphal Book of Tobit. There the sacred and the profane are intimately associated in the figure of the angel himself, who seems at once realistic and supernatural. The buoyant precision of the movement cannot but recall the Baroque dynamism and virtuosity of the painter's youthful art. Little by little Rembrandt would abandon this style in favor of more concentrated effects and a more interior vision. As Germain Bazin has remarked, "his Protestantism came forward in his religious painting, causing him to reject all the iconographical, dogmatic, hagiographic, and rhetorical traditions that in the 17th century, more than ever, interposed themselves in the imagination of the Catholic painter between God and man. Stripped of all historical character, the décor, like the costumes, places us on a plane of evangical simplicity."

right: Rembrandt's *Three Crosses* constitutes a grandiose composition, one of the universal masterpieces of engraving, in which the artist succeeded in giving the drama of Golgotha an expression of incomparable simplicity. The scene is bathed in an atmosphere of crepuscular light that seems to descend upon the martyrs through the long vertical strokes of drypoint. Without emphasis or solemnity, the crosses are surrounded by ordinary human beings, and yet we feel ourselves in the presence of an important event, one mysteriously linked to the whole of creation. Claudel sensed "that quite special atmosphere emanating from the paintings and prints of Rembrandt, [an atmosphere] of dream, something dormant, confined, and taciturn, a sort of disturbance of the night, a kind of mental acidity struggling with a darkness that before our very eyes continues its corroding process. . . . No longer is the present offered; it is an invitation to remember. . . ."

Breaking free of crepuscular shadows,
Rembrandt's figures live out a drama
mysteriously allied to the whole of Christianity

Rembrandt van Rijn. *Three Crosses*. 1653. Holland. Etching, height 2.70m/8′10¼″.

In glaze upon glaze
of transparent paint,
Rembrandt builds
a trap for light
and catches the inner life
of material existence

left: *The Flayed Ox* is one of Rembrandt's most spectacular works, a real challenge to taste and decorum. "A picture," the artist wrote, "is not made to be sniffed. Draw back, for the smell of painting is not healthy." In structuring his subject with huge strokes of thick paint, Rembrandt put an end to the kind of carefully detailed still life long venerated by the Dutch. "This work," notes Charles Sterling, "marked by that supreme inner synthesis which the greatest masters attain in their old age, is a statement proclaiming the imperial power of art over nature. Rarely has the spiritual content that enters into and transforms an object been made so evident, so triumphant. The sordid butcher's cave is illuminated by the gold and ruby of a bloody carcas. Here, even dead meat exudes the formidable energy of life, which can be felt in the massiveness of the chest and in the pathetic extension of the limbs. A flayed ox becomes pictorial material of the rarest sort." The meats of Goya and Soutine, the street stalls of Daumier, and many of Dubuffet's pictures derive from this painting, which Delacroix loved and copied.

right: The *Self-Portrait* of 1660 may be the most astonishing of the sixty paintings (not counting either drawings or etchings) that Rembrandt devoted to his own image, creating, throughout his long life, a veritable journal in which he scrutinized his physical decrepitude with an avidity bordering on masochism. When he undertook the present work the artist had almost reached the end of his days. Worse, he had just been evicted, following bankruptcy, from his beautiful house on Judenbreedesstraat. With absolute candor, he portrayed himself just as he was, hiding nothing of his unhappy face, but, more important, leading us behind appearances into his inner consciousness, the source of the expression heavy with experience and sorrow, of the worried brow and the bitter smile—all so symptomatic of a soul in torment. The sobriety of the color, the broad and supple technique, the concentration of light upon the face serve to exalt the power and the truth of that searching eye, a vision so much more concerned for the soul than for the senses.

Rembrandt van Rijn.
Self-Portrait (detail). 1660.
Holland. Canvas, 1.11 × 0.85m/3′7¾″ × 2′9½″.

Rembrandt van Rijn (1606–69). *The Flayed Ox.* 1655. Holland. Panel, 0.94 × 0.64m/3′1″ × 2′1¼″.

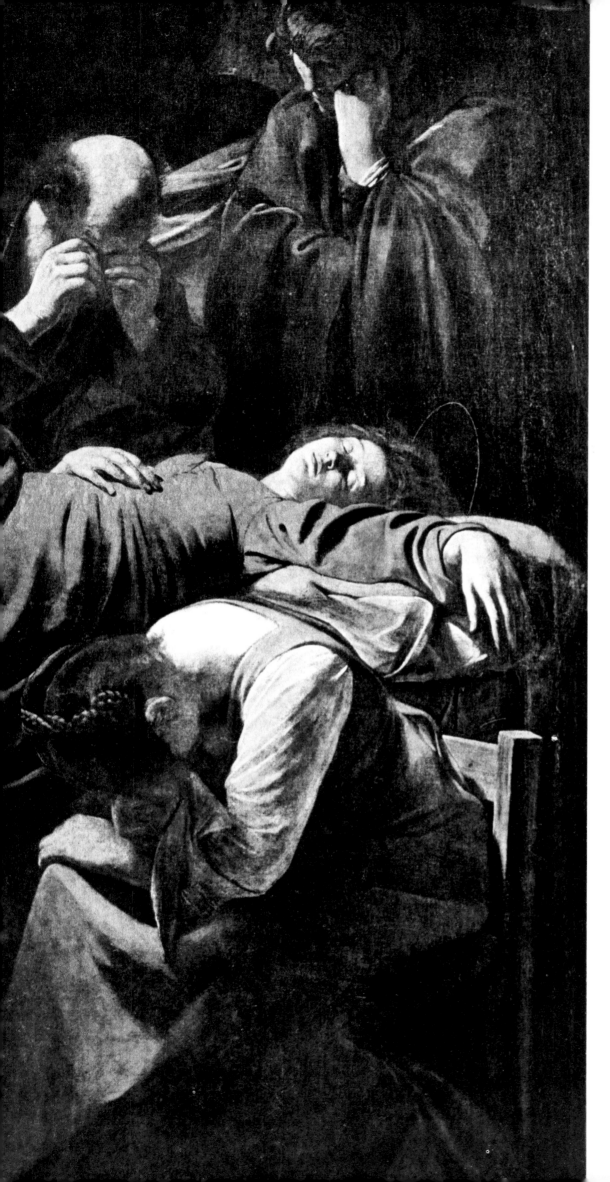

A sovereign light sections Renaissance space and brings dramatic realism to painting

right: La Tour's *Vigilant Magdalene* expresses the 17th century's great devotion to the "perfect lover of Christ." Although nurtured by the realism of Caravaggio, the French master achieved his own artistic independence through a carefully deliberated mystical austerity. Illumination is limited to a single flame, which all about it creates a highly contrasted play of light and dark. Depth too is quite willfully restricted, with the result that the figure seems to emerge from an almost surreal night, an atmosphere conducive to the kind of meditation and prayer that Pascal would soon advocate. All movements and dramatic attitudes have been excluded. In this silent picture, a human being, her head cupped in one hand, contemplates her own nothingness. The painting simply breathes spirituality, which recalls the nascent quarrels of quietism and the Jansenist movement.

left: *Death of the Virgin*, painted for the church of Santa Maria della Scala del Trastevere in Rome, is without doubt the most important picture by Caravaggio to be found outside Italy. From the time of its execution, the work has given rise to countless controversies, beginning with its rejection by the sponsoring chapter, which considered the painting indecent. "The ecclesiastical circles in Rome," Germain Bazin tells us, "accused Caravaggio of having made the Virgin a very common type. There were those who contended that the artist had used as his model a swollen cadaver reclaimed from drowning in the Tiber. Others went so far as to say that he had worked from a prostitute in the Ortaccio quarter. This was an unjust accusation, since the model seems in fact to have been the same one who posed for the *Madonna dei Palafrenieri*—a certain Lena, a poor but honest person." On the other hand, the canvas was enthusiastically received by Rome's artists, who demanded that it be exhibited from the 4th to the 14th of April 1607. It was then that Rubens, while in the service of the Duke of Mantua, recommended that the latter acquire Caravaggio's great picture. Subsequently, it was sold to Charles I of England, then bought by the banker Jabach, who conveyed it to Louis XIV. The realism in the treatment of the Virgin, which once provoked so many objections, no longer shocks. Magnificently ordered around the reclining form, the composition seems, by virtue of the introspective mood it creates, one of the most religiously inspired of all those created by Caravaggio.

Caravaggio (1573–1610).
Death of the Virgin (detail). 1505–06.
Canvas, 3.69 × 2.45m/12′1¼″ × 8′½″.

Georges de La Tour (1593–1652). *The Vigilant Magdalene* (detail). c. 1630–35. France. 1.28 × 0.94m/4′2½″ × 3′1″.

Diffuse, radiant, undulating, light becomes the unifying factor in the landscapes of Claude Lorrain

The seaport was the favorite subject of Claude Lorrain, who gave it many and varied interpretations. It enabled him to express a new conception of light, which here streams in from the distance, invades the vastness of the sky, and comes to expire at the feet of the foreground figures, who, thus back-lighted, contemplate the sunset. A melancholic pantheism dominates this work. Nature expands and "the eye breathes" in this larger universe. By means of the light, which rakes the crests of waves, the artist makes us feel the subtle and profound links that, transcending the everyday agitations of life, bind humanity to the eternal mystery of the world. In the 18th century the English would virtually adopt Claude as their own. The painter of evening nostalgia, he prefigured England's Romantic landscapists, who in turn would influence French 19th-century painting. A rich and fertile art that works slowly, the painting of Claude would inspire Constable to emulation.

Claude Lorrain (1600–82).
Seaport in Fog. 1646. France.
Canvas, 1.05 × 1.50m/3′5¼″ × 4′11″.

Claude Lorrain (1600–82). *Seascape with Setting Sun* (detail). c. 1633. France. 0.33 × 0.42m/1'1" × 1'4½".

Beginning with his earliest work, Claude Lorrain developed his favorite medium—light. Born at Chamagne, in Lorraine, and then apprenticed to a pastry chef, he traveled at the age of thirteen to Rome, where the upper classes eagerly sought kitchen assistants recruited in France. Taking employment with a painter, Augustino Tassi, the young Frenchman passed almost imperceptibly from the kitchen to the studio, where he soon made himself an indispensable assistant. He even dared to paint a picture. Fifteen years later, the former scullery boy would be famous everywhere in Europe, all the while remaining in the Eternal City, where he died at the age of 82. Throughout his long career, Claude worked on commission for a clientele of kings, nobles, and ecclesiastics with whom he discussed the formats, subjects, and prices (very high) of his pictures before ever commencing to paint. In the *Seascape with Setting Sun* of 1633 (above), light serves to bring out detail in the foreground, but loses focus for the trees, and then dissolves into mist and vapor in the distance. The same process can be seen in the *Siege of La Rochelle* (right), where the battle, viewed from a low hill, is fringed about with scatters of crimson uniforms that endow the entire picture with freshness and vitality. Meanwhile, historical fact dictated the disposition of the military figures in the foreground.

208

Bathing nature
in the unifying poetry
of light and atmosphere,
Claude Lorrain transcends
the agitations of 17th-century Europe

Claude Lorrain. *The Siege of La Rochelle by Louis XIV*. c. 1631. Copper, 0.28 × 0.42m/11″ × 1′4½″.

To reinforce its power,
absolute monarchy demands to be presented
in heroic and aloof portraiture

Hyacinthe Rigaud (1659–1743). *Philip V of Spain*. 1700. France. Canvas, 2.30 × 1.55m/7'6½" × 5'1".

left: *Philip V*, painted by Rigaud at the request of Louis XV before his grandson's departure for Spain (between November 15 and December 10, 1700), is an official work in which a virtuoso handling of fabrics and metal compensates for the lack of invention. The young King seems posed upon the threshold of some artificial grotto that surrounds him like a halo of majesty. Along with François de Troy and Nicolas de Largillière, Hyacinthe Rigaud, "king of painters and painter of kings," contributed to the revival of French portraiture that began in 1680. "As his atelier," writes Pierre Francastel, "he maintained a veritable portrait factory with numerous collaborators working under his direction." He reserved his "entirely original figures," totally painted by his own hand, to the most important subjects: monarchs, provincial notables, official artists, all of whom are invariably shown with the symbols of their function and rank. Rigaud's was a painting of state, of the "grand manner," which would soon be supplanted by the "little manner" executed in pastel by such 18th-century masters as Quentin de La Tour and Chardin.

right: The *Portrait of Louis XIV* is a priceless document from the reign of *le Roi-Soleil*. The monarch seems to be about forty years old. "It is possible," notes the specialist Jacques Thuillier, "that the court painter, just when he was beginning his work on [Versailles' Hall of Mirrors], may have asked the King for a few moments." His pastel permits us to have an intimate exchange with the royal subject. Rarely does one see him close up, with his vital and sensitive profile, the imperious nobility of his bearing. "Here," Thuillier adds, "Le Brun joins the great masters of pastel, to such a degree is his notation sure and succinct. The tinted paper is left bare almost throughout, with only a few touches of rose to model the face, a bit of gray-green chalk to define the profile, plus some black or brown to suggest the perruque." Le Brun, who was Louis XIV's official painter, would direct the court's artistic projects for twenty years, doing so with the domineering power of a despot. It was he who would create the great success of the works at Versailles, addressing himself to the slightest details, here placing a fountain and there a statue, combining marble and bronze, fresco and stucco. Pupil of Vouet and influenced by Poussin, he came to be the very symbol of classicism, the great *metteur en scène* ("stage designer") of the Sun King's reign. After Colbert's death in 1683, a cabal formed against Le Brun, for Louvois preferred the mediocre Mignard.

Charles Le Brun (1619–90).
Louis XIV. France.
Pastel on gray-beige paper, 0.52 × 0.40m/1'8½" × 1'3¾".

Nicolas Poussin. *The Triumph of Flora* (detail).

Subtly balancing
order and emotion,
Poussin revives
the legends
of classical antiquity

Nicolas Poussin. *The Triumph of Flora* (detail).

Nicolas Poussin (1594–1665). *Triumph of Flora.* c 1626–27. France. Canvas, 1.65 × 2.41m/5'5" × 7'11".

Triumph of Flora partakes of Poussin's happy mode, as opposed to the tragic mode in which the French classicist created his epidemics and massacres. The painting here constitutes an anthology of bucolic themes borrowed from Ovid and Virgil. Seated upon a wagon and crowned by a pair of flying *amours,* Flora is drawn forward, accompanied by the armored Ajax, who offers the goddess his shield filled with blossoms. At the extreme left, Venus wears a diadem of white and red roses as she dances with still other *amours.* Adonis follows just behind. Clytia, the nymph loved by Apollo, falls to her knees in the foreground, gathering heliotrope. The general precedent for the picture is Titian in his bacchanals, but France's greatest 17th-century master arrived at an inimitable manner all his own. The colors, for instance, seem muted until slowly they yield their richness to the patient eye. In the same way, the details emerge little by little as in a palimpsest, all forming part of an impeccable composition in which everything has been calculated. "I have neglected nothing," Poussin volunteered.

And in front of a canvas he had just completed: "These are not things that can be done while whistling." No one since Uccello or Piero della Francesca could so thoroughly fix the gestures of life and suspend them outside time, halfway between nature and an intellectual construction. Poussin's art consists of a delicate balance between immediate perceptions—recorded at random in a notebook while walking in the street—and their incorporation into an ideal structure. "One can see in the delightful *Triumph of Flora,*" writes Pierre Francastel, "the most accomplished product of this method, a curious mixture of antique-romantic reminiscences and the experience of living in the Tuileries garden, where Poussin occupied a small house that he liked." "Truly," said his contemporary, the Italian sculptor Bernini, "this man kneeling spectacularly before his easel is a great storyteller. . . ."

Baugin (1610–63). *Dessert of Biscuits.* c. 1630.
France. Panel, 0.40 × 0.52m/1′3¾″ × 1′8½″.

above: *Dessert of Biscuits* is one of the four still lifes signed by Baugin, a mysterious artist about whom we know only that he lived in Paris in 1630. The extreme rigor and the classical, even Cartesian character of the arrangement have quite justly made the painting famous. A plastic sense of rare quality enabled Baugin to balance the compact and the transparent, the dense and the light, the luminous and the dark. To the fragility of the biscuits responds the solidity of the table, and to the delicacy of the glass, the squat roundness of the carafe. "This musical feeling for formal relationships," notes the specialist Charles Sterling, "this quiet refinement and extreme sobriety place Baugin among the greatest of France's 18th-century painters. He succeeded in establishing an equilibrium of quotidian reality and abstract beauty, in which he honored the secular vision of the art and civilization of his country. He is the only French painter in the 17th century who evokes the modesty and harmonious grace of Chardin."

right: In the upper left corner of Philippe de Champaigne's *Ex-voto* appears a long Latin inscription composed by Arnauld, the Jansenist theologian associated with the nuns of Port-Royal. The painting was presented by the artist to Port-Royal in 1662 for the purpose of commemorating the miraculous cure, on January 7, 1662, of his daughter, Sister Catherine de Sainte-Suzanne, who had been paralyzed in both legs. The miracle occurred at the end of a novena conducted by the Port-Royal community, of which Sister Catherine was a member. Champaigne executed the painting between January 22 and June 15, doing so as an act of thanksgiving. He represented the moment when Mother Agnès Arnauld, while praying beside the victim, felt the certainty of a miracle. An austere, somewhat stiff, and remarkably spare work, it reflects the artist's deep and abiding faith. With the tonal range restricted and the poses simplified, a mystical atmosphere permeates the composition. Nothing draws our attention from the two portraits. "The strict geometry of a cell that a long inscription . . . keeps from becoming a true environment," writes Jacques Thuillier, "corresponds to the calm rhythm of the draperies, which evoke the praying figures of the Middle Ages. No gesture and no apparition, just a simple ray of light with nothing of the supernatural about it. The miracle—indeed every physical aspect of the scene— is expressed only through its inner dimension."

Philippe de Champaigne (1602–74). *Ex-voto.* 1662.
France. Canvas, 1.65 × 2.23m/5′5″ × 7′3¾″.

In spare and economical compositions,
artists find the plastic equivalents of Jansenism's puritan spirituality

Baroque or reserved, mythic or commonplace, 17th-century painting is governed by the artist's warmth of feeling

Simon Vouet (1590–1649). *Abundance.* c. 1640. France. Canvas, 1.70 × 1.24m/5′7″ × 4′¾″.

left: Simon Vouet's *Abundance,* which old inventories identified as "Victory crowned with laurel holding the infant Louis XIII in her arms," belonged originally to a decorative suite prepared in all likelihood for the new château at Saint-Germain-en-Laye. The style suggests a date close to 1640. Vouet, during his sojourn in Italy (1612–27), and following his discovery of Caravaggio, became aware of the works of the great Italian decorators, soon adopting their light colors and Baroque rhythms. What one admires here is the panache and directness of the artist's new approach. The composition is a vigorous one, anchored to a large reverse curve at the center (the yellow cape), which contrasts with the severity of the architecture suggested in the background.

right: *The Lacemaker,* whose model would have been the artist's wife, is part of a series of paintings each of which represents a single, bust-length figure. Dress, style, and correspondence with other works all suggest that this carefully detailed yet monumental work may have been executed around 1644. Vermeer had a genius for using a tiny format so as to create a sense of mysterious intimacy, an effect further emphasized by the simplicity of the subject, the modesty of the activity, the stability of the light, and the richness of the carefully deliberated brushwork, which seems to caress the canvas with the greatest tenderness. As in almost all his pictures, Vermeer consciously chose an ephemeral moment, enclosing it in a structure firm enough to seem immutable. What he presents is an infinitesimal parcel of time suspended, or trapped, in a painting where everything—cushions, furniture—represents solidity, duration, weight. The tension, or secret life, of this painting comes from the contrast realized by the artist between a maximum of permanence and a maximum of momentariness.

Jan Vermeer (1632–75). *The Lacemaker*. c. 1664. Holland. Canvas, 0.24 × 0.21 m/9½″ × 8¼″.

The Age of Enlightenment, Revolution, and Neoclassicism
18th Century

With the death of Louis XIV, on September 1, 1715, France lost its supremacy in Europe. Now peace was sought through a balance of power, in which France, certainly, constituted one of the polar forces. But the other pole moved northward, toward the real victors in the concluding wars, towards the nations for which the future opened: Prussia, whose Elector gained the title of King; and, more important, England, a true conqueror that would use power only to maintain the stability necessary to commerce. For the first time, in fact, peace was made primarily for economic reasons. Commercial treaties formed part of political treaties, as trade franchises and transport monopolies came into being. The expansion of European influence throughout the known world, a consequence of Renaissance exploration and discovery, now became a reality, causing Europeans to think globally even in their relationships with one another.

If the political situation of Europe underwent radical change, a much older evolution—that of society in general —gained new momentum. The 18th century, by comparison with the 17th, would be a period marked by mounting tension. The capitalism of trade and manufacturing made considerable progress, fostering at the heart of each country a rich bourgeoisie that, through the agency of the great financiers, began to be an extremely important factor of contemporary life. Naturally, this restructuring of society, which occurred everywhere in Europe, would have its effect upon the world of art.

The Rococo

The *gloire* of the Sun King had erected for all Europe the very model of a stately, heroic art. But even in France itself the style depended upon the continual restraints imposed by the court and its representatives. As time passed and society changed, the restraints became more and more difficult to maintain. Thus, the demise of Louis XIV produced a veritable explosion, with society liberating itself in every direction. The old King's grandeur gave way under the demand for an art of ornament and pleasure. Architects renounced immense rooms all linked together in the most rigid and inconvenient way. Indeed, it was convenience and comfort themselves that would become the order of the day, calling for small apartments in which, for the first time, fireplaces were located so as to make them more effective in producing heat.

The King and his great nobles were no longer the sole source of commissions, as life in society succeeded life at court. Now paintings would be acquired not merely for the embellishment of state rooms but also for the sake of collecting and for the pleasure they could give. Themes also changed, becoming more intimate and charming. A more amusing and gracious mythology invaded art, as frolicking troups of cupids, nymphs, and nereids chased away the grand compositions of warring gods.

This great emancipation, or reaction against the rules of Classicism, would express itself in the Rococo style, which broke with the heroic ideal — the conception of a superhuman man—that had motivated the immense compositions derived from antiquity. Replacing majesty with lightness and dignity with intimacy, the Rococo preferred curved over straight lines and sentiment more than reason. Ornament *en rocaille* was brought to France by Gilles-Marie Oppenordt, a decorator of Dutch origin to whom the Regent assigned the design of the interiors of the Palais-Royal. Two formulas governed the Rococo manner: an arabesque in the form of a C closing in upon itself and another in the form of an S that unfolds and splits in two. From the fluidity of these lines—so consonant with the new society's image of itself—would emerge the whole decorative repertoire of the first half of the 18th century, with rocks, shells, reeds, foam, and waves as the principal motifs. Water too seemed an element of the new décor, which is especially evident in the nacreous or pearlescent color harmonies, composed of marine blue, foam white, and a rose suggestive of the translucent sheen of shells. No longer did Mars or Jupiter preside over the arts, but rather Venus, whose triumph received near-universal welcome.

France. Imported from neighboring countries where the long-lingering Baroque of nearby Italy found fertile ground, the Rococo grafted itself upon French Classicism and subsequently facilitated the diffusion of this style throughout Europe. Jean-Antoine Watteau, born in 1684, became, even before the death of Louis XIV, the harbinger of the new style (pages 222, 223). Undoubtedly it was in poetry that he discovered the sensual and sentimental atmosphere so characteristic of the approaching era. But for painting *à l'arabesque,* he would have gone to the studios of Gillot and Audran. Thereafter the *fêtes galantes* that Watteau produced came to seem like the hallmarks of a highly original art of living. Other than this master, Boucher (pages 224, 225) is the most representative of all the Rococo painters.

In *Italy,* where the Baroque tradition began and remained strong, it was the followers of Bernini who espoused Classicism and those of Borromini who took up the Rococo. Painting thrived mainly in Naples and, especially, in Venice, although Pannini practiced in Rome and Magnasco in Genoa. For the Neapolitans, Luca Giordano

and Caravaggio provided the models, while the Venetians produced a brilliant period with the remarkable likes of Tiepolo, Longhi, and Guardi.

Spanish painting went into one of its periodic eclipses, during which the Bourbon monarchs counted on artists imported from France.

Germany, more than any other country, gave the Rococo a triumphant reception. While using whatever motifs might serve their purposes, German architects so exaggerated the distortion of form that they succeeded in achieving a style of marked originality.

By the middle of the 18th century, the Rococo dominated Europe and governed all aspects of the decorative arts. From architecture through objets d'art to utilitarian artifacts, nothing escaped that exuberance born of a new sense of pleasurable living. But this very success would suddenly yield a terrible lassitude, as if everyone had grown weary of fêtes and diversions. Optimism faded as criticism arose and became increasingly sharp in its review of every phase of life. The comic Marivaux was succeeded by the philosophical Diderot and the satirical Beaumarchais. The prospectus for the great *Encyclopédie* appeared in 1750, followed by the first volume in 1751. Now a battle was joined that would give intellectual postures a clearer definition, although no specific political event triggered the struggle, nor do any dates isolate or symbolize the movement. Rather, it was through a slow evolution over a ten-year period, from 1750 to 1760, that the whole collective consciousness of France changed. All the while, the visual arts, those ever-sensitive barometers of the human sensibility, registered and interpreted the mutation. Reacting against an overelaborate art, taste shifted toward a stripped-down style of straight lines, toward a sober, severe style that would persist through Revolution and Empire alike.

Neoclassicism

Once restored to favor, Greco-Roman antiquity inspired a new art. The Classical age, of course, had never been forgotten from the time of its revival by Renaissance Italy. Now, however, a series of publications and discoveries shed a brilliant new light upon the sources of Western civilization, furnishing artists with a great number of fresh models for a complete repertoire of decorative motifs. Excavations uncovered Herculaneum and Pompeii near Naples, and still others in Tuscany revealed much about ancient Etruria. By way of Roman archaeology, another form of monumental expression was discovered: the Egyptian style, which appeared in objects dug up at Hadrian's Villa outside Rome.

Among the *French* there gradually evolved the artistic sensibility that would burst into full flower under Louis XVI, a sensibility that eventually proved perfect for the heroic puritanism of both the Revolution and the Napoleonic Empire.

Sculpture may have been the form in which Neoclassicism received its strongest expression. Pajou was one of the first to realize the new possibilites, doing so by substituting antique draperies for contemporary costume in a series of busts portraying illustrious men. Clodion then created processions of nymphs pursued by the god Pan. Finally, Canova reformulated Classicism into a solemn, voluptuous style that made him the supreme Neoclassical artist.

In painting, the leading "Roman" was incontestably Jacques-Louis David (pages 238, 239, 243), who in drawing more than in color demonstrated to an effete age what virile nobility could be. Helped by a large and gifted atelier —made up of Gérard, Gros, Isabey, Girodet, and Ingres!— David became the literal dictator of the visual arts under the Empire.

It fell to the youngest of these, Jean-Auguste-Dominique Ingres (pages 242, 244, 245), to carry the Davidian torch throughout much of the 19th century. But this truculent defender of linearity and the academic tradition, this "crafty worshiper of Raphael" as Baudelaire called him, blended into the sleekness and chill of his nudes a number of less dispassionate sentiments. In his chained and offended women, the Freudian 20th century would recognize a steamy fantasy life, causing certain Surrealist writers to make Ingres their favorite painter. Théodore Chassériau, the most brilliant follower of Ingres, took up the older master's themes (pages 246, 247) but treated them with the colorism of Ingres' great Romantic rival, Delacroix.

Meanwhile, craftsmen continued to play a major role in the decorative aspect of life. From the middle of the 18th century onward, the straight line would prevail over the curved. The right angles and rectilinearity of the antique formed the very basis of furniture design. As ornaments *à la grecque* — egg-and-dart, pearls, and acanthus leaves — replaced volutes and shells, geometric motifs supplanted floral decorations.

In *England*, the Classical spirit had held more tenaciously than elsewhere. If the Rococo made itself felt in the ornamentation of objects, it never touched architecture, which remained strictly Palladian. Very quickly, therefore, the return to the antique became a return to tradition. Everywhere else in Europe, French artists succeeded, by virtue of native elegance and refinement, in imposing their vision of Classical antiquity.

18th Century

Pre-Romanticism

France. At the same time that the years 1750–60 were witnessing a desire for austerity in reaction against the frivolity of the first half of the century, the same period also saw a parallel development in the return to sentiment, following the long vogue of cold and rather artificial elegance. In both movements, it was simplicity that advanced society valued. Thus, the return to nature and true feeling preached by Jean-Jacques Rousseau began to bear fruit. The fashionable world now drifted away from the salons in search of simpler pleasures and more natural surroundings. The sentimental comedies of Diderot dealt, for the first time since Molière, with the life of the bourgeoisie. Virtue, quite extraordinarily, returned to favor; it became dogma which held that quality could be achieved better in an artless life than in a sophisticated one, and in the country more than in the city. Soon Marie-Antoinette would be living in a cottage, planting porcelain flowers, and playing the milkmaid at the Petit Trianon.

If the antique revival determined style itself, Pre-Romanticism would primarily affect the choice of themes, favoring those of a sentimental nature. Chardin (pages 226–229) became, more by profound, personal affinity than by submission to a new fashion, the painter of middle-class virtues. Not a trace of the maudlin is to be found in his work, whose greatness derives from a true feeling for the details of everyday life and deep appreciation of the richness of the ordinary environment. The splendor of Chardin also lies in the sheer originality and strength of his artistry, realized in a web of free, independent, but carefully juxtaposed strokes, a kind of structural and coloristic facture that would fascinate Cézanne and Matisse. Fra-

gonard (pages 232–234), after having followed Boucher and the painters of elegance in the first half of the century, succumbed to the seductions of sentiment and began painting happy mothers, children at play, and homecoming scenes. Along with these masters, other artists took up the new mode with a good deal more affectation. Greuze, with his scenes taken directly from the bourgeois comedies of Diderot and Nivelle, with his village sentimentality, and with his sensuality parading as innocence, no longer enjoys the critical esteem the 18th century actually accorded to him. Houdon (pages 230, 231) may be the greatest sculptor of the second half of the century. In his portraits of Diderot, Mirabeau, Voltaire, and Rousseau, he revealed himself to be a master capable of penetrating social shells to the inner core of psychological truth.

In *England*, with the works of Zoffany and Ramsay, portraiture retained the primacy it had always held across the Channel. But in the 1750–1800 period it was, above all, Reynolds and Gainsborough who dominated English art. The latter, moreover, was an incomparable landscapist, considered by Reynolds to be "the greatest in England." The English school found itself especially happy in genre scenes inspired by the age's literature of sensibility, which constitutes the sole trait common to both French and English art. Indeed, France went not only to England but also to Germany for the new sense of nature and life that would enter its painting.

In *Spain*, the extraordinary genius of Goya towered above all others at the end of the century. From the small and somewhat mordant scenes at the beginning of his career to the terrifying sabbaths in the "House of the Deaf Man," Goya's visionary, passionate art constituted a magnificent prelude to the Romanticism that would soon roll across the whole of Europe.

With a loaded brush
and a delicate touch
Watteau immortalizes
the autumnal love
and languorous rhythms
of a dying world

The Departure from the Isle of Cythera provided Antoine Watteau with the opportunity to express his melancholy vision of an ephemeral happiness, as precious and unreal as the golden, evanescent landscape that surrounds it. Serving the rarefied conception of the painting is a technique of incredible lightness. "The handling of the surface," explains Germain Bazin, "involving little impasto, resembles the late manner of Rubens, whose *Kermesse* [page 195] Watteau had seen in the royal collections. But Italy too plays its part in this world of illusion, for the general atmosphere of the picture is Venetian, while the bluish mountains in the distance . . . evoke those in the background of Leonardo da Vinci's *Mona Lisa* [page 180] and *Saint Anne* [page 179]." Watteau composed his picture almost cinematically, showing what appear to be the same couples at different, sequential moments in their progress toward the boat. No one has ever spoken so eloquently of this canvas as the Goncourts in their famous *Art of the 18th Century* (1859–75): "Beyond rivers and mountains, paths and gardens, lakes and foundations, the paradise of Watteau appears. It is Cythera under a sky painted with the colors of summer. Near the shore the galley of Cleopatra floats, where the sea is still and the woods hushed. From the grass to the firmament, beating the breathless air with their butterfly wings, a swarm of little cupids fly in every direction. . . . It is love, but a poetic love, one that dreams and reflects, a modern love, with its longing and its crown of melancholy. Yes, at the heart of this work of Watteau's, some slow, vague harmony murmurs among all the gay words, some musical and sweetly contagious sadness permeates these *fêtes galantes.* Although akin to the allure of Venice, a quite special poetry—veiled and yearning—beguiles and charms the spirit."

Antoine Watteau (1684–1721). *The Departure from the Isle of Cythera* (details). 1717. France. Canvas, 1.28 × 1.93m/4'2½" × 6'4".

Reflected in the charm and grace of these casual beauties is the golden age of women — the 18th century

The glorification of female beauty became the favorite enterprise of French 18th-century painting. The sanguine drawing where in one magnificent arabesque Watteau summarizes the whole fragile tenderness of the feminine body is one of the most important works in the Louvre's Cabinet des Dessins. The infinitely soft contours and the contrasted play of sanguine and charcoal create a movement of unparalleled elegance, at once contained and spacious. "The hands of Watteau!" exclaimed the Goncourts. "Everyone recognizes them, those sensitive hands, so beautifully tapered, so coquettishly contoured about the handle of a fan or a mandolin, hands whose febrile life the master's pencil has so lovingly translated." Boucher, a fervent admirer of Watteau and Rubens, would adopt their amorous themes but in a more libertine mood. Under his pencil, the forms curve into one another, the bodies alternately revealing and concealing their secret charms. "Who has ever undressed woman more expertly than he?" asked the Goncourts, those fervent 19th-century connoisseurs of the *ancien régime*. "What scaffolding of ripe flesh, of undulating lines, of forms that seem modeled by a caress! How well he mastered the indiscreet pose, the coquetterie of soft attitudes, the provocations of nonchalance lounging full length upon a cloudlike décor, as if on a harem carpet!" In *Diana after Her Bath* Boucher reinforced his decorative gift with the technical strength of a great painter. Against a rather conventional landscape background appears the perfection of still life and the pink opulence of nude figures. "*Diana after Her Bath* is the first picture that truly thrilled me," admitted Renoir. "All my life I have treasured it like a first love."

Antoine Watteau (1684–1721). *Woman, Half-Nude.* France. Charcoal and sanguine on buff paper, 0.28 × 0.23m/11″ × 9″.

François Boucher (1703–70).
Nymph Study. France.
Charcoal and ink
heightened in white and sanguine,
0.26 × 0.36m/10¼″ × 1′2¼″.

224

François Boucher.
Diana after Her Bath (detail). 1742.
France. Canvas, 0.57 × 0.73m/1'10½" × 2'4¾".

François Boucher.
Reclining Nude Seen from the Back.
Drawing on yellow paper, 0.28 × 0.35m/11" × 1'1¾".

By the alchemy of his textures and the science of his composition, Chardin transforms the "little manner" into grand art

In his *Smoking Room* Chardin arranged a few smoker's objects on a marble tabletop. No subject could be simpler, nor any mastery greater. "This magic is beyond comprehension," wrote the astonished Diderot in 1763. "It consists of thick applications of color, one on top of the other, the effect of which works up from the lower layers. . . . Come close and everything appears confused, flattens out, and disappears. Move back and everything assumes form and comes to life." Disposed with rare sobriety, the objects stand out before a stone wall. Between the diagonal of the pipe stem and the mass of the pitcher the artist has created an abstract play of lines. But the rigor of this organization does not suppress the warmth emanating from the humanity associated with everyday objects. The creamy impasto and the brilliance of the color make the light vibrate, causing a sense of human presence and the charm of peaceful life to radiate from this still life. "Chardin, along with Poussin and Claude Lorrain," writes Charles Sterling, "is the pre-19th-century French artist who has had the greatest influence on modern painting. Without him, some of the experiments of Manet and Cézanne would be inconceivable." Malraux confirmed this opinion in *Les Voix du silence:* "Chardin is not a little 18th-century master who is more delicate than his rivals. Like Corot, he is a sweet simplifier. His quiet authority destroys the baroque still life of the Dutch and makes his contemporaries look like decorators. No one in France equals him from the death of Watteau to the Revolution."

Jean-Baptiste Siméon Chardin (1699–1779). *Chest with Utensils. "Smoking Room)*. France. Canvas, 0.32 × 0.42m/1'½" × 1'4½".

In this inventory
of an ordinary kitchen still life,
the catalogue of
a great painter's brilliant gifts

Jean-Baptiste Siméon Chardin (1699–1779). *The Ray* (detail on facing page). Before 1728. France. Canvas, 1.14 × 1.46m/3′9″ × 4′9½″.

The Ray is a youthful masterpiece that brought sudden fame to Chardin and enabled him to enter the Academy before his thirtieth birthday—a most exceptional feat. The brilliant handling of the fish, with its red and pearl-colored abdomen, made a powerful impression upon the officials, who thought, it is said, they were in the presence of a remarkably accomplished still life by a Flemish master. In *The Ray* Chardin invested all his virtuoso gifts and produced a veritable catalogue of substances: cat fur, the gummy moisture of fish, the whiteness of cloth and oysters, the gleaming compactness of pottery. "Drawn with their own light, created with, so to speak, the soul of their colors," wrote the Goncourts, "the things painted by Chardin seem to break free of the canvas and, by who knows what marvelous optical process, assume life in the space between the canvas and the spectator." Cézanne made a drawing after Chardin's *Ray*, and Matisse copied it in oil. No doubt these great modernists would have subscribed to what *le bonhomme* said of his own work: "One proceeds by painting with the hands and with colors, but it is not with colors and hands that one paints—it is with feeling."

A current of naturalism caresses
the hypersensitive surfaces
of Houdon's sculptures,
endowing them with an unsettling truth

right: *Shivering Woman* is a work of exquisite sensibility that challenges the classical conception that we have of Houdon the portraitist. Clutching herself in an endearing attitude, the little nude figure expresses, not without a measure of coquetterie, the whole of feminine fragility. Dense and compact, the modeling evokes the simplifications of Renoir more than the statuary of the 18th century. To the delight of connoisseurs, the traces left by a large rakelike tool make the wax model seem all the more a *belle esquisse* ("beautiful sketch").

left: *Bust of a Woman* is unquestionably the masterwork of 18th-century France's greatest sculptor. The nudity of the shoulders, the casualness of the hair, the dimple, the charm of the smiling countenance show the degree to which the individual portrait had gained naturalness since the beginning of the century. What passes over the physiognomy of this young woman—possibly the artist's wife—is the tremor of real life, the loving care, the intimate perception of Houdon, who no longer wanted to pose a subject wearing all the signs of his or her function, as did Rigaud with his "grand manner," but rather to seize the truth of the human face. His is an art of tactile sensation that astonishes by its acuity. The portraits of Houdon have an immediacy, a precision, and a closeness that end by creating a kind of discomfort. Voltaire, Mirabeau, and Diderot, fixed upon their plinths and looking at us, seem more alive than nature itself.

Jean-Baptiste Houdon. *Bust of a Woman* (detail). c. 1787.
Plaster, height 0.69m/2'3¼".

Jean-Baptiste Houdon (1741–1828). *Shivering Woman.* c. 1793.
France. Wax, 0.28m/11".

Sheer love of sensuous life
animates the virtuoso brush
of Fragonard

Jean-Honoré Fragonard (1732–1806).
Le Feu aux poudres. c. 1767–71.
France. Canvas, 0.38 × 0.45m/1'3" × 1'5¾".

left: *The Bathers* reveals the remarkable brio of Fragonard, who succeeded here in joining his French manner to the churning genius of Rubens. The transparent paint, applied as if in a single stroke, was no doubt inspired, says Germain Bazin, by the handling of the Nereids in Rubens' Marie de' Medici cycle (page 194), which in the 18th century constituted a veritable school for those artists who chose not to follow the "middle road" taught in the official academies. Pupil of Boucher, Fragonard was twenty when his master entered him in the Prix de Rome contest, which he won. The artist would make a happy career with his libertine subjects, achieving fame with *The Swing,* commissioned by a receiver-general for the clergy. But his well-earned reputation as a painter of light subjects long concealed the importance of the role played by Fragonard as "precursor of the masters of 19th-century painting: Gros, Delacroix, Cézanne" (Pierre Francastel).

Jean-Honoré Fragonard. *The Bathers* (detail). Before 1756.
Canvas, 0.64 × 0.80m/2'1¼" × 2'7½".

above: *Le Feu aux poudres* typifies the piquant pictures that earned Fragonard his reputation as a "merry" painter. Here his subject is cupids armed with torches setting fire to the senses of a sleeping beauty. "This is not a man," wrote the Goncourts, "who ever forgot to place at the heart of his picture that which he knew only too well how to open and undo—the bed. The bed—is it not for him the delicious place of woman, the adored theatre, the downy throne of her body? The moment he touches the batiste of the sheets, the crushed pillow, the parted curtains, the disordered couch, he becomes light and flame, life and rapture; he assumes all the gifts of the vigorous attack, the quick and fluent sketch. He enters upon his field of glory." But the Revolution put an end to that rollicking brush. In 1791 Fragonard achieved a reconciliation with David, the Revolutionary council's dictator of fine arts. But with the fall of Robespierre in 1794 the old master lost whatever remained of his official functions. His popularity passed, pictures like those reproduced here sold for as little as seven or eight francs. Fragonard died on August 21, 1806, in a café, the Véry, in the Palais Royal. He had been enjoying an ice.

233

Jean-Honoré Fragonard (1732–1806). *Study : Young Woman Holding a Book*. France.
Canvas, 0.81 × 0.65m/2′8″ × 2′1½″.

above: Fragonard's *Study* is one of four paintings in a decorative series comprising two figures of women and two of men. The latter have inscriptions on their backs that permit us to identify the subjects as the Abbé de Saint-Non and M. de La Bretèche, each painted *en une heure de temps.* The dazzling technique seen above suggests that it too was executed "in an hour's time." The improvisatory and decorative gifts of Fragonard shine in the virtuosity of the quick, light touch and in the fantasy of the costume. "A sketcher of genius," commented the Goncourts, "that is the nature of Fragonard the painter. Without preparation of any kind, he simply glitters. . . . He exceeded himself and everyone else in this daring picture, which captures the impression of things and flings it onto the canvas like an instantaneous image. One hour! No more. He needed only an hour to choose the pose, block out the composition, and proudly finish up these large portraits, where a whole Spanish fantasy was used as a means of clothing contemporaries in the dignity of former times."

right: Guardi's depiction of the Doge's Ship of State departing for the celebration of Ascension is one of a dozen compositions based upon drawings by Canaletto. The vibrant and iridescent atmosphere of Venice is here rendered with incomparable talent. The work is suffused with a light that transfigures the scene into a pre-Impressionist vision. The twelve pictures painted in 1763 as souvenirs of the coronation of Doge Alvise IV Mocenigo were dispersed during the Napoleonic Empire, but only eight are preserved in the Louvre. The feast of the *Bucentaure* ("Ship of State") was the most spectacular of the Venetian ceremonies. Upon a magnificent red galley, the Doge crossed the Lagoon to the Lido and there celebrated the marriage of Venice to the Adriatic, doing so by tossing a lamb into the sea.

Francesco Guardi (1712–93). *Departure of the Doge's Ship of State* (detail). c. 1763.
Venice. Canvas, 0.67 × 1m/2′2½″ × 3′3¼″.

Like magicians, 18th-century painters
find the shimmering virtuosity
with which to capture
the fêtes and frolics of a high-spirited era

The dazzling restraint
of Eros and Psyche
expresses itself
in the pure arabesque
of a balletic embrace

Eros and Psyche quite justly constitutes the most famous work of Canova, who made the plaster model in 1793. The handling of the translucent marble is of an extraordinary quality. Visiting the sculptor's studio in Rome, Marshal Murat noticed the work and ordered it transported to his château in France. Napoleon then bought the piece in 1812. With its extreme elegance, all turns and counterturns, the sculpture stands at the crossroads of two dominant tendencies at the end of the 18th century: Neoclassicism and pre-Romanticism. The rapid development of archaeology (the excavations at Herculaneum date from 1738, those at Pompeii from 1748) had disclosed an unknown, almost exotic Greco-Roman antiquity. Canova reflects this in the smooth and supple rendering of his figures, also in the slightly effete attitudes. But this image of love, at once reserved and rapturous, erotic and cerebral, also anticipates the tumultuous storms of Chateaubriand's *Attala*.

Antonio Canova (1757–1822).
Eros and Psyche (details). 1793. Italy.
Marble, 1.55 × 1.68m/5′1″ × 5′6¼″.

In burning eyes or vacant looks, a reflection of revolutionary times and tragically abridged lives

right: *Countess del Carpio* is considered to be one of the most beautiful portraits of women painted by Francisco Goya. Against the flat plane of the background, he played with black, white, and rose, creating a harmony that recalls Velázquez. A sorrowful and chaste spirituality emanates from the model. Marie Rita Barrenechea, wife of Count del Carpio, who in 1792 became Marquis de la Solana, would die shortly after the portrait was made. "The fine silhouette," remarks Germain Bazin, "seems to come forward, like a phantom, from the abstraction of the unified background. There is even in this simple work, stripped by its spareness of all hallucinating rhetoric, the 'supernatural' stamp that marks all the great masterpieces of Spanish painting. Light as a sylph, the spindle-like body is only a fragile shell containing a soul that one imagines to be ardent."

left: In the portrait of Madame Trudaine it is tempting to see the beautiful Emilie Vernet, a friend of the painter who died tragically during the Revolution. Abandoning his facility gained from a mastery of the antique, David tried to render the interior life of his subject. In this face, with its large, somewhat distracted eyes, it seems possible to sense the grief of a young woman all of whose family fell victim to the unsettled times. Particularly striking is the daring monochrome of the wide red ground. Effected by scumbling, which catches light and endows the canvas with a slow vibration, it serves to reinforce the model's desolate expression.

Jacques-Louis David. (1748–1825).
Madame Trudaine. c. 1790–91. France.
Canvas, 1.30 × 0.98m/4'3¼" × 3'2½".

Francisco Goya (1746–1828).
Countess del Carpio. c. 1791. Spain.
Canvas, 1.81 × 1.22m/5'11¼" × 4'.

241

Jean-Auguste-Dominique Ingres (1786–1867). *Angelica.* c. 1819. France. Canvas, 0.84 × 0.42m/2′ 1½″ × 1′4½″.

A powerful rhetoric appears in painting, the herald of the severe purities of Neoclassicism

left: *Angelica,* painted by Ingres in the same year he did his large *Roger and Angelica,* is undoubtedly, thanks to its simplicity, the most successful of the several variant interpretations that the artist made of this theme from Ariosto. Ingres, "who had no imagination," preferred to repeat the same subjects rather than invent new ones. Here, the background, with its dominant orange, throws into relief the anatomy of a model whose tortured pose is not without its felicities. Baudelaire, one of the 19th century's best critics, pointed out in several magisterial pages the ambiguity evident in France's severe champion of the classical tradition: "Monsieur Ingres is never so happy nor so strong as when his genius comes to grips with the physical charms of youthful beauty.... He is enamored of an ideal that, even in the portrayal of a tiresome adultress, combines the calm solidity of Raphael with the closely observed details of the 'little master'."

right: The *Brutus* of David, commissioned for Louis XVI by his fine arts minister, is the kind of heroic piece based upon Roman history in which the Neoclassical masters loved to evince their morality through sorely tried but exemplary characters. Brutus has just returned home after having condemned his own sons to death for their involvement with the Tarquins, the former kings of Rome whose tyranny Brutus had overthrown. As the bodies of the executed conspirators are brought in, their mother suddenly rises to her feet and, clutching her hysterical daughters, expresses horror at what she sees. David had painted the sons' heads detached from their bodies, but the circumstances of the moment, which were rapidly leading to Revolution, prompted him to represent the victims in a less sensational manner. The Roman mode, so appropriate for both the new French Republic and its aftermath, the Empire, found in David a prestigious champion and a great painter.

Jacques-Louis David (1748–1825).
Lictors Returning to Brutus the Bodies of his Sons (detail).
1789. France. Canvas, 3.25 × 4.25m/10′8″ × 13′11¼″.

Jean-Auguste-Dominique Ingres (1780–1867). *Small Bather*. 1828. France. Canvas, 0.35 × 0.27m/1′1¾″ × 10¾″.

By the power and grace
of his art,
Ingres discloses bourgeois
realities and fantasies
in the time of Louis-Philippe

above: Ingres' *Small Bather,* painted for Madame Coutan, is a new study made twenty years after the *Large Bather* sent from Rome in 1808. Here the figure recalls the attenuated proportions of the *Grande Odalisque,* in which the artist had taken liberties with anatomical reality in order to obtain an elegant arabesque. With its grace derived from the play of lines and the nuances of color, the painting reflects the progress made by Ingres since his youthful works. It can be felt especially in the greater subtlety of both drawing and composition. As always, the master made every effort to conceal his brushwork and produce, like a good classicist, a perfectly smooth film of paint. "The crafty worshiper of Raphael," as Baudelaire called Ingres, considered it "vulgar" for the painter to leave evidence of his manual labor.

right: Ingres painted the portrait of Louis-François Bertin in 1832. After having planned to represent his model standing, the artist, in a stroke of genius, hit upon this seated pose, which does so much to emphasize the power and authority of the actual man. Journalist, politician, and businessman, founder of the *Journal des débats,* Bertin was one of the principal supporters of the liberal bourgeoisie after 1830. The plump hands, pressed hard upon the knees, the forceful and commanding air—everything in the image expresses "that straight and clear reason caught in a pose of robust vulgarity," as the Goncourts put it. For the general public, the portrait of Bertin has come to seem the very symbol of the rise of the rich bourgeoisie in the time of Louis-Philippe.

Jean-Auguste-Dominique Ingres. *Monsieur Bertin*. 1832. France. Canvas, 1.16 × 0.93m/3′9¾″ × 3′1½″.

Intoxicated with the exotic,
Romantic Europe finds fulfillment
in the image of Oriental odalisques

Théodore Chassériau (1819–56).
Apollo and Daphne. 1844.
France. Canvas, 0.53 × 0.35m/1'8¾" × 1'1¾".

Théodore Chassériau. *Venus in a Seascape.*
1838. Canvas, 0.65 × 0.55m/2'1½" × 1'9¾".

The women of Chassériau are distinguishable from
those of his first master, Ingres, by a romantic melancholy that links the artist to the tumultuous genius
of Delacroix. Born in Santo Domingo and early regarded as a child prodigy, Chassériau had a drawing
instructor at the age of nine. At twelve he entered
the studio of Ingres, who exclaimed one day as the
adolescent artist was working from the model:
"Come see, messieurs, come see! This child will be
the Napoleon of painting." When only nineteen he
won a medal at the Salon, and at twenty-four his
friends were the likes of Théophile Gautier and Gérard de Nerval. Meanwhile, Chassériau formulated a
feminine type that would have an enduring effect
upon the 19th century. With their elongated silhouettes and hip-shot poses, his Venuses and Daphnes
seem to embody some obscure secret, "a mysterious
and sad feeling, a certain wild grace, an indefinable
Oriental languor" (Théophile Gautier). But Chassériau died when only thirty-seven, artistically still
evolving. In his writing, he appears to have anticipated certain aspects of Impressionism: "One must
find poetry in actuality; see antiquity through nature; make one's soul visible, true, and fine; see in
heads, while drawing them, eternal beauty; and se-
lect the happy moment."

Théodore Chassériau. *Esther.* 1842.
Canvas, 0.45 × 0.35m/1'5¾" × 1'1¾".

Romantic Tumult, Impressionist Calm, and Modernist Innovation
19th–20th Centuries

Once the Battle of Waterloo (1815) had put an end to the Napoleonic adventure, the consquences of the immense upheaval could be assessed in the calm of a restored peace. The most immediate effects were felt in the political and social spheres. It took longer, however, for intellectual and artistic life to make its response.

Quite remarkably, the artist became independent, free of royal, state, and aristocratic patronage, even of that provided by the old guilds, which had been suppressed by the Revolution. But while the artist no longer felt the constraints of the old system, he also ceased to enjoy its support, guarantees, privileges, and benefits.

Now the sovereign could not play the great decorator of his kingdom. Even before the bourgeois reign of Louis-Philippe, the monarchy lost the preeminent place it had occupied in every aspect of life under the *ancien régime*. In the 18th century the court, independent of the King himself, succeeded in having a broad effect upon the evolution of the arts. Quite simply, the King could no longer spend endless amounts of money, that all-powerful means of making the royal will felt throughout the nation. Already by the end of the old order, the great private fortunes had begun to appear, often among the bourgeoisie, who in fact became wealthy enough to rival the monarch. In the 19th century, the phenomenon would become general. The rapid advance of industry placed the money of the realm in the hands of the ever-rising and growing middleclass.

Emancipated from control by a centralized power, the artist had to submit to the laws of supply and demand, a demand that could come from nowhere but the public at large. Maecenas was dead. Succeeding the enlightened, intelligent protector was the enthusiast or collector who could help the artist without, however, being able to impose his own taste. But the new system had its own despotism, for the collector found himself forced to accept the artist's vision, all the while that both art and patron often fell victim to the tyranny of fashion.

If the artist had gained his independence, art itself was not yet entirely free. The only protection left to the artist was that offered by the Académie des Beaux-Arts. But this institution, which had been founded to help and inspire artists, now became a constraint, an impediment, and the conservatory of outmoded forms. Academicism had assumed a decidedly pejorative meaning. And this occurred just when, under the impact of the Revolution and the first tremors of nascent Romanticism, the artist took self-expression as his primary objective. The myth of liberty conquered the creative individual, causing him to fall in love with his own personality as translated by original and ever-renewing artistic means.

Thereafter, the entire history of the 19th century would be that of the artist's struggle to escape not only the constraints of official commissions but also the patronage of collectors formed in the academic tradition. "Schools" or styles became nothing more than loose relationships among artists who shared certain affinities.

The great movements of art and thought would generally cross frontiers and would seem to leave national expressions nothing but their own interpretation of common themes.

Romanticism

As we have seen, a Pre-Romantic sensibility developed halfway through the 18th century. With its sources close to those that were traditional in Germany and England, Romanticism had no difficulty taking root there. It proved quite otherwise in France. Literary Romanticism broke through in 1820, the year that Lamartine's *Méditations poétiques* appeared in print. Although the Romantic war waged in the visual arts had commenced earlier, it took longer for it to win a definitive victory. The Classicism of David and Gros was violently attacked in 1817, but unlike the situation in literature, academic art still constituted an important force. At every Salon—1817, 1819, 1824, 1927 —the battle raged, with Romanticism emerging ever-more triumphant after each new encounter.

Romanticism challenged Neoclassicism in, above all else, its choice of subject matter, with preference given to the Middle Ages, the Renaissance, or even contemporary history over antiquity. Romanticism then departed from the academic tradition in spirit, which sought to express, not permanent values, but, on the contrary, impressions of the most subjective and fleeting nature. Finally, there were distinctions of technique, with color recovering all the importance that David had taken from it and given to line or drawing.

Delacroix (pages 256, 257) is the greatest painter of the French Romantic movement. He achieved this eminence by the richness of his imagination, by his dramatic use of color, and by his taste for violence and escapism. Along with him, the slightly older Théodore Géricault (pages 252, 254) helped to affirm the dark power of human passions. The new movement also claimed a number of minor masters, including Descamps, Constantin Guys, and Gavarni.

From about 1848, a new reaction set in, this time against Romanticism itself. It took the form of resurgent Realism, whose influence quickly spread, expressing itself in two different ways. While granting supremacy to objects and to the faithful imitation of nature, it selected a new kind of subject. The painter's task was to illustrate the realities of workaday life. The artist must reveal the truth of the human condition. It was their proletarian preoccupations that distinguished the 19th-century naturalists from the traditional "painters of reality." Courbet (pages 269, 272) became a kind of *chef d'école* to the movement, at the same time that he served as its chief theoretician. But in fact he was more Realist in his themes than in his handling, which retained several traces of Romanticism. Millet and Daumier (pages 266, 267) became the other great painters who attempted to translate their social ideals into art. Carpeaux gave Realism its finest sculptor, after whom came Dalou, along with his strong literary or socialist notions.

A special place must be reserved for the truly remarkable landscape painting that emerged at this time and that in certain respects seemed, by virtue of its realism, to anticipate Impressionism. The art of Corot (page 272) is remote from Impressionism; still, this artist brought a genuine poetry even to the most precise of his early Italian works, well before the more vaporous style that he formulated in the second half of his career. Around Corot gathered a gifted circle—generally known as the Barbizon School— composed of Paul Huet, Théodore Rousseau, Dupré, Diaz, and Daubigny (page 273).

Among the founders of 19th-century painting were, of course, the great English masters: Constable, Bonington (page 258), and Turner (page 259), who in fact may have been the most direct precursors of the Impressionists.

Impressionism

Naturally, resistance developed to Realism—to that pretended total submission to objective truth—and it arose in the very bosom of the movement itself. Such great progenitors of Impressionism as Degas (pages 282, 283, 308, 309) and Manet (pages 268, 275) began as strict Realists. At the outset of their careers, Renoir (pages 277–279), Gauguin (pages 292, 293), Cézanne (pages 274, 280, 281, 296), and Toulouse-Lautrec (304, 306, 307) recorded impressions that were slightly more subjective only in theme and in a certain subtlety of light or touch. Then, there were the great Monet (pages 294, 295, 300–303) and Seurat (pages 290, 291, 305) who transcended simple objectivity by drawing upon theories derived from a new analysis of natural phenomena.

The term Impressionist originated in the witticism of a journalist ridiculing the title of a painting by Monet—*Impression, soleil levant*— presented at the first so-called Impressionist Salon, held at Nadar's photography studio in 1874. For ten years, Monet and his friends had worked as a group, with each member retaining his own distinct personality, but with all bent upon creating an art that would give the modern world a vision based upon the sincerity of the painter. The scandal caused by *Olympia* at the 1865 Salon had rallied the young innovators around Manet. Thus, during Impressionism's formative years, this artist served as older master and respected counselor. But after the Franco-Prussian War (1870), Monet assumed the leadership role. Installed at Argenteuil, he drew his associates about him and made possible the dynamic explosion of Impressionist painting after 1873.

Among the landscapists of the group two tendencies can be detected. The first appears in the art of Pissarro and Sisley, which seems to derive from Courbet and Corot and to retain from Realism a certain firmness of form enveloped in light. The other, bolder tendency was that of Monet, who, having found his first model in Boudin, led Renoir and Caillebotte towards a representation of the world in which the play of light and its reflection would make painted objects seem dissolved and deprived of all weight and density. Even Manet, who made fun of *peinture claire* ("light-toned painting"), would come and paint at Argenteuil. There he portrayed Monet at work in his boat near the Seine embankment. It was on this floating studio that the group's leader and the most doctrinaire of the Impressionists studied—*en plein air* ("out-of-doors"), close to his motif—the variations presented by the same landscape as observed at different times of day. He multiplied the *instantanés de lumière* ("moments of light") and delighted in representing boats with their sails reflected in the shimmering surface of water. Monet indulged his appetite for "rainbow orgies," as a contemporary called the artist's canvases, and fixed forever the incomparable image of summer afternoons on the banks of the Seine, with all their fresh, humid atmosphere.

It was in 1866 that the novelist Emile Zola, who became the Impressionists' defender, had written: "A work of art is a creation seen through a temperament." Such a definition could be applied to any period in the history of art. Still, it seems especially applicable to the Impressionists, who not only developed a new technique utilizing pure hues and high-key tonalities, applied in disengaged strokes so as to suggest the vibration of light, but also transformed the attitude of the artist toward his work. The painter should, above all else, trust his own sensation and by this means create a personal vision of a subject that in itself may have little artistic value.

Beginning with Impressionism, three main impulses would shape the art of the 20th century. For Seurat and his companions—Signac, Luce, and Cross—the physiological conditions that govern painting assumed a crucial importance. Their systematization of the Impressionist procedure of disengaging strokes shifted the artist's interest from the subject painted to the mechanisms of optical perception. Painting began to play with the retina. If Seurat used "pointillism" (also known as Neo-Impressionism) for synthetic purposes, intending that the separate points of color on the canvas should mix in the eye, modern artists would take up a contrary position and endeavor to exploit the properties of painting in order to disassociate forms themselves and pulverize the painting surface. The simultaneous contrasts of Robert Delaunay and the unsettling games of Op Art are the rebel children of pointillism.

In the art of Gauguin and van Gogh appeared the second direction taken during what later critics called the Post-Impressionist period. Color, which was first employed so as to render objects with the greatest truth to observable reality, gradually became autonomous. The yellow of van Gogh no longer has as its primary mission the representation of a chair; instead, it serves, by way of its unprecedented density, to speak of "terrible human passions." In this arose a psychology of color, which Kandinsky would later codify in his book *Concerning the Spiritual in Art* (1912). Gauguin, in an interview, explained this conception of the power of pure color: "With some subject borrowed from life or nature as my pretext, I use arrangements of lines and colors to obtain symphonies and harmonies representing nothing absolutely *real* in the popular sense of the word, directly expressing no idea whatever, but that should provoke thought the way music does, without the help of ideas or images, simply by the mysterious affinities that exist between our brains and such colors and lines."

After Impressionism

From this current flowed two new streams. Fauvism retained the traditional, Renaissance conception of space, but took every liberty in regard to color, creating red beaches, green faces, and blue trees. The Nabis, meanwhile, favored a decorative flatness and the juxtaposition on the canvas of broad, monochrome surfaces, the purpose of which is not to give the effect of space but rather to compose colored ensembles liberated from all immediate reality. In 1890 Maurice Denis, a key Nabi, explained his

group's art in one famous sentence: "Remember that a picture—before it is a battle horse, a nude woman, or some anecdote—is essentially a flat surface covered with colors arranged in a certain order." Matisse, the leader of the Fauves ("Wild Beasts") and Kandinsky found themselves at the intersection of the two currents of pure color. From there Kandinsky took the route to abstraction once he decided, in 1910, to "do without subject matter."

Finally, the third broad tendency that anticipated modern art came from Cézanne. The "solitary of Aix" challenged nothing less than the linear perspective that had governed painting for the past five centuries. In its place, he created an ambiguous space of variable depths, in which each stroke can be read simultaneously as *très loin* ("far away"), or *très près* ("very close"). The rational hierarchies of Renaissance space failed to be verified by the actuality of visual experience. Cézanne did not see a house 500 meters away; rather, he saw a red spot vibrating in sunlight. He therefore placed the equivalent of that spot on his canvas without worrying whether it was "logical" or whether it came "forward of the canvas." At the same time, in order to better take account of the object, Cézanne endeavored to show not only the façade of the house but also its side walls. He frontalized, advancing toward the picture plane the lateral flanks of Sainte-Victoire mountain. He depicted at once both the profile and the top of a coffee pot. In the 20th century the Cubists would systematize Cézanne's approach to the motif, simultaneously showing all aspects of an object, which they then juxtaposed and superimposed on the canvas. A guitar by Picasso is seen from the front, from the side, from above, and from below, all in the same picture. With the end of Renaissance monocular vision, an entire conception of painting perished. From the springboard of Seurat, van Gogh, Gauguin, and Cézanne, the art of the 20th century would launch forth.

In a suspended gallop
over a green English track,
Géricault discovers
the symbol for
the Romantic anguish
of a lost generation,
the heirs of
the Napoleonic era

The Derby at Epsom is a magisterial painting that impresses both by the Romantic amplitude of its subject and by the bold handling that would have a profound effect upon Manet and Degas. Owing to the apparent futility of the event—England's famous horse race, which here seems frozen in time—a fantastic run through a storm succeeds in symbolizing the anxieties of a whole generation. Born at the height of the French Revolution, and twenty-one years old when fate caught up with Napoleon—"the greatest man to come into the world since Julius Caesar" (Stendhal)—Géricault embodied the feverish sensibility of an era that turned back upon itself. Dead at thirty-two, after a dozen years of frenzied activity, he was one of painting's great liberators. The Epsom lawn, where the green nuances are here and there created with separate touches, rather than mixed on the palette, had its origin in the innovations of Constable and would in turn influence Delacroix quite directly. This artist wrote in his journal after hearing of Géricault's untimely death: "What a different destiny seemed to be promised by such physical power, such a fiery imagination."

Théodore Géricault (1791–1824). *The Derby at Epsom.* 1821. France. Canvas 0.9¹ × 1.22m/3′¼″ × 4′.

A surging tumult of bodies
registers the storms of the Romantic soul.
To express the power of human passion,
French art rediscovers
the *terribilità* of Michelangelo

Géricault's *Raft of the Medusa* had its inspiration in a contemporary event: the sinking of the frigate *Medusa* in June 1816, which generated violent attacks against the colonial minister, a royalist who allegedly had allowed the ship to be captained by an incompetent officer then out of service for 25 years. After 12 days adrift on a makeshift raft abandoned by the main lifeboat, 149 passengers had dwindled to 15 survivors. The sufferings of all were extreme. Géricault addressed himself to the tragic event with a vengeance, preparing his subject by means of exhaustive research, especially into the more morbid details of the experience. Throughout the spring and summer of 1818—when he was only 28—the artist made sketches and drawings from patients in the Beaujon Hospital and from cadavers in the morgue. He even had all his hair cut off so as to be more immune to worldly temptation. While endlessly interrogating the rescued, he had the *Medusa*'s carpenter build a scale model of the fateful raft. Fully 49 drawings and paintings by Géricault have come down from this heroic enterprise. Reproduced on the opposite page is one of the four principal studies that the artist prepared before launching into the final, definitive version seen below. Some viewers consider the study more moving by virtue of its incompletion. Introduced at the Salon of 1819, *The Raft of the Medusa* caused a scandal. And this was true despite the fact that the work is solidly classical in its structure and organization, as well as in its sculpturesque figures, recalling both Michelangelo and Caravaggio. The young Delacroix, who served as a model, can be seen in the figure lying face down in the foreground, his left arm extended.

Théodore Géricault. *Sketch for the Raft of the Medusa.* 1818.
Canvas, 0.83 × 0.65m/2′8¾″ × 2′1½″.

Théodore Géricault (1791–1821). *The Raft of the Medusa.* 1819. France. Canvas, 4.90 × 7.16m/16′1″ × 23′6″.

Eugène Delacroix (1798–1863).
Arabian Horses Fighting in a Stable (detail).
1860. France.
Canvas, 0.64 × 0.81m/2′1¼″ × 2′9″.

In scenes of fighting animals Eugène Delacroix found a release for the tumultuous passions that made him the French Rubens. The explosive freedom of the brushwork and the dizzy rhythms of the composition give his bestiary art—which he cultivated throughout his life—an incomparable lightness that anticipated lyrical abstraction. "If," he said, "you haven't enough skill to sketch a man as he jumps from a fourth-story window and falls to the ground, you will never produce big machines."

Eugène Delacroix.
Horse Attacked by a Lioness. c. 1840.
Canvas, 0.34 × 0.43m/1′1½″ × 1′5″.

Eugène Delacroix.
Tiger Hunt (detail). 1854.
Canvas, 0.74 × 0.93m/2′5¼″ × 3′¾″.

An African bestiary
provides Delacroix
with the iconography
of a tempestuous epic

Richard Bonington (1801–28). *View of the Normandy Coast.* 1823. England. Canvas, 4.50 × 3.80m/14′9¼ × 12′5½″.

Artists enraptured with nature
express its
palpitating life
through color-filled
light and atmosphere

J.M.W. Turner (1775–1851). *Landscape.* After 1830. England. Canvas, 0.94 × 1.23m/3′1″ × 4′.

left: *View of the Normandy Coast,* above all else, reflects the powerful fascination that Franco-British artists felt, around 1820, a good half-century before Impressionism, for the shifting skies over Rouen, Honfleur, and Le Havre. "Why ever," cried the generation of John Constable, "do we prefer dark and dirty old canvases to the works of God?" Richard Bonington, the son of an English businessman established in France, became the period's prodigy. For the landscapes he painted in Normandy, after nature, Bonington developed an oil technique that allowed him to achieve effects resembling those possible in watercolor—brilliance, immediacy, and a fresh, airy, "breathing" quality. The friend of Delacroix and Lawrence, Bonington would serve as a link between the artists of England and France, playing a role that would prove enormously important in the birth of a new and highly fluent painting, blond in tonality, transparent, and with light as its principal theme. But this master died at twenty-six, the victim of tuberculosis. "You are the monarch of your domain, and even Raphael has not achieved what you have," Delacroix wrote to Bonington. More than thirty years later, in 1861, the French artist confirmed this estimate: "In my opinion, no one in the modernist movement, or perhaps even before, has ever been capable of such lightness of facture, which transforms his works into diamonds, ravishing the eye and doing so quite apart from all subject matter and all imitation."

above: This *Landscape,* which the Louvre acquired in 1967, dates from late in the career of J.M.W. Turner. No one went further than this artist in the dissolution of form, and no one felt more keenly how each particle of matter participates in the cosmic continuum of perpetual mutation. Turner was a fervent admirer of Claude Lorrain (pages 206–09), and he even specified in his will that two of his own works should hang together in London's National Gallery with a pair of admired canvases by the great 17th-century French master. Turner's technique initiated the "informal" and *nuagiste* ("misty") manner that would triumph in France during the 1850s. As Louvre curator François Mathey has remarked: "Fleeing the soot and tar, the whole industrial scene, he endeavored to rediscover divine light, the source of life. The landscapes of Turner are like a hymn of thanksgiving, sung by the blind man who has recovered his sight."

Seeking his source
in the gaudiness
of an imagined Orient,
Delacroix pretends
to history painting
but achieves an opera
of savage lyricism

Eugène Delacroix (1798–1863). *Death of Sardanapalus* (detail on facing page). 1827. France. Canvas, 3.95 × 4.96m/12'11½" × 16'3¼".

Delacroix found the subject for *Death of Sardanapalus* in a verse tragedy by Lord Byron, published in 1821 and dedicated to Goethe. Besieged in his capital, the Assyrian monarch ordered the throats cut of all his women, servants, pages, dogs, and everyone else who had ministered to his pleasures. The grand and tormented movement of the composition recalls the art of Tintoretto and Rubens: "Did ever a painted image," wrote Baudelaire, "display a vaster conception of the Asiatic despot than this Sardanapalus, who with his black, braided beard, perishes upon his own pyre, swathed in muslin and lounging like a woman?" The work had a poor reception at the Salon of 1827. "Delacroix," Germain Bazin tells us, "who expected to be decorated for this 'Oriental challenge' to the 'Spartan' pastiches of the Davidian school, felt very let down."

To convey the excitement
of feminine beauty,
Delacroix liberates his brush
and thereby opens
the way to Impressionism

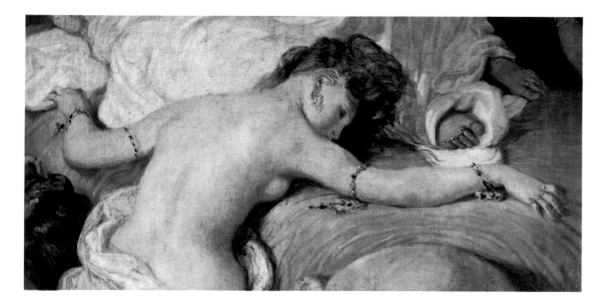

Eugène Delacroix. *Death of Sardanapalus*
(detail of the horse's harness;
see page 261
at the extreme left in the plate).

Sardanapalus, in its details, reveals Delacroix to have been capable of an erotic violence unique in the history of French art. "Give me the mud of the streets," he said, "and I will give you female flesh rendered in the most delicious tints." But the more one enters into the picture reproduced here, the more one is struck by the audacity of a divisionist technique, a technique in which Seurat would perceive the origins of Impressionism. "It is good that the touches [of color] should not be materially fused," explained Delacroix. "From a certain distance they will be seen to fuse naturally, by the law of complementarity that governs them." Baudelaire, Delacroix's ardent defender, would become enthusiastic over the quasi-abstract wonders created by such a palette: "It could be said that this kind of painting, like sorcerers and mesmerizers, projects its thought from a distance. . . . It would seem that the colors think for themselves, independently of the objects they clothe."

Eugène Delacroix. *Death of Sardanapalus* (details).

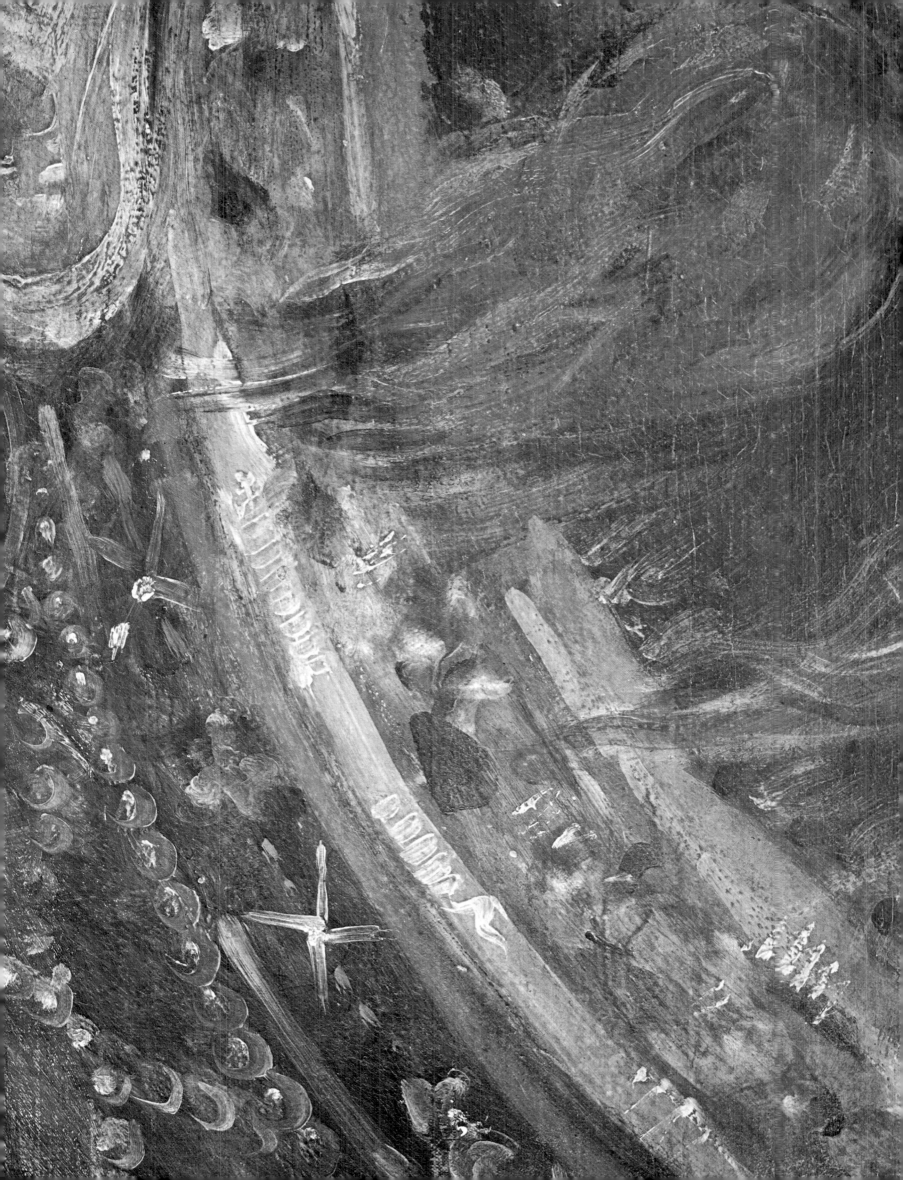

As surfaces collapse
under pressure,
light infiltrates
through broken glazes
and volumes gain in vitality
what they lose in compactness

Jean-Baptiste Carpeaux.
Negress in an Attitude of Revolt. c. 1869.
Terra-cotta, height 0.27m/10¾″.

Jean-Baptiste Carpeaux.
La Patrie. After 1870.
Terra-cotta, height 0.66m/2′2″.

Jean-Baptiste Carpeaux (1827–75). *Crouching Man Wrestling another Figure.* France. Terra-cotta, height 0.19m/7½″.

In the clay "sketches" of Carpeaux we encounter—perhaps even more than in the marbles—the sensibility of the artist's contemporaries. His technique of rolling the damp material in his hands and then working it with his thumbs yielded richly plastic surfaces that seem to vibrate and flicker with shifting lights and shadows, as if in anticipation of the Impressionists and, even closer to us, the late "eaten-away" figures of Giacometti. Whether they sink into the clay with a kind of sensual delight (above) or, on the contrary, burst out of it (right and opposite), the figures of Carpeaux are kneaded into a texture that is unforgettable. Subject and matter seem both to have been fixed at once and in the same stroke, as if the human body were not yet fully liberated from the primordial mud. "This Carpeaux," wrote the Goncourts in 1865, "a nature of nerves, of violence, of exaltation, rough-hewn, always in movement, with flexing muscles and a laborer's eye filled with anger. The fever of genius in the skin of a marble carver." Kept in the reserve for more than thirty years, the three terra-cottas on these facing pages have only recently gained their permanent place in the Pavillon de Flore.

His stroke charged with lightning, Daumier caricatures the absurdities and pleasures of human experience

Honoré Daumier (1808–79). *Crispino and Scapino*. c. 1860. France. Canvas, 0.60 × 0.82m/1′11½″ × 2′8¼″.

Crispino and Scapino discloses Daumier's abiding interest in the theatre, especially in the theatre of Molière. "Like him," remarked Baudelaire, "he gets right to the point. The idea jumps out at the first shot. One look, and we have understood." In regard to the actor, Daumier's view is as modern as that of Degas toward the footlighted dancer, or of the *filles* of Toulouse-Lautrec in the glow of gaslight. The powerful work reproduced here, in which everything not essential has been sacrificed, offers one of the best surviving examples of the artist's style—drawing that simplifies forms, accentuates characters, and transforms actors into general types. "That caricaturist has a bit of Michelangelo's blood in his veins," said Balzac.

Honoré Daumier.
Don Quixote and the Dead Mule. c. 1865–68.
Canvas, 1.32 × 0.54m/4'4" × 1'9¼".

Honoré Daumier. *The Parade* (detail). Pencil, sanguine, and watercolor, 0.26 × 0.36m/10¼" × 1'2¼".

above: Daumier painted his *Don Quixote* as a decoration for the house acquired in 1860 by his neighbor Daubigny at Auvers-sur-Oise. Cervantes had no great currency among artists until 1863, when Gustave Doré experienced an enormous success with his *Don Quixote,* an edition of 370 engravings. Daumier, whose idealist temperament could easily identify with the "Knight of the Sad Countenance," took up one of Doré's engravings and, transforming it completely, painted the picture seen above. It illustrates no more than a few lines: "When they had almost completed their journey around the mountain, they came to the edge of a stream and there found a dead mule, half devoured by wolves and crows, but still wearing its saddle and bridle." The painter handled the scene with dramatic sobriety. Appearing at the top of the picture, the two figures of the Don and Sancho Panza stumble upon the mule in the foreground, where nothing has been allowed to distract from the brutal encounter. The severe geometry of the *mise en page,* the authority of the great lines that *cale* or "lock in" the composition—everything denotes the late period of Daumier, a bold, quick, and powerful master whose genius would not be recognized until after his death.

right: In *The Parade,* a trenchant observation on the diversions of the Parisian lower classes, Daumier used all his fluency and ease, giving full expression to a love of burlesque and caricature. In his lifetime, the artist was known for his magnificent lithographs and the wholesome wickedness of his socio-political satire. But the importance of Daumier the sculptor and painter did not emerge until after his death. Tracking down stupidity and excess, he described a human comedy in which everyone puts on a costume and plays a role—real actors but also the bourgeois, the magistrates, the doctors. Along with Courbet and Millet, he brought to the realities of everyday life a new acuity, the lessons of which would not be lost.

267

As Courbet and Manet
spear the real,
they extract the very juice
of quotidian experience,
claiming to be reporters,
not beauticians

Gustave Courbet (1819–77). *Burial at Ornans* (details). 1849.
France. Canvas, 3.14 × 6.63m/10'3½" × 21'9".

above and right: *Burial at Ornans* is a grandiose mural devoted to provincial France in the middle of the 19th century, with each figure a portrait. At age thirty-six, Courbet solemnly saluted his native region, displaying the roots that attached him to the country of his ancestors. One of the century's best critics, Gustave Geffroy, commented thus on Courbet's *Burial:* "Never has a more grave or beautiful page been dedicated in homage to the dead. Each face among those present expresses the idea of farewell." But *Burial* also constitutes a manifesto of realism. For Courbet, "whose remarkable beginnings have recently assumed the character of an insurrection" (Baudelaire), it was a question of affirming once and for all that art should give up the fantasies of the imagination. "I hold," he would say, "that painting is an essentially concrete art, and should exist only in the representation of real and palpable things. . . . An invisible, abstract object has no place in painting."

left: *The Balcony,* one of the manifesto-canvases in which Manet, in spite of himself, seemed to defy the establishment, was painted in 1868–69. Placed at the center of an artistic battle by two scandals—*Déjeuner sur l'herbe* and *Olympia*—over which no one was more dumbfounded than the artist himself, the bourgeois, peaceful, refined Manet, who dreamed of the Legion of Honor and a Salon medal, was soon consecrated as high priest of the Impressionist revolution. "When visitors [to the exhibition] see the name Manet, they try to burst out laughing," wrote Zola in the year *The Balcony* appeared. "But the canvases are there, light-toned, luminous, seeming to look out with grave and proud disdain. [The spectators] leave, uncomfortable, not knowing what they should think, moved in spite of themselves by the severe voice of talent." Received with derision, *The Balcony* had its source in Goya. It is an attempt to capture, from the exterior, several people posed between two strongly contrasting lights—the deep shadow of the apartment interior and the raw illumination of open air. The young painter Berthe Morisot sat for the central figure (facing page). A great friend of Manet, she wrote to her sister in 1869: "I found Manet . . . looking confused; he asked me to go see his painting, because he dared not take it further. . . . He laughed, somewhat nervously, all the while assuring me both that the picture was very bad and that it would have a great success. . . . I am more strange than beautiful. . . . It seems that the epithet *femme fatale* has circulated among the curious."

Edouard Manet (1832–83). *The Balcony* (detail). 1868–69.
France. Canvas, 1.69 × 1.25m/6'5¼" × 4'1¼".

Antoine-Louis Barye (1796–1875). *Crouched Lion Watching a Prey*. France. Plaster and wax, 0.17 × 0.39m/6¾″ × 1′3¼″.

above: *Crouched Lion* provides an introduction to the salient qualities of the oeuvre created by Antoine-Louis Barye. The greatest of all French *animaliers*, the artist had a genius for integrating keen observation with a wild lyricism that seems all the more liberated when seen against its contemporary background—a society increasingly constrained by the forces of industrialization. The nature depicted by Barye is not that evoked by Jean-Jacques Rousseau, but rather the world of unceasing conflict in which the various species pitilessly prey upon, confront, and kill one another. It is a realm of adventure and instinct, in marked contrast to the bureaucratic organization described by the age's Romantic novelists—Stendhal in *Lucien Leuwen* or Balzac in *César Birotteau*. In preparation for his sculptures, Barye spent his days watching the caged beasts in the Jardin des Plantes. There he made countless drawings and quick studies in the hope of capturing the creature's movements, attitudes, and anatomical structure. The animal kingdom may never have been more passionately analyzed and transposed. One of the artist's biographers could write: "We should be happy that Bayre won none of his competitions and that instead of going to Rome, and submitting to the doctrines of the Villa Medici, he found himself reduced to taking a daily walk in the Zoological Gardens."

right: *Lion's Head* by Eugène Delacroix reveals what an admirable draftsman the great Romantic painter was. The very opposite of the classically pure, linear, static Ingres, Delacroix is vibrant, dynamic, and devoted to the expression of surging vitality, in its most direct and energetic form. His watercolor-loaded brush brings to intense life the head of a lion the artist had studied in the Jardin des Plantes. But for all the realism of the method and the image, the creature has here become a fabulous animal and the very symbol of Romanticism.

In the passions of caged beasts,
the artists of industrial society
see the symbol of their lost freedom

Eugène Delacroix (1798–1863). *Lion's Head*. France. Watercolor over graphite, heightened with white gouache, 0.18 × 0.19m/7″ × 7½″.

Water, its reflections and movement
give artists the sense of
constantly changing nature.
Observing this perpetual metamorphosis,
they anticipate the end
of art dedicated to immutability

Camille Corot (1796–1875).
Bridge at Narni. 1826. France.
Paper mounted on canvas, 0.34 × 0.48m/1'1½" × 1'7".

Charles-François Daubigny (1817–78).
Sunset on the Oise (detail). 1865. France.
Canvas, 0.39 × 0.67m/1'3¼" × 2'2½".

right: *Sunset on the Oise* contains virtually all the qualities of Impressionism. The ephemeral moment, refracted light, water, a scene in Ile-de-France—all the themes that would make Monet one of art's great giants are here set forth by a modest master who, at age 21, was earning his bread by decorating candy boxes 20 sous a piece. In 1857, a small inheritance permitted Daubigny to realize a project that also prefigured the methods of the Impressionists. He had himself built a canal boat—the *Botin*— surmounted by a small cabin covered with wide stripes of different colors. On this craft he would live a wandering existence along the waterways in the region around Paris, exploring the Seine basin and painting "impressions" of an extraordinary freshness.

left: *Bridge at Narni* represents a subject whose wild beauty enchanted Corot during his Italian sojourn in 1826. Painted from direct observation, it gave the artist a study that became his submission to the Salon of 1827. Whereas the final version in oil evokes Claude Lorrain, the study, with its sustained tonality and marked contrasts, is the record of the kind of first impression that the artist would always urge young painters never to forget. In Corot's opinion, the initial impression constitutes the most important factor of landscape painting. Especially remarkable in the work reproduced here is the audacious handling of the hillside on the right, where the long vertical strokes seem to announce the method of Cézanne (page 280). The Louvre is fortunate in owning 134 paintings by Corot.

left: *Stormy Sea,* painted in 1870 just before the drama of the Commune and the artist's exile in Switzerland, reveals in Courbet "the powerful worker, the wild and patient will" that Baudelaire had discerned. Peasant and hunter, Courbet wanted to embrace nature whole and complete and hoped to render its true substance as closely as possible. "In painting," notes René Huyghe, "he did not think; he asked only that his hand reconstitute in colored impastoes what his eye registered." Once when he was asked about a painting in progress, Courbet stood back and gave the work a good look before identifying his subject: "It's a bundle of firewood!" Odilon Redon described him "with his large, sweet eyes that lit up his debonair physiognomy, which pride, like an electrical charge, brought to life. 'I will take a gun, in spite of my genius,' he said during the war as the enemy was invading. Praise changed him, dominated him; once praised, he became a child that anyone could lead."

Gustave Courbet (1819–77).
Stormy Sea. 1870. France.
Canvas, 1.17 × 1.60m/3'10" × 5'3".

For Manet and Cézanne, the voluptuous abundance of women
holds the purity and radiance of light

Paul Cézanne (1839–1906). *A Modern Olympia*. 1873. France. Canvas, 0.46 × 0.55m/1'6" × 1'9¾".

above: *A Modern Olympia*, shot through with an impetuous, zigzagging rhythm, marks the transition that Cézanne made into a mature style from the heavily impastoed brushwork of his early efforts. During 1872–73 the artist stayed at Auvers so as to spend every day at the side of "the humble and colossal Pissarro," an experience that accelerated Cézanne's progress toward a painting light in both tonality and application. "It is useless to close form," explained Pissarro. "Precise, dry drawing detracts from the impression of the whole; it destroys all the 'sensations.' One must not fix the contours of things." *A Modern Olympia,* which parodies Manet's *Olympia,* only to prove more erotic than the original, evokes through its spatial disposition the objects of Cézanne's greatest admiration—Veronese and Tintoretto. At the same time, the artist's deft touch makes one think of the virtuosity of Fragonard. When exhibited at the first Impressionist show in 1874, *A Modern Olympia* was received with utter derision by a hostile and uncomprehending public—which simply reinforced Cézanne's propensity for solitude.

right: *Blond with Nude Bust* reveals the startling mastery with which Manet assimilated the lessons of his junior contemporaries, the Impressionists. In 1874, at the advice of Berthe Morisot, his pupil, Manet began to follow these modernists into the open air. Soon his palette took on a lighter and more joyous tonality. "The principal subject of a painting," he said, "is light." And it is light that radiates throughout the ample forms of this nude, the rich delicacy of whose flesh is set off by a virtuoso play of loose brushwork designed to represent a fringe of clothing. The painterly colorism of Titian, for whom Manet had a profound admiration, found a modern reincarnation in works like *Blond with Nude Bust.*

Edouard Manet (1832–83). *Blond Model with Nude Bust.* c. 1875–78. France. Canvas. 0.62 × 0.52m/2′½″ × 1′8½″.

Alfred Sisley (1839–99). *Flood at Port Marly* (detail). 1876. England-France. Canvas, 0.60 × 0.81m/1′11½″ × 2′8″.

above: *Flood at Port-Marly,* dating from 1876, is certainly the best of the several pictures that Alfred Sisley painted of this subject—water and light reflected in it—which meant much to the Impressionists. Pissarro and Monet made countless studies of the changing, amorphous, reflective character of water. Sisley, however, painted his surrounding countryside with a serene contemplation that is unique to him. Here, he seems absolutely immersed in the beauty of the scene. Totally attentive to the unceasing dialogue between sky and light-struck water, he was able to express his sensibility with a delicacy close to that of Corot. In this very year—1876—the powerful critic Albert Wolf visited the Impressionist Exhibition, where Sisley figured large, and in *Le Figaro* denounced the "five or six lunatics, including one woman, a group of wretches overcome by the folly of ambition. . . . There are those who burst out laughing in front of their things. As for myself, I feel quite sad."

right: *The Path Mounting into the High Grass* was probably painted at Ville d'Avray around 1876–78. The influence of Monet can be felt in motif and manner alike, which can hardly surprise since the two artists had worked together at Argenteuil throughout much of 1874. In the painting reproduced here Renoir translated into the true language of Impressionism the sparkle of light on vegetation, revealing that he had become a great colorist, capable of making his tones vibrate, mainly through the touches of sonorous red that animate the dominant green. The technique is a complex one, uniting the divisionist stroke of Impressionism with the luminous brushwork of the French 18th century, which Renoir very much admired.

Taking their easels
into the open air,
painters make direct contact with
a favorite subject — nature —
recording their most fleeting
and momentary impressions

Auguste Renoir (1841–1919). *Path Mounting into the High Grass.* c. 1876–78. France. Canvas, 0.49 × 0.74m/1'7¼" × 2'5¼".

With his glittering brush
and rainbow palette,
Renoir seizes the vitality
of an age
dappled in clear light
and blue shadow

right: *The Swing*, executed at the same time as *Le Moulin de la Galette* (left)—one worked on in the morning, the other in the afternoon—is a virtuoso demonstration of the possibilities for animating a subject by means of light. Thanks to the trees that filter daylight into random patches of color, the artist succeeded in pulverizing the forms and in transforming the young woman's dress into an immaterial reflection. That "modern goddess, silken, satiny, velvet-like, particolored with clothes and ribbons," to quote Gustave Geffroy, the great critic of Impressionism, appeals to us as the very symbol of *joie de vivre:* "[Renoir] may be the only painter," said Octave Mirbeau, "who never produced a sad picture."

left: *Le Moulin de la Galette,* the café on the Butte Montmartre frequented by artists and *grisettes,* pleased Renoir by its happy atmosphere. Having sold a painting, he moved nearby, at 78 Rue Cortot, so as to be able to work on the spot. "This canvas," recalled Georges Rivière, friend of Renoir and Cézanne, "we transported every day from the Rue Cortot to the Moulin, since the painting was executed entirely on site. It did not always proceed without problems. . . ." Renoir admitted to difficulties in composing a scene with so many figures. However, the picture he created is widely celebrated, and justly so, for it admirably evokes a motley Sunday crowd of Parisians who look as if they came straight out of a story by de Maupassant. Sunlight, filtering through the trees, dapples the blue and pink of the dresses, causing every color to vibrate. "For me," said Renoir, "a picture should be something likeable, joyous and pretty, yes pretty. . . . There are enough annoying things in life without our creating still more." When he was still a student, his teacher, Gleyre, commented: "It is no doubt merely to amuse yourself that you try to paint?" Renoir: "Monsieur, if it did not amuse me, I would not do it."

Auguste Renoir (1841–1919).
Le Moulin de la Galette (detail). 1876.
France. Canvas, 1.31 × 1.75m/4′3½″ × 5′9″.

Auguste Renoir. *The Swing.* 1876. Canvas, 0.92 × 0.73m/3′1¼″ × 2′4¾″.

Paul Cézanne (1839–1906). *The Maincy Bridge.* 1879. France. Canvas, 0.60 × 0.73m/1′11½″ × 2′4¾″.

In his revisualization
of nature
as a scaffolding
of floating planes,
Cézanne nullifies
a half-millennium
of Renaissance space

right: The *Self-Portrait* of Cézanne, manificent in its density, is a recent acquisition at the Louvre. Simply encrusted with thick, pasty medium, and almost sculpted in its material, the painting expresses the artist's structural instincts and his longing for a painting "solid and durable like the art of the museums." "I am," he said, "the primitive of the way I have created." It would be twenty-five years before the Cézannian revolution triumphed in France. In 1887 Huysmanns still spoke of "an artist with diseased retinas." Père Tanguy, a merchant of art supplies, sold Cézanne's pictures at fixed prices: forty francs for the small ones and one hundred francs for the large.

left: *The Maincy Bridge* was painted by Cézanne during his stay at Melun, from June 3, 1879, to February 25, 1880. If the motif is Impressionist, the conception of perspective is something entirely new. Applying paint as flat, disengaged planes, he "hollowed out" a space that is ambiguous. Each stroke or plane invites several different readings. Depth is not established once and for all; rather, it floats. The artist simply refused to enclose his landscape or to define it as static. His eye told him that the world is mobile and constantly changing, that nothing is fixed in nature—and that the whole of his effort should be directed toward describing the unstable nature of reality. All this—everything he saw—is what Cézanne called his *petite sensation.* "Cézanne was right," said the painter Emile Bernard a quarter of a century later. "It is not great painting if the picture plane remains flat; objects must turn and recede into space; they must live. Therein lies the magic of our art."

Paul Cézanne. *Self-Portrait.* c. 1875. Canvas, 0.64 × 0.53m/2′1¼′ × 1′8¾″.

Edgar Degas (1834–1917). *Two Bathers on the Grass.* c. 1890–95. France. Pastel, 0.70 × 0.68m/2'3½" × 2'2¾".

Cutting his figures
at the framing edge,
Degas achieves the realism
of the candid camera

above and right: The pastels of women must be counted among the best art created by Degas. Taking his lead from photography, which he loved, Degas developed a new conception of the pictorial field in painting, which liberated him to brutalize the composition of a scene, if necessary, in order to enhance the expressiveness of the whole. In *Two Bathers on the Grass,* where the models, as almost always in Degas, are seen from a steep angle, the work looks like a detail arbitrarily isolated from a larger canvas. It is precisely this imaginary extension beyond the edge or frame that Degas wanted the spectator to experience. Much criticized, however, is the candor with which Degas portrayed women in the privacy of their toilettes. "It is the human animal tending to itself. . . . Until now the nude has always been presented in poses that assumed an audience. But my women are simple, honest human beings, concerned about nothing but their physical existence. . . . It is as if you were watching them through a keyhole. . . ."

Edgar Degas.
Woman Combing Her Hair. c. 1887–90.
Pastel, 0.82 × 0.57m/2'8¼" × 1'10½".

left: The *Study of Hands* painted by Degas in 1868 discloses the meticulous care exercised by the artist in the elaboration of his work. In 1859–60, when only twenty-two, Degas painted a large Ingres-type portrait of the Belleli family. But having failed to do the hands of the Baroness to his satisfaction, the artist resolved, almost a decade later, to correct the faulty detail. Meanwhile, in 1861, while copying David in the Louvre, Degas met Manet and in him an art totally liberated from classicism. Out of this came the unusual freedom of Degas' study, in which the veined hands of the model are rendered with stunning craftsmanship and heightened with the muted brilliance of a reddish fabric. Even though the study includes two unrelated sketches, arbitrarily juxtaposed on the same canvas, Degas must have been particularly pleased with the result, since he signed it (upper right corner). "A picture," he said, "is something that requires as much trickery and vice as does the perpetration of a crime. Fake it and then add a touch of nature. . . ."

Edgar Degas. *Study of Hands for the Belleli Family Portrait.* 1868. Canvas, 0.38 × 0.46m/1'3" × 1'6".

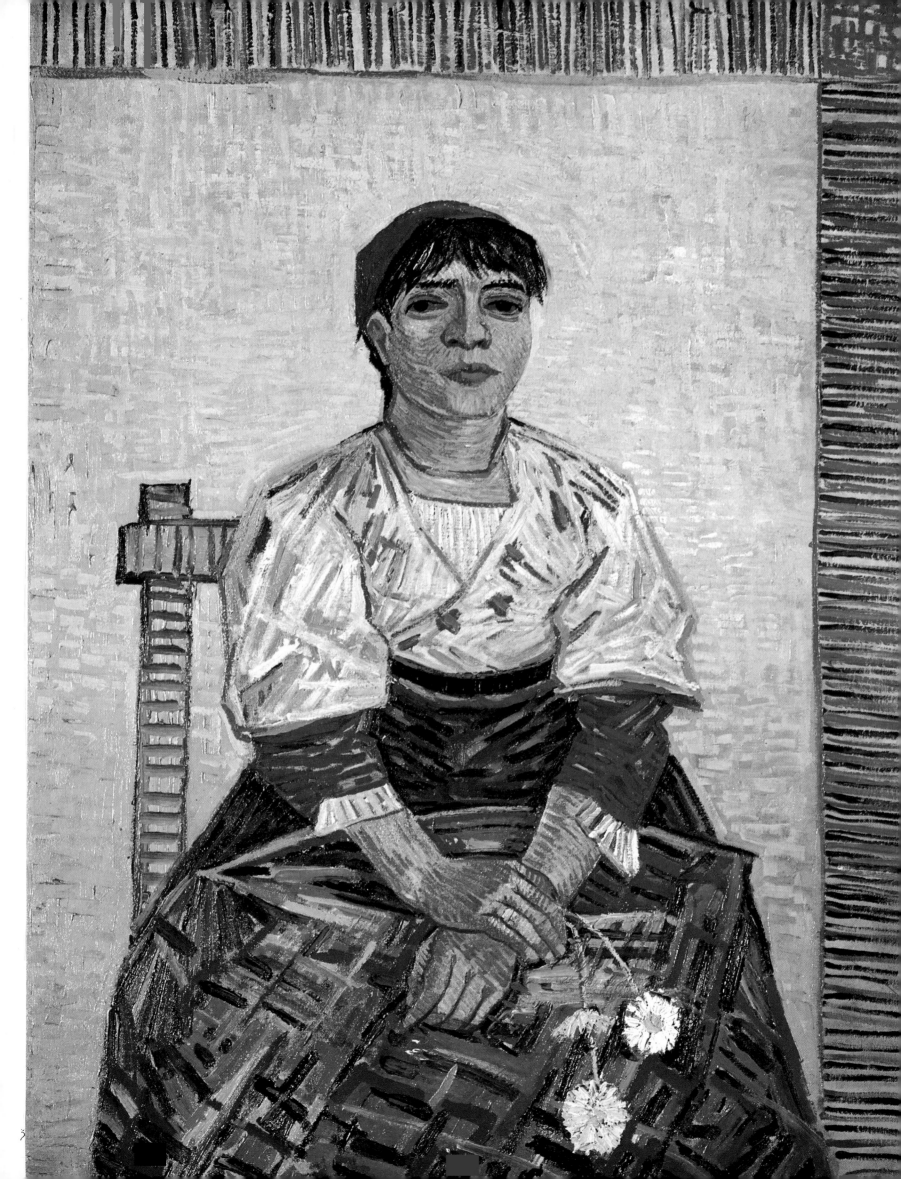

The shrieking color
and vehement brushwork
of van Gogh
shatter the nuanced art
traditional to France

An Italian Woman, which dates from van Gogh's Parisian period, is a picture of almost stupefying chromatic brilliance. Barely had the artist heard about the pointillist divisionism of the Neo-Impressionists than he took up the technique with a passion that reveals the whole excess of his character. Painted without shading, placed off center by a crudely rendered fringe or border—to which the chair back seems to offer a muted response—the composition close up (right), discloses a broad scaffolding of colored hatches, the boldness of which would not be exceeded by either Vlaminck or Derain. In the impetuosity of this French conversion can be felt the stormy fate of van Gogh. But also to be found here is the origin of an entire movement, for after van Gogh, color would disengage from description and cease to express anything but itself, its power to aggress physically upon the human retina. Even beyond Fauvism, van Gogh anticipated Kandinsky and Mondrian. "I envy the Japanese," he wrote, "the extreme simplicity of everything they do. . . . They create a figure in a few sure strokes, as if it were no more difficult than buttoning a jacket."

Vincent van Gogh (1853–90).
An Italian Woman (la Segatori?). 1887.
Holland-France. Canvas, 0.81 × 0.60m./2'8" × 1'11¾".

Vincent van Gogh. *An Italian Woman (la Segatori?)*. Detail.

Freed from the constraints of reason, van Gogh uses arbitrary distortions to express "terrible human passions"

Vincent van Gogh (1853–90). *Vincent's Room in Arles.* 1889. Holland-France. Canvas, 0.56 × 0.74m/1′10″ × 2′5¼″.

above: For his room in Arles van Gogh made virtuoso use of "the high-key yellow" that haunts the whole of his work. The exaggerated perspective—comparable to what could be obtained in modern photography with a wide-angle lens—heightens the anxiety emanating from the empty room, a void that is made all the more moving by the doubling of most of its contents: two chairs, two pillows, two portraits on the wall. "It is simply my bedroom," he wrote. "Color alone should do it and, with its simplicity giving a grand style to things, be suggestive of rest or of sleep in general. In the end, the scene should calm the mind or even more the imagination." Van Gogh would paint several versions of this picture. That reproduced here dates from 1889, during the time the artist spent in the hospital at Saint-Rémy, where he had voluntarily placed himself under treatment. In such an environment and in one year van Gogh painted a hundred canvases.

right: This *Self-Portrait,* very likely painted in the hospital at Saint-Rémy, seems composed of one continuous movement, as if the background and the clothing were made of the same texture. Bonded to a flat plane covered with dancing, flamelike strokes, the gaze—unforgettable in its fixity—constitutes the very image of Vincent's rage to express and his struggle against the impossible, experienced in an atmosphere of nervous tension and anxiety that from time to time plunged the artist into madness. In this radical painting, only the white of the shirt and the vivid red of the beard interrupt the unity of a blue-lilac palette. "I would like to do portraits that a century later might appear like apparitions," wrote van Gogh to his sister.

286

Vincent van Gogh. *Self-Portrait.* 1899. Canvas 0.65 × 0.54m/2'1½" × 1'9¼".

Under the pressure
of a convulsive brush,
forms swell and burst
as nature totters
on the brink of chaos

Vincent van Gogh (1853–90). *The Garden of Dr. Gachet.* May 27, 1890. Holland-France. Canvas, 0.73 × 0.52m/2′4¾″ × 1′8½″.

left: *The Garden of Dr. Gachet,* painted by van Gogh one week after his arrival in Auvers, only a short while before his suicide, is a convulsed landscape in which the chaos of nature, seen with a visionary eye, is controlled by nothing but a stroke that here attains a mastery and a daring possible only for the very greatest artists. "Vincent often adopted," remarks Jean Leymarie, "a high vantage point, thereby collapsing space and heightening the tension between near and far, governed as they are by different axes and rhythms." It is an effect that the painter achieved with unusual power in this canvas. The main mass of the foreground—the sinuous yew tree at the center and the adjacent yucca with its pointed leaves—seems almost rammed from behind by the aggressive perpendicular of the roof. A muscular hatching structures the picture, at the same time that the texture proves unsettling in the sheer acrobatics of its application. In the only article published about van Gogh in his lifetime, Georges-Albert Aurier, in 1890, described "a strange nature, at once true and yet almost supernatural, a nature in which beings and things, shadows and lights, forms and lights, forms and colors—all leap out as if desperately determined to roar their own essential song, doing so in the most intense timbres, at their most fiercely high-pitched." This was a time when the paintings of van Gogh could be bought for forty francs, but no one wanted them. Eighty years later, in 1970, a painting by the Dutch master sold in New York for more than a million dollars.

right: *The Church at Auvers,* dating from June 1890, is one of the last canvases painted by van Gogh, who would die at the end of July, saying to those who attempted to save him: "It's useless. The sadness will last all my life." We know, from a letter he wrote to his sister, how the artist himself regarded this work, which had been created in a state of high excitement: "I have a large picture of the village church, in which the building seems purplish against a sky of deep and simple blue, a pure cobalt in which the stained-glass windows appear like patches of ultramarine, while the roof is violet and partly covered in orange. . . . In the foreground, a bit of flowering green and sand sun-brightened to pink." Intense colors joined with torsioned drawing become a paroxysm of expression wherein explodes the whole poignant drama lived out by van Gogh in the Ile-de-France countryside. For the artist: "Auvers, it has a grave beauty."

Vincent van Gogh. *The Church at Auvers.* 1890.
Canvas, 0.94 × 0.74m/3′1″ × 2′5¼″.

Through a screen
of tiny dots of pure color
emerges drawing and modeling
of incomparable refinement

Georges Seurat (1859–91). *Model from the Back 1887*. France. Panel, 0.25 × 0.16/9¾″ × 6¼″.

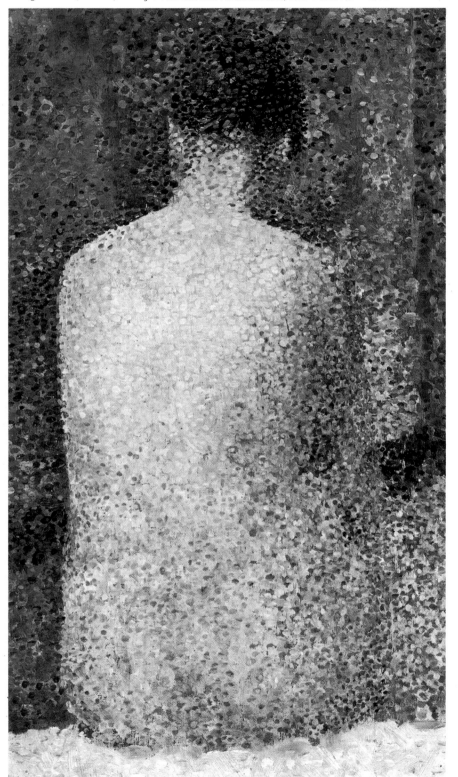

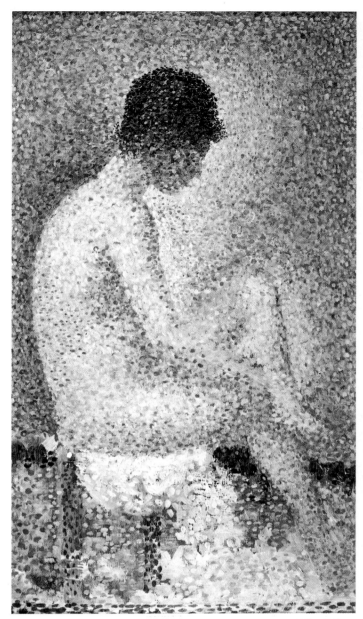

Georges Seurat. *Model in Profile*. 1887. France. Panel, 0.25 × 0.16m/9¾″ × 6¼″.

The *Poseuses* ("Models") from behind and in profile were painted in 1887 while Seurat was preparing the large composition of the same title that now belongs to the Barnes Collection in Merion, Pennsylvania. The little paintings, which are of an exquisite refinement, capture the very essence of "pointillism." The strokes are all the same size, and each contains only the purest hue. Applied side by side and with infinite patience, they effect a kind of optical velvet. Seurat would take a year to complete the large *Poseuses,* which measures 2 × 2 meters. That "turbulent mass of tiny spots," as Félix Fénéon phrased it, recomposes on the retina into vivid color as the viewer moves away from the painting. When observed under a microscope, the Louvre's *Poseuses,* remarked Germain Bazin, "reveal that the touches are not so much juxtaposed as disposed in different layers and linked together like the weave of a fabric. The sense of absolute purity emerging from these works evokes Vermeer." Rarely does one see in French painting a more serene mood, a more allusive delicacy. Depending on the viewer's distance, the subject seems either to take form or to dissolve. Seurat, by deliberately exploiting the mechanisms of visual perception, opened the door to Delaunay and optical art.

Georges Seurat. *Model in Profile* (detail).

In a flat, decorative art
of synthetic colors and shapes,
Gauguin creates the symbol
of fin-de-siècle Europe's
longing for the Arkadian paradise

Arearea dates from Gauguin's first voyage to Tahiti, which occurred in 1891. At that time the artist already stood out as the leader of Synthetism, and an entire generation followed him when he denounced those who, like Monet, "see nothing but matter, with a mindless eye," who "search in what the eye sees and not in the mysterious center of thought." Gauguin wanted the right "to dare all." Anticipating abstraction, he declared that a picture "should provoke thought the way music provokes thought, without the support of ideas or images, simply by the mysterious affinities that exist between our brains and certain arrangements of colors and lines." Taking refuge in Tahiti, Gauguin began stigmatizing "the old ways of Europe, the expression of degenerate races. . . . My feet, in constant contact with pebbles, have hardened and become accustomed to the soil, and my body, which is almost always nude, does not suffer from the sun. Bit by bit civilization leaves me. I commence to think simply, to have only slight dislike for my fellow beings—still better, to love. I have the full joy of a free life, animal and human." It is the sensual wonder before nature that we see translated in *Arearea*. Nourished by Japan and Egypt, Gauguin's decorative style, with its large flat planes of color and its antirealist audacity—as in the red dog—acquired an unrivaled splendor in Tahiti.

Paul Gauguin (1848–1903). *Arearea.* 1892. France. Canvas, 0.75 × 0.93m/2′5½″ × 3′1½″.

With his riveting powers
of visual perception
Monet focuses all his intensity
upon one subject
(the façade of Rouen Cathedral)
and achieves
a great pictorial adventure
—a series recording
the ever-changing effects of light

Claude Monet (1840–1926). *Rouen Cathedral;*
Main Portals; Morning Sun; Harmony in Blue. 1894.
France. Canvas, 0.91 × 0.63m/2′11¾″ × 2′¾″.

Claude Monet. *Rouen Cathedral;*
Main Portals and the Albane Tower; Morning Light; Harmony in White.
1894. France. Canvas, 1.06 × 0.73 m/3′5¾″ × 2′½″.

Claude Monet. *Rouen Cathedral;
Main Portals; Gray Weather.* 1894.
Canvas, 1 × 0.65m/3′3¼″ × 2′1½″.

Claude Monet. *Rouen Cathedral; Main Portals and the Albane Tower; Full Sunlight; Harmony in Blue and Gold.* 1894.
Canvas, 1.07 × 0.73m/3′6″ × 2′4¾″.

The *Cathedrals* of Monet are among the most radical breakthroughs made by Impressionism. "The anxious observer of minute-by-minute differences," as Gustave Geffroy characterized Monet, pursued his ideas about light with an intensity bordering on the maniacal. He attempted to trap the ephemeral and the impalpable in a series of twenty-eight canvases representing the same subject at various times of day. This motif no longer belongs to the world of tangible things, but derives from the play of natural elements. In February 1892 Monet rented a room above the shop "Au Caprice" facing the cathedral in Rouen. He would live there for months on end, with the window open so that he could scrutinize the façade opposite, switching, according to the hour, from one canvas to another. "His painting," notes Germain Bazin, "became a sort of cement, as if to imitate the very material of old stones." Exhibited in 1895 at the Durand-Ruel Gallery, the *Cathedral* series had a great success. The enthusiastic Georges Clémenceau, then an art critic, wrote in *La Justice:* "Each new moment of each variable day constitutes, by virtue of the changing light, a new state of an object that has never existed, and that will never exist. . . . The stonework itself lives, and one feels it mutating from the life it once had to the life that will follow."

By collapsing perspective, Cézanne destroys the visual habits of centuries, but builds the foundations of a new kind of pictorial art—Cubism

above: *Still Life with Onions*, executed around 1895–1900, clearly shows, in its compositional freedom and in the faceting of its volumes, the influence of watercolor on Cézanne's technique. The calculated imprecision of the contours enhances the motif's pulsating luminosity. The tilt of the plate in the foreground, like the vertical rigidity of the transparent glass, proves the stubbornness with which Cézanne wanted to be true to his first impression—"to give the image what we see, forgetting all that has previously come before us." And it is the same man who, while doing the portrait of Vollard, exclaimed, after fifteen sessions with the model: "Understand a little, Monsieur Vollard, the contour escapes me. . . ."

right: *The Woman with the Coffee Pot* has the characteristics of the most beautiful and mysterious of Cézanne's works. The style places the picture at the climax of the artist's classic period, or around 1890. Here one can discern a new attitude toward the motif. As the cup clearly shows, Cézanne painted the same scene from different points of view, examining things both in profile and from above, as if the artist had worked first sitting down and then standing up. Thus, while the woman's bust is represented frontally, her wide apron looks like a flat or isometric projection. "The same subject," explained Cézanne in 1906, "viewed from a different angle, offers a study of the greatest interest, so varied that I think I could remain busy for months, by simply leaning somewhat to the right and then to the left." This way of moving about an object would fascinate the Cubists, giving them in fact the very basis of their aesthetic. Developing the Cézannian process, they learned to record on the same canvas many separate approaches to the same object, thus again shattering Renaissance one-point perspective.

Paul Cézanne (1839–1906). *Still Life with Onions* (detail). c. 1895–1900. France. Canvas, 0.66 × 0.82m/2′2″ × 2′8¼″.

Paul Cézanne. *The Woman with the Coffee Pot.* 1890. Canvas, 1.30 × 0.97m/4′3¼″ × 3′2¼″.

With his pulsating,
luminous planes,
Cézanne creates a new kind
of pictorial unity,
in which the human image,
like near and far distance,
partakes of the same vitality,
substance, and structure

Bathers, one of the most vibrant studies produced by Cézanne, demonstrates his eagerness to mix all of nature's elements on the same canvas and to "marry the curves of women to the shoulders of hills." Here again, it is the density of forms and the presumed stability of reality that are questioned. With his prophetic sensibility, the Master of Aix discerned, beyond the illusory separateness of things, the great molecular chaos that within an overall order confounds animal with vegetable with mineral. "My eyes," he said, "are so glued to the point I am looking at that I think they will start to bleed." Two years before his death, the artist would write to Vollard: "I work doggedly; I glimpse the Promise Land. Shall I be like the great leader of the Hebrews, or shall I be able to enter?" At the time of *Bathers,* Cézanne remained an unknown figure of astonishing modesty. "He is not vain, Monsieur Rodin, he shook my hand! . . . A decorated man!" Cézanne cried during a visit to Monet in 1894. Ten years later, his uncompromising art would dominate European painting.

Paul Cézanne (1839–1906). *Bathers.* c. 1890–94. France. Canvas, 0.22 × 0.33m/3¾" × 1'1".

From the
airy young women
of his maturity
to the
aqueous abstractions
of his old age,
Monet has
one objective—
the dissolution
of form in light

Woman with Umbrella, miraculously transparent and subtle, constitutes a triumph for the "painter of air." Touched by Monet's brush, beings and things alike acquire a vaporous and immaterial texture. In this canvas of 1886, the view from below gives us a sense of joining the model in her metamorphosis, in her levitation toward ether. Gustave Geffroy, who was not only Monet's friend and privileged observer but also his principal critic, pointed out how, "accumulating touches with prodigious sureness, knowing exactly which phenomena of light they corresponded to . . . [Monet] built up the figures of his airy, rhythmical young women in sheer, thin stages, under a golden sun and passing clouds. The new thing here is the evaporation of objects, the melting away of contours, a delicious encounter of surfaces and atmosphere.

Claude Monet (1840–1926).
Woman with Umbrella (detail). 1886.
Canvas, 1.31 × 0.88m/4'3½" × 2'10¾".

right: The *Self-Portrait* of 1917, given to the Louvre
by Monet's friend Georges Clémenceau, is a particularly moving witness to the old age of the patriarch
of Giverny. The leading exponent of Impressionism,
Monet would be the last survivor and the determined
continuator of an aesthetic he had formulated a half-
century earlier. Until his death in 1926, all the while
that a whole series of schools developed in reaction
against his art (Synthetism, Fauvism, Cubism, Surrealism), Monet went on imperturbably scrutinizing
the infinite play of light and cloud on water and flowers. The *Self-Portrait* dates precisely from the period
when, at the height of the war, the artist painted the
vast environment of waterlilies that today is installed
in the Orangerie. One could believe that the violet
tonalities of this work were reflected on the broad,
calm face of the artist and thus captured by him in
his own portrayal. "Monet, I add him to the Louvre!"
exclaimed Cézanne one day. But it was the end of the
19th century before this admiration could be shared
by a majority of art lovers. In 1894 the academic
painter Gérôme wrote, in regard to the Caillebotte
bequest (sixty-seven Impressionist paintings): "For
the state to accept such filth, there would have to be
a very great moral decline." Gérôme reiterated his
position at the 1900 Universal Exhibition, standing
in the way of the French President as he tried to enter
the Impressionist gallery: "Stop, Monsieur le Prési-
dent, here is the shame of France."

right and overleaf: The *Waterlilies* of the Orangerie
are the apotheosis of Monet, his Sistine Chapel.
Nineteen panels, distributed throughout two large
oval rooms and arranged according to the artist's in-
structions, compose what today we call an environment. "Together the paintings represent a tour of
the pond [at Giverny]," explained Gustave Geffroy
on behalf of Monet, "and should be placed low on
the gallery walls so as to be viewed from above, exactly as if it were the real surface of water and the
encircling bank." Surrounded by an infinitely varied
play of "impressions" in every color, the visitor feels
himself immersed in an ambience, almost in a deep,
mysterious, and limitless depth. The waterlily theme
occupied Monet for a quarter of a century. In 1890
he wrote: "I have again taken up things that are impossible to do—water with grass undulating at the
bottom. . . . It is wonderful to see, but to try to paint
it is to go mad." In 1908, just before exhibiting a first
series on the waterlily theme, Monet admitted to
Geffroy: "These landscapes of water and reflections
have become an obsession. It is beyond the strength
of an old man, yet I want to succeed in rendering
what I see there. I have destroyed some [canvases]. I
commence others. . . . And I hope that so much effort will produce something." At Giverny the artist
obtained permission to divert a river, the little Epte,
in order to fill a special pond in which he would plant
willow, bamboo, and rhododendron. He also sowed
the pool with waterlilies. A team of gardeners per-
manently attended this "painting in space." It is
there that Monet would live from 1883 until his
death in 1926. And it is there that the painter's old
friend Georges Clémenceau, nine days after the
1918 victory, would come to receive in the name of
France the prestigious gift made by Claude Monet.

Claude Monet. *Self-Portrait*. 1917. Canvas, 0.70 × 0.55m/2′3½″ × 1′9¾″.

Claude Monet. *Waterlilies, Setting Sun* (see detail overleaf). 1914–18. Canvas, 1.97 × 5.94m/6′5½″ × 19′5¾″.

Subjecting the pirouettes
of the circus
to their aesthetic systems,
Seurat and Lautrec
create arrested arabesques
that reflect tensions
in a time of
rapidly shifting values

right: *The Circus* is the last canvas painted by Seurat before his death at age thirty-two from angina pectoris. As if aware that his life would not be long, the young artist achieved a complete artistic evolution within a very few years. We have only to compare the scrupulous realism and static qualities of the *Poseuses* of 1887 (pages 290–91) with the obsessive arabesques of *The Circus* in order to understand the artist's inner crisis. Seurat gave up the naturalistic objectives of Impressionism and moved toward a linear, more formal art, in which a careful concern for composition prevails over interest in the observed moment. Inscribing the complexity of his curves upon a highly regulated background of verticals and horizontals, the artist obtained a richly contrasted effect that made him one of the fathers of early 20th-century art. After Seurat's death, *The Circus* was sold by Signac to an American collector, John Quinn, on the condition that he leave it to the Louvre, which was done in 1927. Thus France finally acquired one of the monumental canvases of Georges Seurat.

left: *La Clownesse Cha-U-Kao* portrays one of the more picturesque performers at the Moulin Rouge. Lautrec several times made her the subject of his comic interpretations of the stage. The most intimate of the depictions is the one given here, but it is also a magnificent bit of painting. Made up of low-value colors, the background is slashed across with the exploding brilliance of a yellow crescent, whose hue is continued in the bow crowning the hat. Altogether, this color theme clashes like cymbals in the general harmony of the work. The figures of Lautrec, said Gustave Moreau, "are painted in absinthe." The

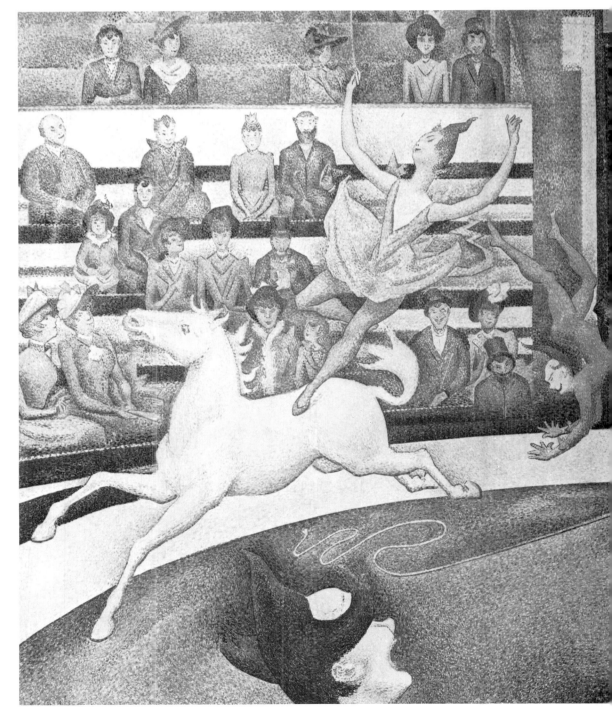

Henri de Toulouse-Lautrec (1864–1901).
La Clownesse Cha-U-Kao. 1895.
Cardboard, 0.64 × 0.49m/2'1¼" × 1'7¼".

Georges Seurat (1859–91). *The Circus* (detail). 1891. France. Canvas, 1.86 × 1.51m/6'1½" × 4'11½".

left: *Jane Avril Dancing* is one of the many studies made by Toulouse-Lautrec at the Moulin Rouge, where the dancer portrayed was an extremely popular star. On several occasions she posed for the artist whose spirit and drawing she appreciated. On his part, Lautrec felt drawn by the sad grace and the strong character of this very personal artist who knew how to match her dances with costumes of unusual color. Here she appears in full movement, drawn more than painted on a cardboard support that somewhat mutes the colors. This kind of painting, vigorously carried off by a powerful brush, reveals the influence of Degas. If Lautrec adds something harsh in the brushwork, something more "modern" in the subject, he nonetheless recalls Degas in the off-center framing and in the bold rendering of the dancer.

right: *La Goulue Dancing* is a tribute to Louise Weber—called "The Glutton" because of her fabled appetite—who was one of Lautrec's favorite models, in hundreds of drawings, lithographs, and posters. A former laundress, she had begun at the Bobino and then moved to the Moulin de la Galette. In 1890 she formed a troop with *la Môme Fromage* ("The Cheese Kid"), *Nini Patte-en-l'Air* ("Nini the Kicker"), *Grille-d'Egout* ("Sewer Trap"), and *Torpille* ("Torpedo"), who together performed at the Moulin Rouge. But their success did not last, and La Goulue finally opened a booth at a public fair (le Trône). Having become very fat, she concentrated exclusively on belly dancing. Lautrec painted two large panels as decorations for her new establishment. In the one opposite, he shows the star in an Egyptian dance, covered in transparent gauze and doing her number before the most sophisticated audience in Paris: on the right the critic Félix Fénéon, whose goatee and finicky style were already famous (he called La Goulue *une sauteuse à arachnéennes pattes*—" a jumper with cobweb-light feet"), Oscar Wilde (at the center, wearing his top hot), Jane Avril (with her celebrated black hat), and finally Lautrec himself, a tiny figure wedged in between La Goulue and Fénéon. One cannot but be struck by the sovereign ease of the draftsmanship and the artist's facility in dealing with large surfaces. The smaller forms—the pianist and the tambourine player—are bitingly sketched, realized as if in one swift stroke of the brush. Degas, who was generally spare with compliments, would simply say to Lautrec: *Vous êtes du bâtiment* ("you are a member of an exclusive fraternity").

Henri de Toulouse-Lautrec (1864–1901).
Jane Avril Dancing. France.
Cardboard, 0.85 × 0.45m/2'9½" × 1'5¾".

With an electric and febrile stroke,
Toulouse-Lautrec captures
the raffish rhythms of bourgeois low life

Henri de Toulouse-Lautrec. *La Goulue Dancing.* 1895. Canvas, 2.85 × 3m/9′4¼″ × 9′10″.

Edgar Degas (1834–1917).
Dancer. c. 1890–95. France.
Bronze, height 0.46m/1'6".

The *Dancers* of Degas form part of a secret oeuvre, which the artist never showed. "Left in the studio," explains Michel Beaulieu, curator of the Louvre's sculpture department, "these sketches deteriorated, sometimes fell victim to their maker's wrath, and even more to his lack of technique. A deplorable technician, Degas constructed his armatures with miscellaneous materials, tying willy-nilly with rags and strings, and heavily overloading the frames. Discouraged by clay—by its grit and damp cloths—and disgusted by plastiline, the artist decided to use wax. Conceiving the notion that he could make the wax himself, he mixed tallow and various colorants, which together had the effect of rendering the material very friable, irremediably dooming the statuettes to destruction." But sixty-three have been saved and cast in bronze. All the *Dancers* embody a desire to seize movement in its most difficult and tense moment, as if the artist sought to preserve those delicate passages where the body all but comes apart and finally, without affectation, reveals the truth of its structure.

Edgar Degas.
Dancer. c. 1877–83.
Bronze, height 0.46m/1'6".

Edgar Degas.
Dancer. 1882.
Bronze, height 0.44m/1'5¼".

Through
his systematic analysis
of balance and movement,
Degas reveals
the dancer's dislocated grace

Edgar Degas. *Dancer.* c. 1877–83. Bronze, height 0.46m/1'6".

Rousseau's *War* was the product of two influences: a propaganda campaign launched in 1889, and certain Renaissance paintings, by Uccello and Carpaccio for instance, that the artist had carefully analyzed from postcards and visits to the Louvre. But the Douanier ("Customs Officer"), as he was called for his job as a toll-taker in Paris, added to his sources a unique quality all his own—a powerful sense of design that endows his volumes with great immediacy, physical presence, and impact. Fernand Léger would remember the Douanier's art in his first Cubist compositions, and Robert Delaunay counted himself among the most fervent admirers of the old "primitive." In his fifties Rousseau retired from his minor, low-paying job so as to devote full time to painting. His first exhibition had come only in 1885, when he was in his mid-forties. Subsequently a friend of Apollinaire and Picasso, he became one of the most picturesque and authentic "characters" at the Bateau-Lavoir, where in 1908 his friends honored him with a legendary banquet given in Picasso's rooms. "Few artists," wrote Apollinaire, "have suffered more scorn in their lifetime than the Douanier, and few men could remain so calm in the face of such an avalanche of raillery and abuse. . . . That serenity, of course, was nothing more than pride. The Douanier understood his own strength. He even let it be known once or twice that he was the greatest painter of his generation. It is possible that in this respect, as in several others, he was not entirely wrong."

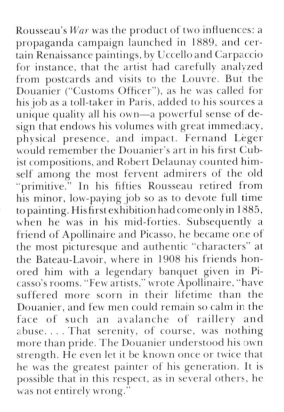

Through the naïveté of what
he considers to be the epitome of academic painting,
the Douanier Rousseau anticipates
both the fantasy and the abstraction
of 20th-century painting

Henri Rousseau, called *Le Douanier* (1844–1910). *War and the Cavalcade of Discord.* 1894. France. Canvas, 1.14 × 1.95m/3'9" × 6'4¾".

Guide to the Louvre and Its Collections

Historical Plan of the Louvre and Tuileries Palaces

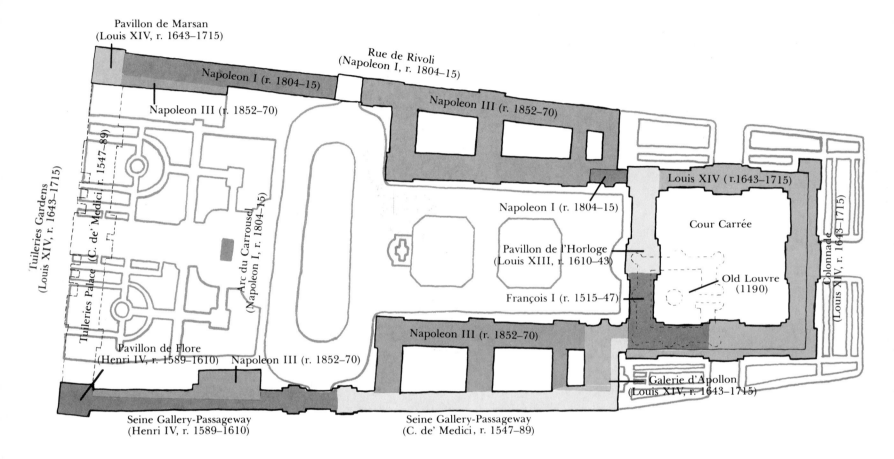

Pavillon de Marsan
(Louis XIV, r. 1643–1715)

Rue de Rivoli
(Napoleon I, r. 1804–15)

Napoleon I (r. 1804–15)

Napoleon III (r. 1852–70)

Napoleon III (r. 1852–70)

Tuileries Gardens
(Louis XIV, r. 1643–1715)

Tuileries Palace (C. de' Medici r. 1547–89)

Arc du Carrousel
(Napoleon I, r. 1804–15)

Louis XIV (r.1643–1715)

Cour Carrée

Napoleon I (r. 1804–15)

Pavillon de l'Horloge
(Louis XIII, r. 1610–43)

Old Louvre
(1190)

Colonnade
(Louis XIV, r. 1643–1715)

François I (r. 1515–47)

Pavillon de Flore
(Henri IV, r. 1589–1610)   Napoleon III (r. 1852–70)

Napoleon III (r. 1852–70)

Galerie d'Apollon
(Louis XIV, r. 1643–1715)

Seine Gallery-Passageway
(Henri IV, r. 1589–1610)

Seine Gallery-Passageway
(C. de' Medici, r. 1547–89)

Ground Floor

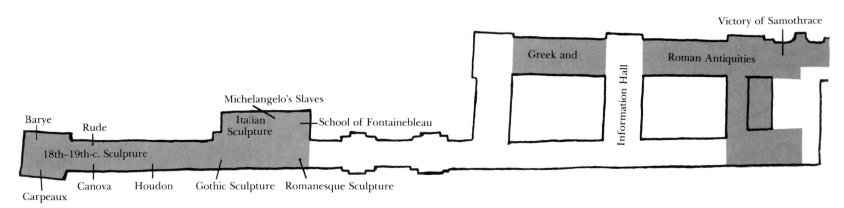

Victory of Samothrace

Greek and   Roman Antiquities

Information Hall

Michelangelo's Slaves

Italian
Sculpture   School of Fontainebleau

Barye   Rude

18th–19th-c. Sculpture

Carpeaux   Canova   Houdon   Gothic Sculpture   Romanesque Sculpture

Ground Floor

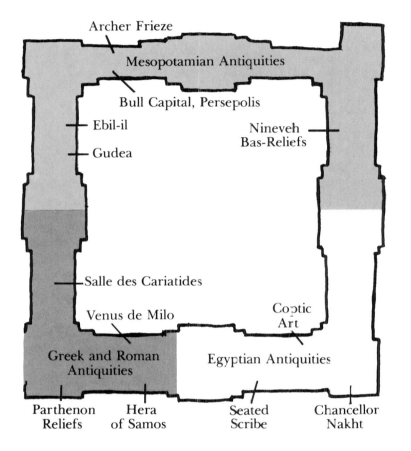

Archer Frieze

Mesopotamian Antiquities

Bull Capital, Persepolis

Ebil-il

Gudea

Nineveh
Bas-Reliefs

Salle des Cariatides

Coptic
Art

Venus de Milo

Greek and Roman
Antiquities

Egyptian Antiquities

Parthenon   Hera   Seated   Chancellor
Reliefs   of Samos   Scribe   Nakht

First Floor

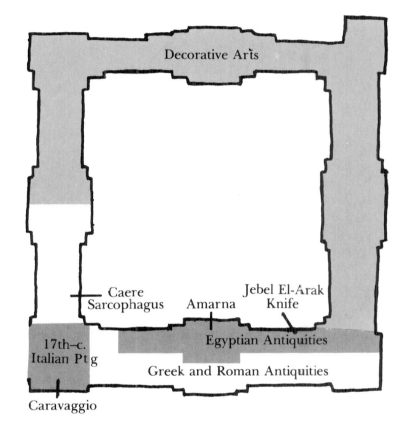

Decorative Arts

Caere
Sarcophagus

Amarna

Jebel El-Arak
Knife

17th–c.
Italian Ptg

Egyptian Antiquities

Greek and Roman Antiquities

Caravaggio

First Floor

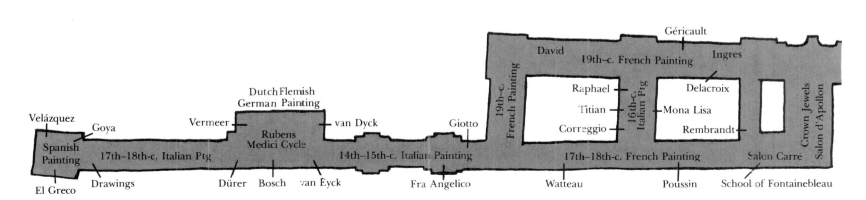

Géricault

David   19th–c. French Painting   Ingres

Dutch Flemish
German Painting

Raphael   Delacroix

Titian   Mona Lisa

Correggio   Rembrandt

Velázquez

Goya

Vermeer   van Dyck   Giotto

19th–c.
French Painting

16th–c.
Italian Ptg

Crown Jewels
Salon d'Apollon

Spanish
Painting

17th–18th-c. Italian Ptg

Rubens
Medici Cycle

14th–15th-c. Italian Painting

17th–18th-c. French Painting

Salon Carré

El Greco   Drawings   Dürer   Bosch   van Eyck   Fra Angelico   Watteau   Poussin   School of Fontainebleau

The Tuileries,
a ghostly presence
and glorious gardens
at the heart of Paris

Only through old paintings and photographs can we know the Tuileries Palace, which was gutted by fire during the Commune of 1871. But by the time of the building's destruction, little remained of the edifice put up in the 16th century by Philibert Delorme and Jean Brullant for Catherine de' Medici, who died long before the palace was completed even according to the original plans. When in the late 16th century Du Cerceau took over the project for Henri IV, he began a process of expansion that under Le Vau, in 1664–66, resulted in a structure vast beyond anything contemplated by the Medici Queen. Working to satisfy Louis XIV's thirst for *gloire,* Le Vau rebuilt the central pavilion almost totally, crowning it with an imperial dome and adding to the ad-

jacent one-story wings both an upper floor and an attic. The wings also gained porticoes supporting terraces that ran from the central pavilion to the lateral pavilions. In the 19th century the terraces would be built up with supplementary apartments. In the courtyard on the Louvre side of the Tuileries, Napoleon I commissioned the Arc de Triomphe du Carrousel, which served as a heroic gate to the palace. The famous and wonderful Tuileries Gardens, created by Le Nôtre in the 17th century, have survived intact, leading the eye along their central axis across pools and patterned plantings to the Champs-Elysées and on up to the climactic Arc de Triomphe de l'Etoile over a mile away.

Photographic Credits